Destitute Patriots

Destitute Patriots

Bertie County in the War of 1812

Gerald W. Thomas

Office of Archives and History
North Carolina Department of Cultural Resources
Raleigh
2012

North Carolina Department of Cultural Resources
Linda A. Carlisle
Secretary

Office of Archives and History
Jeffrey J. Crow
Deputy Secretary

Division of Historical Resources
David L. S. Brook
Director

Historical Publications Section
Donna E. Kelly
Administrator

Front cover: Drawing by Walter Manton of the imprint made by the 1782 die (original) of the Great Seal of the United States. File courtesy of Wikipedia Commons.

Printed by Data Reproductions

Contents

Maps, Illustrations, and Tables

Foreword

In order to commemorate the bicentennial of the War of 1812, Gerald W. Thomas has written *Destitute Patriots: Bertie County in the War of 1812*. Briefly chronicling the war at the national, state, and county levels, the author places Bertie County in context and uses it as a microcosm of the conflict's impact, albeit limited, in North Carolina.

Between June 1812 and February 1815, a total of 241 Bertie County men served either in the United States Army or the North Carolina detached militia companies called into service by the federal government. With only a short-lived British naval raid at Ocracoke, most of Bertie's troops were assigned to Norfolk and never fired a shot at the British. Any casualties were the result of exposure and disease. Poor communication and a breakdown in bureaucracy led to inadequate arms and deplorable conditions for the citizen soldiers. Nevertheless, these "Destitute Patriots" heeded the call to serve their country, just as their predecessors had done during the American Revolution.

Mr. Thomas is a graduate of East Carolina University and a retired federal executive. In 1996 he wrote *Divided Allegiances: Bertie County during the Civil War* for the Office of Archives and History, and he is currently working on a volume about Bertie County during the Revolutionary War. Robert M. Topkins, former editor with the section, edited and indexed the book. Susan Trimble typeset the text, prepared all of the maps, and designed the cover. Lisa Bailey applied her considerable proofreading skills to the text, and I saw the work through press.

I would like to acknowledge the generous personal donation by Carol Canales, president of the North Carolina chapter of the United States Daughters of 1812, for the publication of this book.

Donna E. Kelly, Administrator
Historical Publications Section

Preface

My interest in the contributions of Bertie County citizens during the War of 1812 stems primarily from the knowledge that nearly all of my lineal ancestors who lived during that period in our nation's history resided in the county. Two of my direct ancestors—Charney Cale and David White—served in the United States Army and in North Carolina's detached militia during the war. Another ten men who were relatives of my lineal ancestors (brothers, cousins, etc.) likewise actively served.

While across the country many citizens vehemently opposed the conflict, the citizens of Bertie County generally supported war against Great Britain. The county's white male population (those persons who could vote) tended to sustain the pro-war Republican Party and the war efforts of President James Madison's administration, but that support did not translate into substantial enlistments in the army. During the first eighteen months of the conflict, only twenty-six men offered their services to the army. While recruiters from southeastern Virginia eventually visited the county during the early months of 1814 and achieved a higher degree of success in coaxing men to sign up than had previously been the case, during the whole of the war only eighty-four men signed on for army service. Of those men, thirteen were rejected (apparently for medical and physical reasons) and did not serve. A few of Bertie County's soldiers, members of the Tenth Regiment United States Infantry, were sent to the active war front along the Canadian border. Once there, however, they were involved in virtually no combat against the British. Only one Bertie County resident, Pvt. William Avis, sustained a wound during service along the border. The majority of the county's army members served at Norfolk, Virginia, and were involved in no combat.

Two companies of detached militia from Bertie County were called into service during the war. Capt. Augustin Pugh's artillery company spent six days at Edenton during July 1813, following the British raid at Ocracoke and the ensuing panic that consumed eastern North Carolina. Pugh's company deployed a second time in October 1813, this time to Currituck County to assist in curtailing illegal and treasonable trade between certain citizens of that county and British forces cruising off the coast. Pugh's company spent four months on that tour.

In late September 1814, Capt. Jonathan H. Jacocks's infantry company deployed to Gates Court House, where more than eighty of its members were combined with militiamen from other counties to constitute a company. Brig. Gen. Jeremiah Slade dismissed Jacocks and gave Capt. James Iredell of Chowan County command of the company he had assembled. About 80 percent of the company's members were men whom Captain Jacocks had marched from Windsor. The company was assigned to the First Regiment (McDonald's) North Carolina Militia (Detached). The regiment marched to Norfolk in early October 1814 and assisted in the defense of that city until almost the end of the war. The regiment, including the Bertie County men, suffered greatly for want of clothes, blankets, and sufficient shelter. While the regiment was involved in no combat, it lost 212 members (eleven of whom were Bertie County residents) to the ravages of illness and disease.

North Carolina was not a theater of combat during the war. Therefore, this book does not present accounts of grand military maneuvers, ferocious battles, or gallant bayonet charges. Rather, it recounts and documents the contributions made by Bertie County citizens in the context of the war as it unfolded in eastern North Carolina. The county, a constituent community along the expansive waterways of the eastern sector of the state, was a "small player" in the war. Mostly, its citizens reacted to events that transpired along the state's coastline and to calls made upon its leaders and militia commanders from state officials in Raleigh. In short, the experiences of the county's citizens represent a microcosm of much of the rest of the eastern sector of the state—a community not sufficiently large in population, commercial output, or economic impact to influence events significantly but whose citizens were patriotic in support of the nation's cause and reacted emotionally to the events.

Both the regular army and North Carolina's detached militia encountered extreme obstacles and problems in providing essential items needed to raise, organize, arm, train, and sustain fighting forces. Overwhelming deficiencies and problems in logistical networks created grave shortages of arms, munitions, clothing, camp equipment, medical stores, supplies, and provisions. Furthermore, the troops often were not paid for their services. For example, the members of Captain Pugh's Bertie County militia company were not paid for their two tenures of service in 1813 until February 1816, almost a year after the war formally concluded and nearly two years after they were discharged from active service.

While British ships cruised the coast of North Carolina, beginning in 1813 and continuing throughout the war, no large-scale invasions or raids occurred. In short, North Carolina was not a high-value target to the British—it was principally a rural state with no large cities, harbors, or commercial interests (such as those found in other states on the Atlantic seaboard). The federal government's financial and military resources were highly strained during the war, and officials logically dedicated most of such resources to the northern sectors and the active campaigns there. In a large measure, the departments of war and navy's defensive strategies for eastern North Carolina were to tolerate British raids, since to the enemy there was no strategic value in invading North Carolina. Officials in the nation's capital were of the opinion that any British raids that might occur would be of short duration, resulting primarily in depredations against small communities.

Any history of a specific topic represents a record of the relevant events that occurred and a historian or author's interpretation and/or analysis of those events based on the documentary evidence available and examined. To this end, I have relied heavily on four primary categories of records to prepare this book: (1) North Carolina governors' letters and papers; (2) records of the North Carolina adjutant general's office; (3) secretary of war letters; and (4) secretary of the navy letters.

I have prepared this history specifically for readers with a special interest (genealogical or historical) in Bertie County. I have provided names, dates, and locations whenever the sources were sufficiently detailed. I sincerely hope that my effort has uncovered some facts and perspectives heretofore unknown to us, many of whom are descendants of those Bertie County patriots who experienced the "Second War of Independence" nearly two centuries ago.

Gerald W. Thomas

CHAPTER 1

"Dire Necessity" to Arms

On November 20, 1811, a group of "the respectable citizens" of Bertie County gathered at the courthouse in Windsor to discuss the worrisome situation in which the United States found itself. The men who gathered in Windsor on that day—members of the Democratic-Republican Party—were concerned and highly aroused over the ever deepening crisis that consumed the nation.[1] The youthful American republic had been embroiled with Great Britain in turbulent relations for years, and in the fall of 1811 ominous "war clouds" were fervently boiling on the political horizon. The United States was actively preparing for an armed confrontation with its "Mother Nation," Great Britain.[2]

The Revolutionary War, which gave birth to the American nation, formally concluded on September 3, 1783, when the United States and Great Britain signed the final peace treaty in Paris.[3] With the conclusion of the war, Americans and their leaders began constructing the foundational tenets that would form the bases for governing the country, protecting newly achieved freedoms, and sustaining a democratic society. As an independent and sovereign entity, the country naturally felt that it had earned the recognition and respect of the nations of the world. The country fully expected to conduct its affairs—both internally and internationally—without interference and disturbance from other nations. Nevertheless, Great Britain and France antagonized and bullied the Americans. The threat of war had loomed since shortly after the turn of the nineteenth century. Great Britain and France had resumed hostilities with each other in 1803, and Americans had been caught in the Anglo-Franco cross fire. Determined to weaken one another, the belligerents tried to disrupt each other's maritime trade with neutral countries, including the United States.[4]

Great Britain's naval forces had continually interfered with United States commercial vessels as they plied the seas. The British time and time again had boarded American ships to snatch away—or "impress"—British-born sailors. Although impressments—a practice as old as the Royal Navy—were supposed to be limited to British subjects, by accident or design thousands of Americans (including North Carolinians) were dragged from their vessels by the British. Impressments became so common that, according to one estimate, in the six-year period from 1804 through 1810, almost 5,000 sailors had been forcibly removed from American ships—including 1,361 whom the British later freed after acknowledging they were American citizens. While British officials were willing to release impressed Americans, such releases were made only after satisfactory proof of the American sailors' citizenship had been delivered through diplomatic channels, a process that often took years. In the meantime, American victims of impressments were forced to serve aboard British warships, where they were exposed to the rigors of harsh discipline and all the dangers of war not of their own country's making.[5]

War nearly occurred in the summer of 1807 as Americans became enraged after the British frigate *Leopard* fired upon the American frigate *Chesapeake*. The *Chesapeake*, unprepared for an armed confrontation, struck its colors and surrendered after being fired upon. The incident occurred on June 22 in the Atlantic Ocean immediately off Norfolk, Virginia, and resulted in the killing of three United States crewmen. Americans clamored for war upon learning that the British, after firing upon the vessel, had boarded it and seized three American crewmen and a lone British sailor.[6]

Four weeks after the *Leopard-Chesapeake* incident, a "large number" of the citizens of Bertie County—angered by the British warship's attack and other "unfriendly & hostile dispositions manifested by the government of Great-Britain towards the U. States"—met at the courthouse in Windsor. Those in attendance sought to express openly their resentment toward the British. They appointed Jonathan Jacocks to chair the meeting and Joseph Hunter Bryan to serve as secretary. A committee of seven county residents—William Cherry, Simon Turner, Whitmell Hill Pugh, Prentis Law, Jeremiah Devan, William Burlingham, and Joseph Hunter Bryan—was appointed to draw up "resolutions expressive of the meeting." The gathering, through a report prepared by the committee, expressed "emotions of anxious concern, mingled with indignation" over Great Britain's actions toward the American republic, "notwithstanding the uniform and unremitting exertions" of the United States "to preserve the relations of peace, good understanding and friendly commercial intercourse." The Bertie County residents asserted their resentment that the nation's commerce had been "interrupted and oppressed by the illegal searches, captures for trial & adjudication of our merchantmen (peacefully pursuing a lawful commerce) by the armed ships of his Britannic Majesty."

On June 22, 1807, the British warship *Leopard* attacked the American frigate *Chesapeake*, shown here, in the Atlantic Ocean immediately off Norfolk. A number of the *Chesapeake*'s crewmen were killed and captured during the incident. Americans exploded in indignation at the British action, and many called for war. Bertie County residents publicly expressed their anger and resentment toward the British during a meeting at the courthouse in Windsor on July 20. They issued to North Carolina governor Nathaniel Alexander a decree declaring that they would support any measures of retaliation taken by American leaders against the British. Image courtesy of the Naval Historical Foundation, Washington, D.C.

Those attending the meeting unanimously approved three resolutions directly related to the *Leopard–Chesapeake* affair. The measures

- viewed with "the most warm and heartfelt indignation the outrageous, and in point of atrocity the unparalleled attack made upon the U[nited] States frigate Chesapeake, unprepared and almost defenceless, in a state of profound peace, by his Britannic Majesty's ship of war Leopard";
- concurred with the "firm, manly and patriotic conduct of the citizens of Norfolk & Portsmouth in resenting this daring outrage upon the honour and rights of the American people, merits and obtains our unlimited approbation, and should instruct our fellow citizens elsewhere, to be prepared against the insidious & unexpected warfare usually practised by Great Britain"; and

- "most cordially" approved of the conduct of President Thomas Jefferson in dealing with the *Leopard-Chesapeake* affair, and reposed the "utmost confidence in his wisdom, firmness and energy," and promised to "cordially co-operate in any measures of retaliation, redress or revenge adopted by the constitutional authorities of the country, and pledge for this purpose or fortunes and our lives."

The meeting's report was transmitted to President Jefferson and North Carolina's governor, Nathaniel Alexander.[7]

Shortly after the "war scare" associated with the *Leopard-Chesapeake* affair, another contentious issue surfaced—the British Orders in Council. The orders were a series of decrees issued by the British government to control neutral trade with the European continent. Issued in January and November 1807, the orders were retaliatory actions against Napoleon's Berlin Decree of November 1806. Napoleon's measure proclaimed the British Isles to be in a state of blockade by land and sea. The British orders of January banned neutral trade from ports controlled by Great Britain's enemies. The November orders further directed all neutral ships to stop at British ports or be subjected to search by British authorities. All vessels were liable to capture and confiscation, and additionally, the British ordered neutral ships to pay duties and obtain licenses for trade with its enemy (France and its allies). Napoleon reacted by issuing the Milan Decree of December 1807, which extended France's embargo to neutral countries' trade with Great Britain. Jointly, the British and Napoleonic orders and decrees greatly hampered Americans' free trade with the European continent. The British defended their Orders in Council as a necessary response to Napoleon's decrees, but that position did little to pacify Americans who thought the European belligerents were using war as a pretext for looting American commerce. American losses were considerable. Between 1807 and 1812, Great Britain, France, and their allies seized approximately nine hundred American ships.[8]

In the early nineteenth century, Windsor was an active inland port of commerce for Bertie County with at least ten vessels claiming the town as their home port. Merchant vessels used Windsor, situated on the Cashie River, to deliver goods and ship exports, primarily agricultural commodities and forestry products. Prior to early 1808, the port town of Edenton—directly across the Chowan River from the eastern boundary of Bertie County—was the official point of entry for commercial vessels entering the upper Albemarle Sound region. Windsor was a port of delivery under the Edenton customs office. Merchant vessels originating in or destined for Windsor were required to stop in Edenton so that the government collector could assess and collect duties on goods, wares, and merchandise. On April 25, 1808, Congress subdivided the Edenton district and established Plymouth as a separate district. Plymouth, like Windsor, had been a port of delivery in the Edenton district prior to the congressional action. The Plymouth district included the Roanoke and Cashie rivers, as well as all the creeks and harbors interconnected with those waterways. Windsor and Skewarky (present-day Williamston) were designated as ports of delivery under Plymouth. Levi Blount, a Plymouth businessman, was appointed collector for the newly established district, with his office at Plymouth.[9]

Caught in a vise between the two European antagonists and the growing infringements on American rights, the United States—primarily as a result of Republican insistence—responded by imposing its own series of economic sanctions against the two powers. In November 1806 Congress enacted a partial non-importation act that prohibited certain British imports. More than a year later, in December 1807, Congress enacted a general embargo that eliminated exports and trade with other nations of the world, but in March 1809 Congress repealed both measures and substituted a non-intercourse act that prohibited all trade with Britain, France, and their colonies. Congress repealed this law in 1810 and in 1811 imposed a non-importation act that barred all British imports.[10] Those measures, intended to win concessions from Great Britain and France, failed to yield the desired results. No concessions were won from either country. Instead, the laws resulted in severely damaging the American economy, under-mining the nation's prosperity, and depriving the central government of much-needed revenue from trade. American imports, which had peaked at $108 million in 1807, plummeted to $22 million in 1808.[11]

Those Bertie County merchants who produced goods and commodities for export to foreign countries experienced the negative impact on American shipping resulting from the British Orders in Council and the French decrees, as well as the American embargo. While no records delineating the actual seizure and confiscation by British ships of goods originating from Bertie County are available, it is very conceivable that a negative impact of some degree occurred. Likewise, the subsequent embargo measures would have detrimentally affected the county residents' production and export of goods. To illustrate, the port of Edenton reportedly cleared only four or so ships a week under the embargo law, but when President James Madison proclaimed commerce with Britain again open in 1809, the number jumped to eleven per week.[12]

Two other developments contributed to the deterioration of Anglo-American relations in 1811. The first—the *Little Belt* incident—a kind of *Leopard-Chesapeake* affair in reverse, in which the American warship *President* on May 18, 1811, off Cape Henry, fired upon the British warship *Little Belt*, killing and wounding thirty-two members of its crew. The second was the outbreak of an Indian war on the nation's northwest frontier. An Indian federation headed by the Shawnee brothers, Tecumseh and Tenskwatawa (better known as "The Prophet"), was determined to renounce the ways of whites and prevent further encroachments on its lands. Most Americans were convinced that British officials in Canada were behind the Indian conspiracy. On November 7, 1811, Gen. William Henry Harrison defeated the Indians in the battle of Tippecanoe (in present-day Indiana), but Indian depredations continued to render the entire northwest frontier unsafe.[13]

In the fall of 1811, a defiant mood swept through the nation's capital. On November 4, 1811, the Twelfth Congress—known to history as "the War Congress"—convened amid ever escalating rhetoric and talk of war with Great Britain. A new group of "youngblood" legislators took their seats in that body and embarked on a legislative session dominated in both the Senate and the House of Representatives by Republicans. Led primarily by firebrand southerners—particularly John C. Calhoun of South Carolina and Henry Clay of Kentucky—the Republican majority came to subjugate Capitol Hill with its oratory, despite Federalist skepticism over the "war talk."[14]

On November 5, President Madison, also a Republican, sent his annual message to Congress. The president recounted the various transgressions that Great Britain had committed against the United States and accused the British of making "war on our lawful commerce." He stated that "the period is arrived, which claims from the Legislative G[u]ardians of the National rights, a system for more ample provisions for maintaining them." The president laid out his expectations of Congress: with the "evidence of hostile inflexibility in trampling on rights which no Independent Nation can relinquish; Congress will feel the duty of putting the United States into armour, and an attitude demanded by the crisis, and corresponding with the national spirit and expectations." Madison concluded by expressing his "deep sense of the crisis in which you are assembled" and his "confidence in a wise and honorable result to your deliberations."[15]

News and accounts of the stressed relationship, adversarial actions, and related unrest between the United States and Great Britain were brought to

In the Twelfth Congress, Representatives John C. Calhoun (of South Carolina) and Henry Clay (of Kentucky) were predominant spokesmen and leaders of the so-called "War Hawks," a group of legislators from the southern and western states who demanded an aggressive national policy toward Great Britain. Employing fiery oratory and carefully reasoned arguments, Calhoun and Clay (who was elected as Speaker of the House of Representatives) were instrumental in the movement toward war against the British. Image of Calhoun courtesy of the Library of Congress, Washington, D.C.; portrait of Clay courtesy of the *Dictionary of American Portraits*, 119.

the citizens of Bertie County primarily through the newspapers of the day, principally the *Edenton Gazette,* the *Raleigh Register and North Carolina Gazette,* the *Raleigh Minerva*, and other regional prints. The papers routinely reprinted articles and accounts of events that appeared in newspapers of the major cities of the United States, including Boston, New York, Philadelphia, Baltimore, Washington, Norfolk, and Charleston.[16] In addition, communications from the North Carolina adjutant general in Raleigh to the commanding officer of the Bertie County militia indirectly conveyed relevant information concerning certain military matters to the county's residents.

On November 20, 1811—slightly more than two weeks after the "War Congress" convened—prominent Bertie County Republicans assembled to discuss the "potential armed confrontation with Great Britain" and frame resolutions conveying their sentiments and positions. Richard Poindexter,

President James Madison, a member of the Democratic-Republican Party, led the United States during the War of 1812 and the period immediately preceding it. Goaded by the "War Congress," Madison in early November 1811 delivered his annual message to that body, in which he called for the country to prepare for war against Great Britain. Before the end of that month, a committee of Bertie County residents wrote to the president and expressed their adamant support for the government in whatever course it decided to take in dealing with the British. Image courtesy of the White House Historical Association, Washington, D.C.

minister of Sandy Run Baptist Church in the western sector of the county, chaired the meeting, and Jonathan H. Jacocks, a prominent planter and militia officer from Windsor, served as secretary. Whitmell H. Pugh, Joseph Hunter Bryan, James W. Warburton, James Palmer, Jonathan R. Leggett, and John Webb comprised a committee that formally prepared resolutions to be transmitted to President Madison, as follows:

The Republicans of Windsor and its vicinity, called together by a just sense of the awful crisis which overclouds our political horizon, feel it their duty to declare that though they have long witnessed with painful regret, the unfriendly spirit in which the British Orders of Council were dictated, they never ceased fondly to hope "That the scrupulous regard to justice, the protracted moderation, and the multiplied efforts of the U. States to substitute for the accumulating dangers to peace of the two countries the mutual advantages of re-established friendship and confidence," would, independent of the manifest, unjust and hostile policy which gave them birth, ultimately cause their removal. Disappointed in this, their just expectation, and deeply lamenting the dire necessity which is about to clad our country in arms, not only to obtain indemnity for past wrongs so long and so patiently borne, but to oppose the execution of measures, no less derogatory to the honor of Great-Britain, than injurious to our interest and destructive to our rights as an independent nation, rights which we never can, never ought, and never will relinquish.

Be it therefore Resolved. As the sense of this meeting, that the indispensable condition assigned by the British Envoy, as necessary to the repeal of the Orders in Council, is highly insulting and affords additional evidence of the unfriendly disposition of that power towards the U. States, inasmuch as it requires commercial regulations in different countries of Europe beyond the control of our government, and that they can but view the rigorous execution of these Orders . . . as not only affording evidence of British injustice and determined hostility to the United States, but as actual war both in purpose and effect on our lawful commerce. With this solemn impression, they look forward with anxious solicitude to the future decisions of the General Government; and though they deeply deplore the anticipated evils expected to flow from a state of war, yet they would prefer it, with all its horrors, to submission without a struggle, to measures calculated to endanger our dearest interest and strike directly at our rights as a free and independent nation.

Be it further Resolved, That while they are alive to all the insults and indignities offered us by G. Britain, they are not forgetful that the course pursued by France, since the repeal of her decrees, has not been in unison with her warm professions of friendship and good will, and that the unwarrantable retention of our property, seized and condemned under various pretexts, unfounded in Justice as well as the unexpected restrictions on American commerce, call loudly for corresponding measures of retaliation.

Be it further Resolved, That while they warmly approbate the spirit and tone of the President's late message to both houses of Congress, they pledge their lives, their fortunes and sacred honor, to support the government in whatever course it may in its wisdom adopt as best calculated to secure us from future wrongs, and indemnify us for past injuries, so long and so unjustly sustained.

Be it further Resolved, That a copy of the foregoing resolutions be transmitted to the President of the U. States; and the proceedings of this meeting be published in the Raleigh Register and Edenton Gazette.

Poindexter and Jacocks jointly signed the document. Jacocks transmitted it to the president under a cover letter dated November 26, 1811.[17]

The Bertie County Republicans unequivocally supported the president's position in dealing with Great Britain, while in Raleigh, the North Carolina legislature and the governor were moving to support the president and Congress in the national war measures. The first and foremost concern of the state lawmakers, however, was the inadequate defenses along North Carolina's seaboard. On Christmas Day, Gov. William Hawkins forwarded to President Madison a set of resolutions passed by the General Assembly on December 23 expressing the legislature's concern and conveying resolutions for action by the state's congressional delegation to seek funding from Congress for defending North Carolina's ports and harbors.

> Whereas the warlike attitude by Congress is calculated to awaken in the citizens of North Carolina, an anxious solicitude for their safety and protection: And whereas, from the extent of the territory, population, and trade of this State, she is entitled to rank among the most important States in the Union: And whereas, her seaport Towns are, to the agricultural interests of her citizens, of infinite importance; and are at present in a very defenceless situation.
>
> Resolved therefore, that our Senators in Congress be instructed, and our Representatives requested to use their exertions to obtain from Congress an appropriation of money commensurate with our right, and which may be in the power of Congress to grant, for the purpose of fortifying the ports and harbours within this State.[18]

The following day, Hawkins dispatched another communication to the president conveying resolutions of the General Assembly approved on December 19 in support of Madison's November 5 message to Congress. The governor wrote that the "sentiments [expressed in the message] are such as must gratify the feelings and advance the welfare of a Nation sensible of its rights and determined to maintain and defend its Sovereignty and Independence." Hawkins further conveyed the views of the legislature that "the evils which we have been compelled to endure for years past, have arisen wholly from the unprincipled conduct of the belligerent nations of Europe." Finally, he announced that "we will cheerfully co-operate with the General Government, in the prompt and effectual execution of such measures as may be deemed best calculated to promote the interest, and secure the Union, Liberty, and Independence of the United States."[19]

In the nation's capital, a minority faction of Republicans in Congress—known as the "War Hawks"—adamantly supported the movement of the United States toward a declaration of war against Great Britain. At least twenty-one members of Congress were sufficiently vocal in their pressure for war to be regarded as "War Hawks." This group included three North Carolina Republican congressmen—Representatives William Blackledge, William R. King, and Israel Pickens. Blackledge and King represented districts in the eastern section of the state.[20]

Within Congress, the Republicans, principally from the South and West, were clamoring for war with Great Britain, while the Federalists, primarily New Englanders, opposed the movement to war. However, the Federalists in their deliberations and positions were not as adamant and vocal against the war as the "War Hawks" and the other Republicans generally were in support of it. Even though significant antiwar sentiment

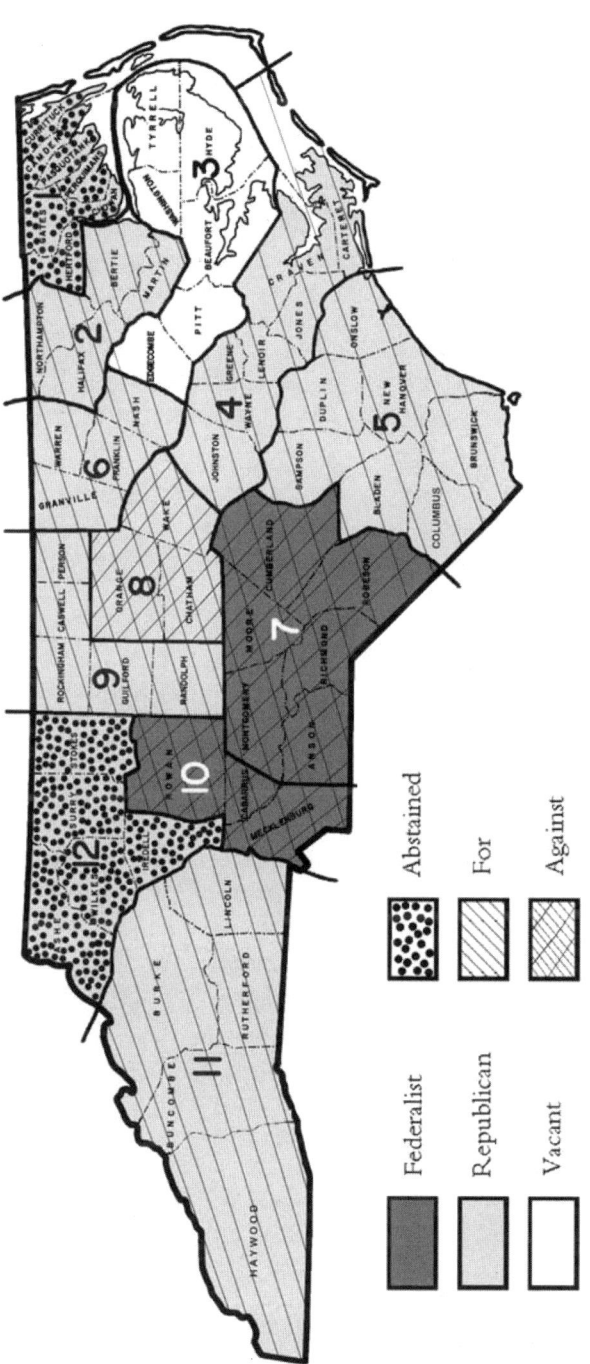

In late 1811 Congress began taking measures to prepare the country for war. At that time North Carolina was represented by eleven Republican and two Federalist legislators. Both of the state's senators were Republicans, as were nine of its representatives. One North Carolina seat in the House of Representatives—that of Thomas Blount (a Republican)—was vacant (Blount having died on February 7, 1812). Willis Alston, a Republican, represented the Second Congressional District (in which Bertie County was situated) and voted for war. The map shown above delineates the political affiliation of North Carolina's representatives to the House, by district, in June 1812. Map adapted from John L. Cheney Jr., ed. *North Carolina Government, 1585–1979: A Narrative and Statistical History* (Raleigh: Department of the Secretary of State, 1981), 666.

William R. King, at the age of twenty-five, was likely the youngest member of the "War Congress" and represented North Carolina's Fifth Congressional District. King, a dedicated Republican, was North Carolina's leading War Hawk and was staunchly supported by his constituents in eastern North Carolina. Image courtesy of the Library of Congress.

existed within the country, Federalist legislators offered only token resistance and actually voted in favor of some war measures. Overall, Congress supported President Madison and began taking defined measures to prepare the nation for hostilities.[21]

In order to prosecute a war against one of the world's most militarily powerful nations, the United States required a substantial army. Americans, in the early nineteenth century, held a deep-rooted fear of standing armies—one of Great Britain's legacies to the American nation. The colonists regarded every man as a trained, armed soldier who was prepared to respond to any emergency when called upon. As such, the colonists believed that there was no need for a professional standing army. As a result, in the fall of 1811 there existed in the youthful country a very small national army comprised of only ten "authorized" regiments of all types of service (infantry, artillery, and dragoons), numbering about 6,000 soldiers. Consequently, the nation relied extensively on the states' citizen soldiers, or militiamen, for defense.[22]

North Carolina law required that "all freemen and apprentices, citizens of this state or of the United States, residing in the state, who are or shall be of the age of eighteen years, and under forty-five years, shall . . . be severally and respectively enrolled in the militia of this state, by the captain or commanding officer of the company within the bounds of whose district . . . such citizen shall reside." Certain persons were exempted from militia duty, including judges and justices of the peace, county sheriffs, physicians and surgeons, ministers, postmasters, and customhouse officers.[23]

The population of militia-age white men in Bertie County in 1811 numbered about 1,000. According to the county's 1810 federal census, 2,415 "free white males" resided in the county, of which 987 were ages sixteen to forty-five years—roughly the age of required militia service in 1812. In total, more than 11,200 persons resided in the county in 1810, of whom more than 6,000 were slaves and thus not subject to militia duty.[24]

In accordance with a 1793 state law, the North Carolina militia was arranged into brigades and divisions. In the fall of 1811 the state's militia consisted of fifteen brigades organized into six divisions.[25] Within Bertie County, one regiment of militia existed, which according to the 1811 annual returns of the North Carolina Adjutant General's Office consisted of thirty-eight officers and 819 noncommissioned officers and privates. The regiment, along with regiments from Hertford, Washington, and Tyrrell counties, was assigned to the Thirteenth Brigade under the command of Brig. Gen. John Scott of Hertford County. The Thirteenth and First Brigades comprised the First Division, commanded by Maj. Gen. Thomas Wynns of Halifax County. The component regiments of the division were from northeastern North Carolina. According to returns, the division contained more than 5,000 citizen soldiers—slightly less than 10 percent of the state's total reported militiamen (50,860) in 1811.[26]

The military competency and readiness of the First Division, including the Bertie regiment, were highly suspect. Each regiment was required by state law to muster "at least" once during each year and to exercise agreeably to established rules of discipline for at least three hours during each muster. While complete records of the Bertie County regiment's musters do not exist, mustering once a year and conducting "discipline exercises" for less than half a day were hardly sufficient to train the men, primarily farm boys, and teach tactics to achieve a competent degree of military efficiency and readiness.[27] During 1811 General Wynns formally reviewed the regiments within the First Division and submitted his observations in his official annual return to North Carolina adjutant general Calvin Jones. Wynns noted that two officers, "teachers of Military tactics, have had schools, or were likely to have them in all Counties composing the first Division. Where these schools have been held many Officers and others, have acquired considerable information and were much improved. . . . But it is to be regretted that a great portion of the Militia are

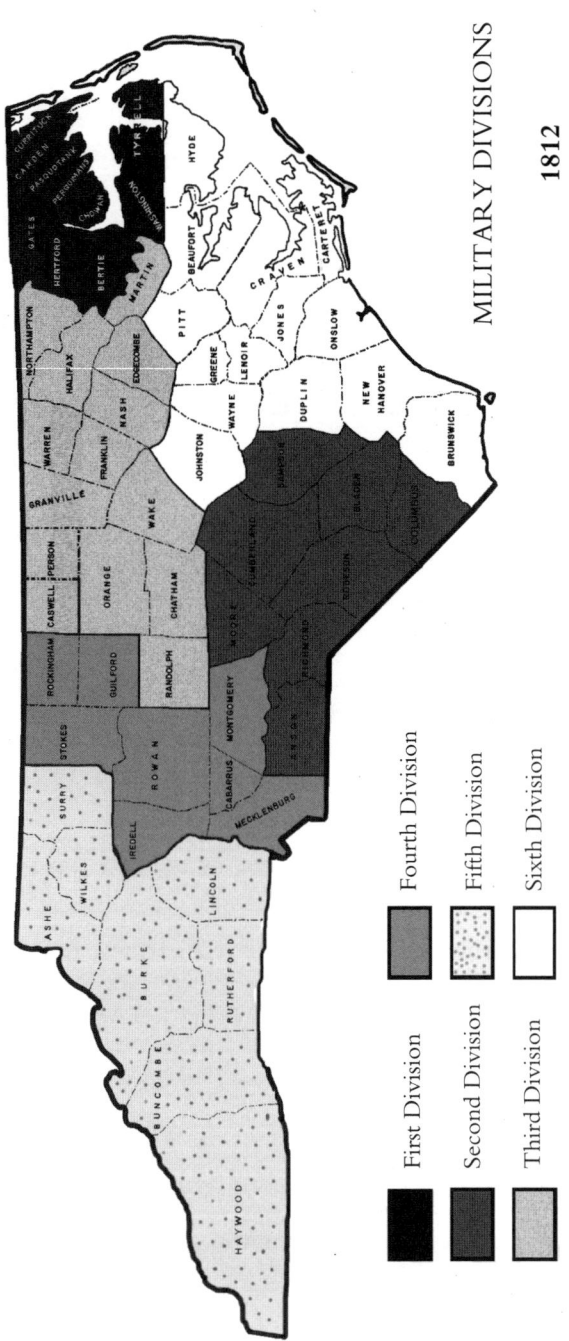

MILITARY DIVISIONS

1812

First Division

Second Division

Third Division

Fourth Division

Fifth Division

Sixth Division

In the fall of 1811, North Carolina's militia forces reportedly totaled almost 55,000 men. Across the state the overall militia organization was comprised of six divisions with fifteen constituent brigades. The Bertie County regiment belonged to the Thirteenth Brigade, First Division. The map shown above illustrates the geographic makeup of North Carolina's militia divisions on the eve of the War of 1812. Map adapted from Cheney, *North Carolina Government*, 670.

very deficient in discipline, which is to be ascribed chiefly to the defects of our Militia Code and the indiscreet adherence to the rule of promotion by seniority."[28]

During the summer of the previous year, the state's adjutant general had questioned the readiness of the Bertie regiment. Jones, accompanied by Generals Wynns and Scott, had reviewed the state's various brigades, including the Thirteenth, about which he had reported that the "Regiment of Bertie . . . is without discipline . . . rather inferior in order and appearance, [but] was in no ways behind in its zeal. Much is expected from the enterprising spirit of the newly appointed Colonel" [Jonathan Jacocks]. Jacocks, a prominent Bertie County planter and father of Jonathan H. Jacocks (participant in the November 20 Republican meeting in Windsor), had been appointed colonel of the Bertie County militia in December 1809.[29]

In addition to the questioned military competency of the members of the First Division, the troops' ability to carry out combat and military actions was severely constrained by a lack of arms. North Carolina law stipulated that every citizen enrolled in the militia was to "provide himself with a good musket, smooth-bored gun or firelock, or with a good rifle, shot-pouch, and powder-horn." Each militiaman was expressly responsible for keeping and preserving his "arms and accoutrements in good order, and in a soldierlike manner."[30] According to division returns, the constituent regiments reported only 3,831 weapons in the hands of the 5,805 militiamen in the fall of 1811—almost 34 percent of the men had no weapons.[31]

The Bertie regiment was likewise inadequately armed, both in numbers and the military quality of its weapons. The regiment's annual return indicated that more than one in five of the militiamen were without personal arms. According to the return, the regiment consisted of 38 officers and 777 staff—sergeants, corporals, and privates—a total of 815 men who would have been required, and expected, to carry arms. Nevertheless, the return reveals that the troops collectively possessed only 536 shotguns—a deficit of 279 weapons, or one for every three members of the regiment.[32] Furthermore, the weapons held by the regiment's members were inferior for military purposes—shotguns loaded with buckshot were effective only at extremely short ranges, hardly the type of weapon desirable in combat. But, to a Bertie County country boy, a shotgun was the most appropriate tool for taking game and "putting meat on the family's table," a more important consideration personally than contingent military duty.

The issue of sufficient military-grade arms for the North Carolina militia was not limited to the Bertie regiment and the First Division. On

December 30 Adjutant General Jones informed President Madison that the "militia of this state would afford good materials for an army" and that "[t]hey have the necessary talents, courage and patriotism but they are very defectively armed. Many are entirely destitute of arms, and of those [arms] reported a great proportion are totally unfit for service. I beg leave to express a wish that this situation of the militia in this respect may obtain the favorable notice of the General Government." Jones added his belief that it was "unquestionably true, that they [the state's militiamen] are ever devoted to their country's service."[33]

Furthermore, on January 12, 1812, Rep. Archibald McBryde of North Carolina's Seventh Congressional District wrote to Secretary of War William Eustis to request that the War Department allow "some arms at Fayetteville (North Carolina) belonging to the United States" to be used by a company of North Carolina militia. Three and one-half months later, Gov. William Hawkins likewise communicated with the secretary for the purpose of effecting "a loan of sufficient arms belonging to the United States deposited at Fayetteville" to arm two North Carolina companies. On May 6 Eustis responded to Hawkins and informed him that the superintendent of military stores at Fayetteville (J. Winslow) had been directed to deliver to the order of the governor "the number of arms necessary for the two companies." Hawkins, upon receiving that information from Eustis, wrote to Winslow and requested that "one hundred and thirty stand of those arms" be delivered to Maj. John Cameron of the North Carolina militia. By June 12 Winslow advised Secretary Eustis of the delivery of the arms and furnished a duplicate receipt for 130 muskets and bayonets.[34]

In April 1808 Congress had acted to begin arming state militias by passing a law that provided $200,000 annually for the manufacture and distribution of arms to those organizations. The arms were to be distributed and apportioned on the basis of the states' annual militia returns submitted to the War Department. One estimate indicated that perhaps less than one-third of the country's citizen soldiers were armed according to law. The funds appropriated annually by Congress for arming the state militias were preposterously insufficient—while as many as 700,000 militiamen were enrolled throughout the states and territories, the authorized funds were sufficient to procure only about 14,000 arms per year.[35] Furthermore, while about $800,000 had been appropriated to fund the purchase of militia arms from 1808 through 1811, one member of Congress, Benjamin Tallmadge of Connecticut, found that only $100,000 had actually been expended for arms and another $100,000 had lapsed (become unavailable

William Hawkins, elected governor by the North Carolina General Assembly in 1811, held the post throughout the War of 1812. Hawkins favored going to war with Great Britain and consistently supported President Madison's administration during the conflict. He strived to keep North Carolina's militiamen ready to march, even though they were often desperately short of necessary supplies and equipment. Image courtesy of the North Carolina State Archives, Office of Archives and History, Raleigh, N.C.

for expenditure) because it had not been drawn within the time specified by the law.[36] Clearly, the intent by Congress to place military-grade armaments in the hands of the country's militiamen was not being realized.[37]

In 1812 the North Carolina General Assembly passed a law stipulating that the arms actually received per the April 1808 federal statute were to be distributed to select counties in the eastern sector of the state. The Bertie County regiment and each of the other regiments comprising the First Division were designated to receive sixty-four stands of arms. The governor was responsible for ensuring that the weapons were "forthwith" delivered to the colonels commanding the specified regiments.[38] Col. Thomas Worley, who had succeeded Jonathan Jacocks as commander of the Bertie County militia, in April 1813 received fifty-two weapons, not the sixty-four the state legislators had authorized.[39]

Governor Hawkins, direly in need of arms for the state's militia, called upon the War Department to furnish weapons. On June 3 he wrote Secretary of War Eustis and requested 2,000 stands of arms. Eustis replied five days later, informing the governor that "measures will be taken to deposit two thousand stands of arms at Fort Johnston," near Wilmington. On June 24 Eustis directed Lt. John Erving at Fort Johnston to "deliver to the order" of Governor Hawkins 2,000 arms. That same day, the War Department shipped from Washington, D.C., to Fort Johnston the stated number of arms destined for the North Carolina militia. On June 28, while the shipment of arms from Washington was in transit, Erving wrote to Hawkins that there were at Fort Johnston 152 stands of arms subject to the governor's order.[40] Army-grade weapons would now be available to North Carolina's troops.

Even though the national militia system was the primary force to be relied upon to defend the country, deficiencies in the system were quite evident and clearly known to members of the Twelfth Congress. The state militias were not prepared to fight a war. Years of neglect by the states, or indifference on their part, had resulted in a military force that was not ready for the duties and rigors required during wartime. The problem was not a question of the militias' apparent willingness to fight but rather of their ability to fight. The state militias were simply not adequately trained, organized, and equipped to go to war. In addition to the issue of arms, the militias lacked other rudimentary items required of a military force—clothing/uniforms, camp equipment, tents, blankets, and other military stores.[41]

With war looming, North Carolina's legislature recognized that Congress had failed to provide for a uniform, reliable national militia. In December the legislators in Raleigh passed a resolution complaining that state militias were disciplined "according to the notions that prevail in different parts [of the country] . . . thereby tending to create disorder, rather than a uniformity of Discipline." The legislature instructed its representatives in Congress to work to establish "one detailed and general system . . . to make an improved uniform organization in Military tactics throughout the United States."[42] On December 30 Adjutant General Jones wrote to President Madison that the "discipline of our [North Carolina] militia is improving" but that it was "greatly retarded" by the "antiquated system" of military tactics in effect. Jones concluded that he was "gratified to see that a step has been taken in Congress which I believe is an advance towards a more perfect system of Modern Tactics."[43]

Rep. William Blackledge of North Carolina's Fourth Congressional District had already acted to move Congress to improve the country's military system—army and militia. On December 13, 1811, he introduced in the House of Representatives a resolution requesting President Madison to have prepared "a system of rules and regulations proper to be adopted for training and discipline the regular troops and militia of the United States." The House approved the resolution in revised form four days later and forwarded it to Secretary of War Eustis. On February 18, 1812, Eustis presented to President Madison for consideration "a system of field exercise and maneuvers of Infantry, adapted to the militia and regular troops of the United States, conformable to a resolution of the House of Representatives of 17 Decr 1811."[44]

While the basic tenet of national defense was predominantly rooted in the state militias, Congress well recognized that the country's regular army must be immediately and significantly expanded and enhanced.[45] On December 24, 1811, Congress passed an act to "immediately" complete the nation's existing military establishment. At that time the nation's army, as authorized by previous acts of Congress, consisted of ten regiments—seven of infantry, two of artillery, and one of dragoons.[46] Only eighteen days later, on January 11, 1812, Congress enacted a measure to expand the army, authorizing the raising of ten regiments of infantry, two of artillery, and one of light dragoons.[47]

By March 1812 the War Department was tendering dozens of officer appointments to men throughout the country to fill positions in the recently authorized regiments, or "New Army," as the units collectively were called. Various North Carolina men were tendered officer commissions at this time, primarily to fill vacancies in the Tenth Regiment United States Infantry—a newly authorized regiment to be recruited in North Carolina and Virginia. Secretary of War Eustis offered the colonelcy of the Tenth Regiment to James Wellborn of Wilkesboro. Wellborn was a former state senator and a brigadier general in the North Carolina militia commanding the Ninth Brigade. Wellborn accepted the appointment and on May 15 wrote to Governor Hawkins and resigned his generalship in the state militia.[48]

In March 1812, Rep. Willis Alston of North Carolina's Second Congressional District (which included Bertie County) nominated to the secretary of war William Speller Rhodes of Windsor to be a lieutenant in the Tenth Regiment. On May 12 Secretary Eustis wrote to Rhodes and offered him the position of first lieutenant in the Tenth. Five days later

William Eustis, a prominent Massachusetts politician, served as secretary of war from 1809 through the first six months of the War of 1812. In June 1812 fewer than 7,000 troops were scattered in garrisons across the state under Eustis's tutelage, despite Congress's overexuberant prewar plans to enlarge the army. Overwhelmed by his responsibilities and summarily criticized for the nation's lack of military preparedness, Eustis resigned in December 1812. Image courtesy of the Library of Congress.

Rhodes replied to Eustis and accepted the appointment, declaring "I feel a greate willingness to defend my country['s] cause."[49] Rhodes was the only Bertie County resident to be offered an officer's commission in the army immediately before and during the war.

In the early 1800s, commanders and officers of army regiments were charged with recruiting men to fill the ranks of their regiments; organizing the men into companies; and arming, equipping, and training the troops. While Colonel Wellborn was responsible for superintending the recruiting service for the Tenth Regiment, the War Department appointed him to superintend the overall recruiting service for the "New Army" regiments to be raised in North Carolina, South Carolina, and Georgia. This area— known as the "Southern States" and designated as Recruiting Department Number 2—fell under the command of Maj. Gen. Thomas Pinckney, whose headquarters were at Charleston. Therefore, since the War Department had made Wellborn responsible for recruiting in the three states, he became subordinate to Pinckney. Headquarters for the recruiting department were established at Columbia, South Carolina. Within North Carolina, recruiting rendezvous were established at Salisbury, Fayetteville, and Tarboro. Lt. Col. Benajah White of the Tenth Regiment oversaw the Tarboro location—the closest rendezvous to Bertie County.[50]

While the "War Congress" took a number of significant measures to increase and enhance the army, it was less receptive to passing similar measures for the navy. In early 1812 the nation's navy consisted of only 25 war vessels (10 frigates and 15 other vessels) and 170 gunboats. At that time, not all of the vessels and gunboats were war ready. The country's overall naval defenses were predicated on gunboats, prompting Secretary of the Navy Paul Hamilton to request Congress to authorize the navy to purchase or construct more than twenty warships. On March 5, 1812, the House of Representatives naval committee failed to approve Hamilton's requests for the purchase or construction of ten additional frigates and twelve 74-gun ships. On March 30 Congress authorized President Madison to "cause to be immediately repaired, equipped and put into service" three frigates—the *Chesapeake*, the *Constellation*, and the *Adams*. At that time the three ships were "laid up in ordinary reserve." Congress appropriated $300,000 for the navy to ready the three vessels for war.[51]

By the same statute, Congress directed that the "gun boats now in commission be laid up, and with those not in commission, be distributed in the several harbors of the maritime frontier which are most exposed to attack."[52] In the decade prior to 1812, the United States constructed some 174 gunboats, of which only 62 were in service in the spring of 1812. The gunboats, identified only by number, were narrow-built vessels forty to sixty feet in length and powered by oar and sail. The gunboat program originated with President Thomas Jefferson, a Republican, who with the support of Republican majorities in Congress had opposed a large navy of big ships. Jefferson and his supporters desired a naval force essentially limited to coastal defense.[53]

Gunboats, if properly deployed and utilized, were considered to be an effective means of naval defense for North Carolina's "maritime frontier." The eastern sector of the state is punctuated and indented by five sounds into which flow the major rivers of the Coastal Plain. The sounds— Albemarle, Currituck, Pamlico, Core, and Bogue—are relatively shallow waterways amenable to navigation and patrol by gunboats. In 1812 a shallow inlet through Currituck Banks—Currituck Inlet (closed by a storm in the 1820s)—provided access to Currituck Sound and the Elizabeth City region. Ocracoke Inlet was the primary ocean-access port for the state, followed by ports at Wilmington, Beaufort, and, to a much lesser extent, Swansboro. Gunboats strategically positioned at the inlets and ports, in conjunction with militia and/or army companies, presumably could protect the state's shipping interests and defend the waterways and inland port towns (such as New Bern, Washington, Plymouth, and Edenton) against British war vessels.

By the spring of 1812 Congress instituted measures to build up the army and to a lesser extent, the navy. It was imperative that the country's predominant defensive military force—the state militias—be readied for war. On April 10, 1812, Congress passed an act to authorize the president to require the executives of the states and territories to "take effectual measures to organize, arm and equip according to law, and hold in readiness to march at a moment's warning, their respective proportions of one hundred thousand militia, officers included."[54]

Five days after passage of the act, Secretary of War Eustis wrote to Governor Hawkins and informed him that North Carolina's quota of the 100,000 militia was 7,000 troops. Eustis advised the governor that the state's share of troops should be organized and readied "within the shortest period that circumstances will permit."[55] Governor Hawkins replied to the secretary on April 24, assuring him that he (Hawkins) would give the necessary orders "to cause the requisition to be complied with, and . . . to have the quota to be raised by this State in readiness, well organized and in a situation to be useful when their services are required in the field."[56]

On April 27 Hawkins ordered Adjutant General Jones to "proceed without delay to distribute the necessary orders" to cause the requested requisition to be made "as speedily as possible."[57] Two days later Jones issued general orders to the state's militia commanders stipulating that North Carolina's 7,000-man quota was to be detached from the state's militia, organized, armed, equipped, and held in readiness to march "at a moment's warning." He charged the state's fifteen brigadier generals to furnish their defined quota of troops and organize them into companies and regiments. Jones further ordered that eight regiments be organized across the state, of which one regiment was to be detached from the First and Thirteenth Brigades (First Division). The Thirteenth Brigade, including the Bertie County regiment, was to furnish 296 troops.[58] Brigadier General Scott ordered Col. Thomas Worley, commandant of the Bertie County regiment, to furnish one company of troops for the state's "detached militia."[59]

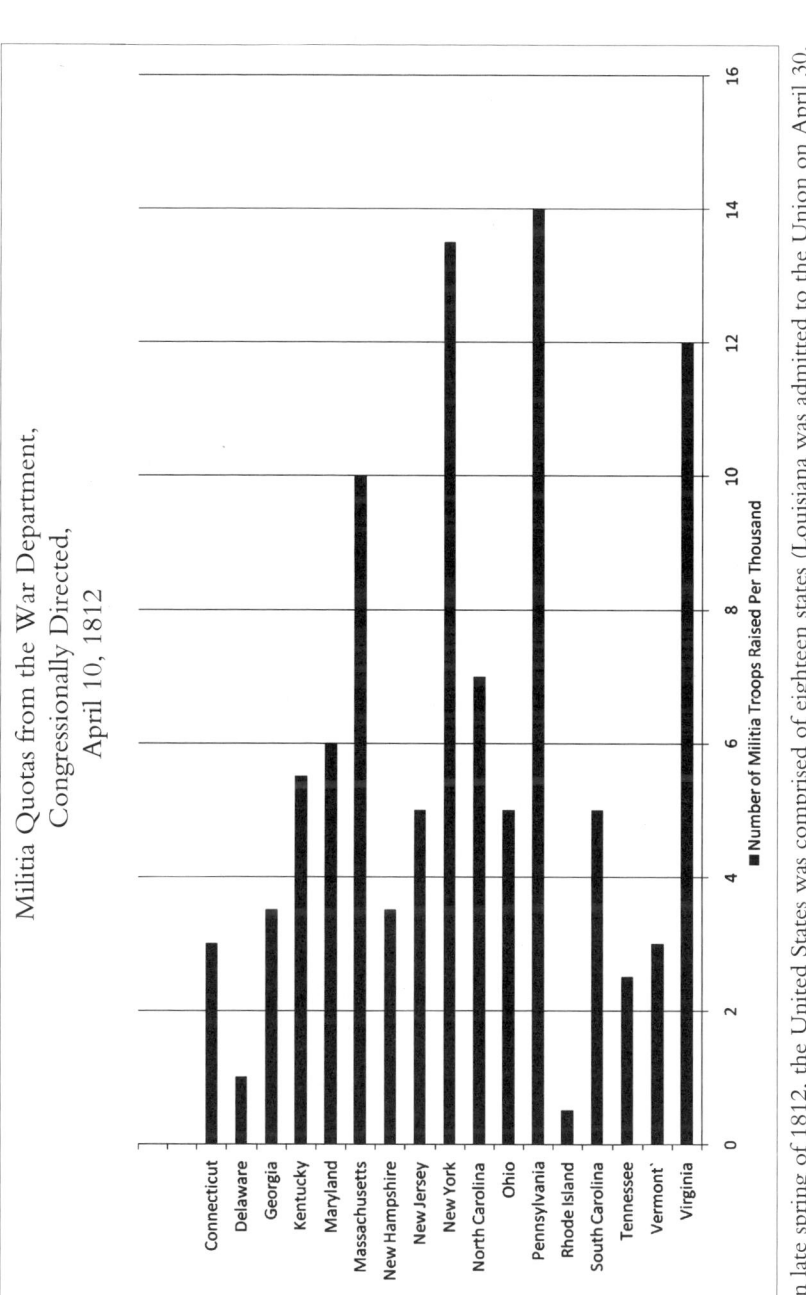

Militia Quotas from the War Department, Congressionally Directed, April 10, 1812

■ Number of Militia Troops Raised Per Thousand

In late spring of 1812, the United States was comprised of eighteen states (Louisiana was admitted to the Union on April 30, 1812) and five territories. On April 10, 1812, Congress directed that 100,000 militiamen be raised in the states and territories and placed in a state of readiness to march when called upon. The graph shown above depicts the states and the number of militiamen requested by the War Department to be raised from each, pursuant to Congress's mandate. Data obtained from *United States Statutes at Large* 2 (1845): 705–706.

On April 30 Jones informed Hawkins that he had "proceeded without delay" to prepare general orders to the state's brigadier and major generals to organize North Carolina's detached militia. In total, the detachment was to be comprised of 5,920 infantrymen, 350 artillerymen, 350 cavalrymen, and 380 riflemen.[60] Across the state, militia commanders began mustering their troops and organizing their designated portions of the state's quota of detached militia.

The Bertie County militia regiment consisted of eighteen companies under the command of Thomas Worley, who was appointed colonel by the state General Assembly on December 18, 1811. (Worley succeeded Col. Jonathan Jacocks, who had died a year earlier.) William Watford and Joel Hyman served as majors of the regiment. Upon receipt of the orders to organize a company of the county's militia from the regiment, these three officers mustered the troops in Windsor and effectuated the detachment. They initially sought volunteers to form the company, but, to the extent that a sufficient number of such recruits was not attained, subsequently "drafted" men into the regiment to complete the company. Joseph Hunter Bryan was designated captain; Augustin Pugh, lieutenant; and Joel Hyman, ensign. The company contained 108 members, including the three officers, and was one of five companies placed in the artillery service of the state's quota of detached militia.[61] The Bertie County "patriots" stood ready to serve their country in whatever manner that might be ordered.

As the spring of 1812 progressed, the United States continued to ready its war posture. Diplomatically, the nation was reaching a "breaking point" in its tumultuous relationship with Great Britain. In Washington, congressional deliberations intensified on the issue of going to war. On May 21 North Carolina "War Hawk" congressman William Blackledge wrote to Secretary of the Navy Paul Hamilton that "[t]he push is now [at] hand when I hope the Declaration of War is to be brought before Congress."[62] War seemed inevitable—just a matter of time.

On June 1 President Madison sent his war message to Congress. He recounted in summary form the principal incidents of British aggression and interference with American affairs that had transpired for almost a decade: impressments; interference with commerce and neutral trade; blockades of American ports and coastline; violations of neutral rights; and hostile actions. He concluded: "Whether the United States shall continue passive under these progressive usurpations and these accumulating wrongs, or, opposing force to force in defense of their national rights, shall commit a just cause into the hands of the Almighty Disposer of Events." The decision of whether or not to go to war was to be ultimately decided by Congress, a decision that the Constitution "so confides" to that legislative body.[63]

On June 4 the House of Representatives voted 79 to 49 for war. Six North Carolina representatives—Willis Alston, William Blackledge, James Cochran, William R. King, Nathaniel Macon, and Israel Pickens (all Republicans)—voted for war. Three of the state's congressmen—Archibald McBryde and Joseph Pearson (both Federalists), and Richard Stanford (Republican)—voted against war, and two—Lemuel Sawyer and Meshack Franklin (both Republicans)—abstained.[64]

On June 17 the Senate voted 19 to 13 for war. Both North Carolina Republican senators—Jesse Franklin and James Turner—voted in the majority.[65] The following day the United States formally declared war against Great Britain (and Ireland and their dependencies):

Be it enacted by the Senate and House of Representatives of the United States of America in Congress assembled, That war be and the same is hereby declared to exist between the United Kingdom of Great Britain and Ireland and the dependencies thereof, and the United States of America and their territories; and that the President of the United States is hereby authorized to use the whole land and naval force of the United States to carry the same into effect, and to issue to private armed vessels of the United States commissions or letters of marque and general reprisal, in such form as he shall think proper, and under the seal of the United States, against vessels, goods, and effects of the government of the said United Kingdom of Great Britain of and Ireland, and the subjects thereof.

Approved by Pres. James Madison, June 18, 1812.[66]

The nation's central leadership had declared war against the most formidable military power in the world. The American nation's existence and sovereignty were now at stake.

Notes

1. The Democratic-Republican Party was founded by Thomas Jefferson and James Madison in the early 1790s. Members commonly referred to themselves as "Republicans." Hereafter, the author will similarly use that term to refer to the party and its members. The Republican Party was dominant in the United States from 1800 to 1824. The party's elected presidents were Thomas Jefferson (elected in 1800 and 1804), James Madison (1808 and 1812), and James Monroe (1816 and 1820). The opposition Federalist Party controlled the federal government until 1801. Its only elected president was John Adams (1796). The Federalists continued to oppose Republican policies as the appeal of their party declined. The party broke up in 1816. Sarah J. Purcell, *The Early National Period: An Eyewitness History* (New York: Facts on File, Inc., 2004 by author), 79, 81, 88, 109–110, 151, 230, 239, 278, 336–337, 345, 348–349; David S. Heidler and Jeanne T. Heidler, eds., *Encyclopedia of the War of 1812* (Annapolis: Naval Institute Press, 1997), 318; Gordon S. Wood, *Empire of Liberty: A History of the Early Republic, 1789–1815* (Oxford: Oxford University Press, 2009), 312–313.

2. Raymond Parker Fouts, *Abstracts from the* Edenton Gazette and North Carolina General Advertiser, *Edenton, North Carolina*, 3 vols. (Cocoa, Fla.: GenRec Books, 1993), 2:107 (hereafter cited as Fouts, *Abstracts from the* Edenton Gazette); J. C. A. Stagg et al., eds., *The Papers of James Madison: Presidential Series*, 6 vols. to date (Charlottesville: University of Virginia Press, 1999), 4:36–37 (hereafter cited as *James Madison Presidential Papers*). Numerous scholarly histories and accounts of the War of 1812 present and discuss the various causes that led to the conflict. The author's purpose is not to expound upon the causes in totality or detail but to summarize the more important and galvanizing events and present a brief timeline of their occurrences in relation to contemporaneous events transpiring in Bertie County. See David S. Heidler and Jeanne T. Heidler, *The War of 1812* (Westport, Conn.: Greenwood Press, 2002), xvii–xviii, 1–5; Donald R. Hickey, *The War of 1812: A Short History* (Urbana: University of Illinois Press, 1995), 1–8; Heidler and Heidler, *Encyclopedia of the War of 1812*, 587–590.

3. Peace negotiations began in Paris in April 1782. The parties concluded a preliminary peace treaty on November 30, 1782; the accord was to become effective once Great Britain reached agreements with its other enemies. The United States Congress ratified the preliminary peace treaty on April 15, 1783. American peace commissioners Benjamin Franklin, John Jay, and John Adams signed the final treaty on September 3, ending the American Revolution. Alan Axelrod, *The Real History of the American Revolution: A New Look at the Past* (New York: Sterling Publishing Co., 2007), 344–347.

4. Great Britain and France had faced each other in war during the 1790s. Napoleon I led the French armies, and peace had come between the two countries in 1802. However, Napoleon's expansionist policies led the British to renew the war with France on May 16, 1803. Heidler and Heidler, *Encyclopedia of the War of 1812*, 368–369.

5. Hickey, *The War of 1812*, 12; Heidler and Heidler, *Encyclopedia of the War of 1812*, 252; Anthony S. Pitch, *The Burning of Washington: The British Invasion of 1814* (Annapolis: Naval Institute Press, 1998), 12. The precise number of North Carolina seamen impressed by the British navy cannot be ascertained by existing records. An act passed by

Congress on May 28, 1796, authorized the president to appoint agents at foreign ports who were to "inquire into the situation of such American citizens or others, sailing conformably to the law of nations, under the protection of the American flag [who are] impressed or detained by any foreign power [and] to endeavour, by all legal means, to obtain the release of such American citizens, or others." On March 2, 1799, another act required the secretary of state to submit to Congress an annual statement containing an abstract of records received on impressments. Records generated by the Department of State as a result of the two laws indicate that significant numbers of impressed seamen were registered between 1796 and 1814 by the department's collectors of customs at the ports of Edenton, New Bern, Washington, and Wilmington. *United States Statutes at Large* 1 (1845): 477–478, 732–732; Miscellaneous Lists and Papers Regarding Impressed Seamen, 1796–1814 (microfilm, M1839), Record Group 59, National Archives, Washington, D.C.; Registers of Applications for the Release of Impressed Seamen, 1793–1802, and Related Indexes (microfilm, M2025), Record Group 59, National Archives.

6. Heidler and Heidler, *Encyclopedia of the War of 1812*, 96–97; Hickey, *The War of 1812*, 8.

7. *Raleigh Register and North Carolina Weekly Advertiser*, August 6, 1807; Report of Meeting of the Citizens of Bertie County, July 20, 1807, Nathaniel Alexander, Governors Letter Books, State Archives, Office of Archives and History, Raleigh. Those who attended the meeting likewise resolved that the report be transmitted to the "Committee of Norfolk." The author was unable to locate any records of, or correspondence with, such a body. In response to the British attack, President Jefferson assembled his cabinet to discuss and consider actions to be taken by the United States. Jefferson left the question of war to deliberation by Congress. The president, through Secretary of War Henry Dearborn, requested Gov. William H. Cabell of Virginia to organize and "put in readiness for service at the shortest warning" 100,000 members of that state's militia. Gunboats and fortifications about Norfolk were placed on alert and readied for action. In retaliation, citizens of Norfolk destroyed British naval property. In August, British officials in London finally conceded that the attack was a mistake. War was averted, but many Americans and naval officers yearned for revenge. President Thomas Jefferson to Gen. Henry Dearborn and Albert Gallatin, June 25, 1807; Jefferson to Gov. William H. Cabell, June 29 and July 8, 1807; Jefferson to Vice-Pres. George Clinton, July 6, 1807; Jefferson to Dearborn, July 7, 1807; Jefferson to Naval Officers at the Ports of Norfolk and Portsmouth, Virginia, July 8, 1807; Jefferson to Capt. J. Saunders, Fort Nelson (Norfolk), July 8, 1807; and Jefferson to General Matthews, Virginia Militia, July 8, 1807, all in Albert Ellery Bergh, ed., *The Writings of Thomas Jefferson, Memorial Edition*, 20 vols. (Washington, D.C.: Thomas Jefferson Memorial Association, 1904), 11:255–267; Heidler and Heidler, *Encyclopedia of the War of 1812*, 96–97.

8. Heidler and Heidler, *Encyclopedia of the War of 1812*, 394–395; Hickey, *The War of 1812*, 8.

9. *United States Statutes at Large* 2 (1845): 497; *Washington* (D.C.) *Expositor*, May 21, 1808; Correspondence of the Secretary of the Treasury with Collectors of Customs, 1789–1833 (microfilm, M178), Record Group 36, National Archives; Excerpt from

The Windsor Story—1768–1968, by Harry L. Thompson, online publication by the Windsor Bicentennial Commission, Bertie County NCGenWeb Project Page, www.rootsweb.ancestry.com/~ncbertie/windsor.htm; Record Group 36 Finding Aid, page 145, National Archives.

10. Heidler and Heidler, *Encyclopedia of the War of 1812*, 587; Hickey, *The War of 1812*, 8.

11. Hickey, *The War of 1812*, 9.

12. James H. Broussard, *The Southern Federalists, 1800–1816* (Baton Rouge and London: Louisiana State University Press, 1978), 123. The Albemarle Sound region in northeast North Carolina was a fertile agricultural basin; planters and farmers generally disposed of their surplus agricultural produce in Virginia, principally through the port of Norfolk. See Delbert Harold Gilpatrick, *Jeffersonian Democracy in North Carolina, 1789–1816* (New York: Octagon Books, 1967), 181–182.

13. Hickey, *The War of 1812,* 9.

14. President Madison had called for the special session of Congress on July 24, 1811, specifically to prepare for war with Great Britain. Pitch, *The Burning of Washington*, 13; *James Madison Presidential Papers*, 3:392–393.

15. Madison's "Annual Message to Congress," November 5, 1811, *James Madison Presidential Papers*, 4:1–5.

16. Fouts, *Abstracts from the* Edenton Gazette (see the three volumes generally); see also weekly editions of the *Raleigh Register and North Carolina Gazette*, and the *Raleigh Minerva* published throughout the war. Those papers, as well as other North Carolina journals, were dependent upon the delivery of mail, primarily from northern cities (where war activities were most prevalent), to receive papers with relevant war-related articles for reprint. Naturally, the length of time required for the papers printed "up north" to reach editors in various North Carolina towns often delayed the timely reporting of fresh news. Reporting delays became even more pronounced when interruptions occurred in the mail system.

17. Fouts, *Abstracts from the* Edenton Gazette, 2:107–108; *James Madison Presidential Papers*, 4:36–37. Richard Poindexter was an influential Baptist minister from the western section of the county. Jonathan H. Jacocks, a planter, was an officer in the Bertie County militia and son of the county's former militia colonel, Jonathan Jacocks (who died in December 1810). Whitmell Hill Pugh was a physician and planter who later represented Bertie County in the North Carolina House of Commons in 1813, 1814, and 1815. Joseph Hunter Bryan, an affluent planter, had served in the House of Commons in 1804, 1805, and 1807–1809 and at the time of the subject meeting was a trustee of the University of North Carolina. In 1810 Bryan was defeated in his attempt to gain the Halifax District seat in Congress from the incumbent, Willis Alston. He later served two terms in Congress—from March 1815 to March 1819. James W. Warburton, James Palmer, Jonathan R. Leggett, and John Webb were planters. The author has found no record that President Madison replied to Poindexter and/or Jacocks. Bertie County deed indexes and deeds for cited individuals, Bertie County Register of Deeds Office, Windsor; Jonathan Jacocks's will (Book F, page 181), proved February 1811, Bertie County Office of the Clerk of Court, Windsor; John E. Tyler, "Sandy Run

Baptist Church, Roxobel—A History in Recognition of its Bicentennial, 1759–1950" (Roxobel, N.C.: the author, 1950); John H. Wheeler, *Historical Sketches of North Carolina from 1584 to 1851*, 2 vols. (Philadelphia: Lippincott, Grambo and Co., 1851), 2:34; William S. Powell, ed., *Dictionary of North Carolina Biography*, s.v. "Joseph Hunter Bryan," "Whitmell Hill Pugh."

18. Hawkins to Madison, December 25, 1811, Miscellaneous Letters Received by the Secretary of the Navy, 1801–1884 (microfilm, M124), Record Group 45, National Archives (hereafter cited as Secretary of the Navy—Miscellaneous Letters Received); *James Madison Presidential Papers,* 4:91. The state's principal ports were Ocracoke Inlet, Beaufort, Wilmington/Cape Fear River, and Swansboro. At the time, an inlet (Currituck Inlet) existed through the northern barrier island into Currituck Sound, through which light-draft vessels could navigate, providing access to Elizabeth City. Currituck Inlet was closed by a storm in the 1820s. William S. Powell and Michael Hill, *The North Carolina Gazetteer*, 2nd ed. (Chapel Hill: University of North Carolina Press, 2010), 140.

19. Hawkins to Madison, December 26, 1811, *James Madison Presidential Papers*, 4:92.

20. Heidler and Heidler, *Encyclopedia of the War of 1812*, 541–542. William Blackledge represented the Fourth Congressional District, King the Fifth, and Pickens the Eleventh. Bertie County was situated in the Second Congressional District, represented by Willis Alston—a Republican.

21. Hickey, *The War of 1812*, 11. In 1811 the nation consisted of seventeen states: Delaware, Pennsylvania, New Jersey, Georgia, Connecticut, Massachusetts, Maryland, South Carolina, New Hampshire, Virginia, New York, North Carolina, Rhode Island, Vermont, Kentucky, Tennessee, and Ohio. Territories of the United States included the Mississippi Territory (1798–1817), the Indiana Territory (1800–1816), the Orleans Territory (1804–1812, which became the state of Louisiana and entered the Union in April 1812), the Michigan Territory (1805–1837), the Louisiana Territory (1805–1812, renamed the Missouri Territory (1812–1821), and the Illinois Territory (1809–1818). *The World Book Encyclopedia* (2000 edition), s.v. "Connecticut," "Delaware," "Georgia," "Illinois," "Indiana," "Kentucky," "Louisiana," "Maryland," "Massachusetts," "Michigan," "Mississippi," "Missouri," "New Hampshire," "New Jersey," "New York," "North Carolina," "Ohio," "Pennsylvania," "Rhode Island," "South Carolina," "Tennessee," "United States," "Vermont," "Virginia."

22. C. Edward Skeen, *Citizen Soldiers in the War of 1812* (Lexington: University of Kentucky Press, 1999), 4. On April 12, 1808, Congress had authorized the raising of five regiments of infantry, one regiment of riflemen, one regiment of light infantry, and one regiment of light dragoons (eight regiments in total), in addition to the two regiments that had existed under the "military peace establishment" since 1802. The provisions of the April 1808 act were not completely executed, however. Therefore, while ten army regiments had been "authorized," ten complete regiments had not been raised and placed in the field by the fall of 1811. Adam Seybert, *Statistical Views of the United States of America* (Philadelphia: Thomas Dobson & Son, 1818; New York: Augustus M. Kelley, Publishers, 1970), 560–561; Francis B. Heitman, *Historical Register and Dictionary of the United States Army*, 2 vols. (Washington: Government Printing Office, 1903), 1:81–102.

23. *Laws of the State of North Carolina*, 2 vols. (Raleigh: J. Gales, 1821), 2:1074–1075 (hereafter cited as *North Carolina Laws*).

24. Third Census of the United States, 1810: Bertie County, North Carolina, Population Schedule, National Archives.

25. *North Carolina Laws*, 1:701.

26. The First Brigade, commanded by Brig. Gen. Jeremiah Brite, consisted of militia regiments from Currituck, Camden, Perquimans, Gates, Pasquotank, and Chowan counties. On November 28, 1811, Adj. Gen. Calvin Jones reported to the North Carolina General Assembly that 50,860 militiamen comprised the state's regiments of infantry, per returns received in the Adjutant General's Office (AGO). However, not every county commander had submitted an annual return at the time of Jones's report. According to certain AGO records, approximately 55,000 men comprised North Carolina's militia in 1811. Adjutant General Letters, Orders, Returns: 1807–1812 (AG-1), Records of the Adjutant General's Office, State Archives, Office of Archives and History, Raleigh (hereafter cited as Adjutant General Letters, Orders, and Returns); Adjutant General Militia Returns, Orders of Officers, 1811–1813 (AG-2), Records of the Adjutant General's Office, State Archives, Office of Archives and History (hereafter cited as Adjutant General Militia Returns and Orders); *North Carolina Laws*, 2:1123.

27. *North Carolina Laws*, 2:1078.

28. Adjutant General Militia Returns and Orders.

29. Fouts, *Abstracts from the* Edenton Gazette, 2:27. Colonel Jacocks died on December 2, 1810.

30. *North Carolina Laws*, 2:1075, 1231.

31. Adjutant General Militia Returns and Orders.

32. Adjutant General Letters, Orders, and Returns; Adjutant General Militia Returns and Orders. By law, each North Carolina militia regiment was required to submit an annual return to the brigadier general commanding the brigade to which the regiment belonged before October 25. *North Carolina Laws*, 2:1083.

33. Jones to Madison, December 30, 1811, *James Madison Presidential Papers*, 4:107.

34. McBryde to Eustis, January 12, 1812, Letters Received by the Secretary of War, Unregistered Series, 1789–1861 (microfilm, M222), Record Group 107, National Archives (hereafter cited as Secretary of War—Letters Received [unregistered]); Hawkins to Eustis, April 26, 1812; Eustis to Hawkins, May 6, 1812; Hawkins to Superintendent of Military Stores [J. Winslow], Fayetteville, May 15, 1812, William Hawkins, Governors Letter Books, State Archives, Office of Archives and History (hereafter cited as Hawkins Letter Books). Winslow to Eustis, June 12, 1812, Letters Received by the Secretary of War, Main Series, 1801–1870 (microfilm, M221), Record Group 107, National Archives (hereafter cited as Secretary of War—Letters Received).

35. *United States Statutes at Large* 2 (1845): 490; Skeen, *Citizen Soldiers in the War of 1812*, 12.

36. Skeen, *Citizen Soldiers in the War of 1812*, 24.

37. The army's standard weapon of issue during the war was a .69 caliber smooth-bore musket. This was a muzzle-loaded flintlock that fired a soft lead ball weighing about an ounce. Its effective range was less than 100 yards. See www.visit1812.com/history/USMusket.html.

38. *North Carolina Laws*, 2:1229–1230. The 1812 session of the General Assembly met from November 16 until December 25, 1812.

39. Worley to Hawkins, April 13, 1813, Hawkins Letter Books.

40. Eustis to Hawkins, June 8, 1812; Eustis to Erving, June 24, 1812; Eustis to Hawkins, June 26, 1812; Erving to Hawkins, June 28, 1812, Hawkins Letter Books. The 2,000 arms sent by the War Department to Fort Johnston appear to be in addition to 1,600 weapons sent earlier. On June 15, 1812, Acting Inspector General Alexander Smyth informed Maj. Gen. Thomas Pinckney that 1,600 stands of arms had been forwarded to Fort Johnston. Smyth to Pinckney, June 15, 1812, Letters Sent by the Office of the Adjutant General, Main Series, 1800–1890 (microfilm, M565) Record Group 94, National Archives (hereafter cited as Adjutant General—Letters Sent).

41. Skeen, *Citizen Soldiers in the War of 1812*, 2.

42. Skeen, *Citizen Soldiers in the War of 1812*, 17.

43. Jones to Madison, December 30, 1811, Secretary of War—Letters Received; *James Madison Presidential Papers*, 4:107.

44. *James Madison Presidential Papers*, 4:189. See note 1 at bottom of page.

45. A February 28, 1795, law authorized the president to call forth militia of the states to repel invasions, enforce and execute the laws of the Union, and suppress insurrections. The militia "employed in the service of the United States" was to "be subject to the same rules and articles of war, as the troops [army] of the United States." *United States Statutes at Large* 1 (1845): 424.

46. Col. William H. Powell, U.S. Army, *List of Officers in the Army of the United States from 1779 to 1900* (New York: L. R. Hamersly & Co., 1900), 51–65 (hereafter cited as Powell, *List of Army Officers*); Seybert, *Statistical Views of the United States*, 561; Maj. Gen. Thomas Pinckney to Adj. Gen. Thomas Cushing, September 23, 1812, Letters Received by the Office of the Adjutant General, 1805–1821 (microfilm, M566), Record Group 94, National Archives (hereafter cited as Adjutant General—Letters Received).

47. *United States Statutes at Large* 2 (1845): 669–671.

48. Wellborn to Hawkins, May 15, 1812, Hawkins Letter Books; Powell, *List of Army Officers*, 59; Charles K. Gardner, *A Dictionary of All Officers Who Have Been Commissioned or Have Been Approved in the Army of the United States, 1789–1853* (New York: G. P. Putnam and Company, 1853), s.v. "Wellborn, James," and other persons as noted throughout this book (hereafter cited as Gardner, *Dictionary of Army Officers*). This document lists thousands of officers alphabetically. The author reviewed the document to identify the states of residency and dates of officer appointments for the Tenth Regiment United States Infantry and other regiments as warranted by his research.

49. Alston to Eustis, March 11, 1812, Secretary of War—Letters Received; Rhodes to Eustis, May 17, 1812, Adjutant General—Letters Received. Alston nominated Rhodes in place of William Mears, who declined the officer appointment.

50. Pinckney to Eustis, April 11, 1812; Eustis to Pinckney, April 29, 1812; Col. James Wellborn to Adjutant General, May 23, 1812; Wellborn to Col. Alexander Smyth, Acting Inspector General, June 4 and 13, 1812, Adjutant General—Letters Received;

Pinckney to Eustis, May 18, 1812; Rep. William Blackledge to Eustis, September 5, 1812, Secretary of War—Letters Received; Smyth to Wellborn, June 25, 1812, Adjutant General—Letters Sent; General Orders, Adjutant General's Office, War Department, July 4, 1812, General Orders and Circulars of the War Department and Headquarters of the Army, 1809–1860 (microfilm, M1094), Record Group 94, National Archives (hereafter cited as War Department General Orders and Circulars).

51. *United States Statutes at Large* 2 (1845): 699; Seybert, *Statistical Views of the United States*, 647.

52. *United States Statutes at Large* 2 (1845): 699.

53. Heidler and Heidler, *Encyclopedia of the War of 1812*, 218.

54. *United States Statutes at Large* 2 (1845): 705–706.

55. Eustis to Hawkins, April 15, 1812, Hawkins Letter Books; Letters Sent by the Secretary of War Relating to Military Affairs, 1800–1889 (microfilm, M6), Record Group 107, National Archives (hereafter cited as Secretary of War—Letters Sent).

56. Hawkins to Eustis, April 24, 1812, Secretary of War—Letters Received.

57. Hawkins to Adj. Gen. Calvin Jones, April 27, 1812, Hawkins Letter Books; Adjutant General Militia Returns and Orders.

58. General Orders, Adjutant General, Raleigh, April 29, 1812, Hawkins Letter Books.

59. The Adjutant General records do not contain an explicit order from the brigadier general of the Thirteenth Brigade to Colonel Worley of the Bertie regiment. Nevertheless, the author concluded that such an order was issued inasmuch as Worley, consistent with the overall order issued by Adjutant General Jones, organized a detachment of the county's militia for potential United States service.

60. Jones to Hawkins, April 30, 1812, Hawkins Letter Books.

61. *Muster Rolls of the Soldiers of the War of 1812 Detached from the Militia of North Carolina, in 1812 and 1814* (Raleigh: Ch. C. Raboteau, 1851; Winston-Salem: Barber Printing Company, 1926), 65 (hereafter cited as *Muster Rolls of North Carolina's Detached Militia*); Adjutant General Militia Returns and Orders. The four other companies in the artillery service of the 1812 detached militia were from Wake, Edgecombe, Carteret, and Brunswick counties. *Muster Rolls of North Carolina's Detached Militia*, 63–64, 66.

62. Blackledge to Hamilton, May 21, 1812, Secretary of the Navy—Miscellaneous Letters Received.

63. *James Madison Presidential Papers*, 4:432–438.

64. Heidler and Heidler, *Encyclopedia of the War of 1812*, 571–574, 588. One congressional seat for North Carolina—that of Thomas Blount, who had died in February 1812—was vacant at the time of the vote. The seat was subsequently filled by William Kennedy in 1813.

65. Heidler and Heidler, *Encyclopedia of the War of 1812*, 571–574; Hickey, *The War of 1812*, 16.

66. *United States Statutes at Large* 2 (1845): 755.

Defense of the "Maritime Frontier"

News of the declaration of war against Great Britain reached the residents of Bertie County on June 25. That morning the editors of the *Edenton Gazette* produced an "Extra" of the paper containing the declaration. The paper was immediately distributed to regular subscribers to the journal, including persons residing in Bertie County.[1] With the nation at war, the security and well-being of the county and the remainder of eastern North Carolina rested on the defenses employed by the central government in Washington, D.C., and state leaders in Raleigh to protect the coastal and inland waterways of the state. Any British incursions and raids into the eastern section of the state would be launched from warships arriving along the coast rather than ground troops marching overland.

Bertie County is situated at the confluence of three of North Carolina's most important waterways—the Albemarle Sound and the Chowan and Roanoke rivers. Its location along those waterways, particularly its position at the head of Albemarle Sound, seemingly exposed the county to potential raids and depredations by British forces. In actuality, however, such exposure was hardly a cause for significant alarm among the county's residents, given the "higher-value" economic targets of the port towns along the coast—Ocracoke, Beaufort, and Wilmington—and the inland ports of Washington, New Bern, Edenton, and Plymouth. Indeed, state and local officials considered Edenton, New Bern, and Wilmington very plausible targets because of the presence of banking establishments within these towns. Nevertheless, the common factor that made those locations, and even Bertie County, vulnerable to being visited by British warriors was the network of interconnecting waterways that would provide enemy vessels access should they breach the barrier islands and enter the inland sounds of the state. For residents of coastal eastern North Carolina, the war, should the British bring it to that region, would be one of defensive measures at the state's strategic inlets and ports.

North Carolina officials were naturally concerned over the exposure and vulnerability of the eastern section of the state to British raids and depredation. Indeed, in December 1811 the governor and state's legislature had discussed their concerns with the president as they sought funding from Congress to augment and enhance coastal defenses. During the period of

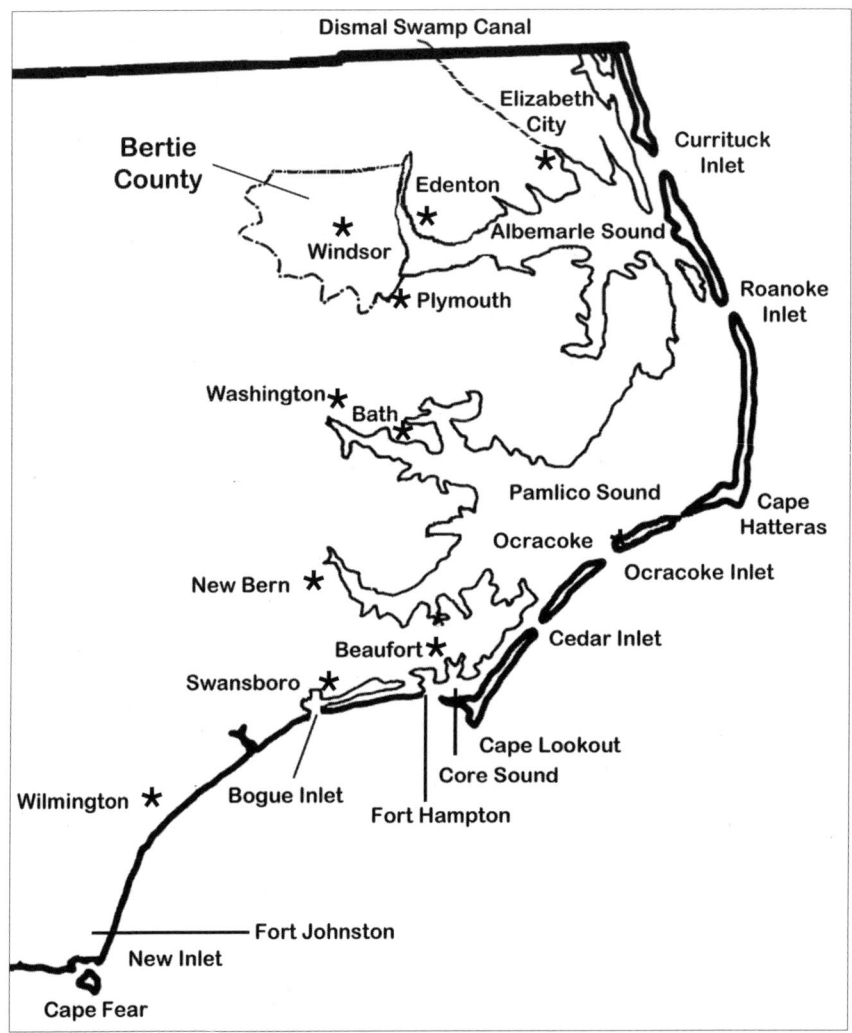

North Carolina's vast coastal region and its resulting exposure to potential raids and incursions by British military forces prompted Governor Hawkins and other state officials to move to bolster defenses in the region. The port communities of Wilmington, Beaufort, Swansboro, and Ocracoke were vulnerable to attack. Furthermore, officials feared that inland port towns were likewise defenseless should British vessels breach coastal defenses and sail into the sounds. Adapted from the Price-Strother 1808 map and the ca. 1812 map of North Carolina "Drawn by S. Lewis Tanner Sc." from UNC Libraries Digital Collections, North Carolina Maps Collection, http://dc.lib.unc.edu.

the buildup to war, Congressman William Blackledge communicated with the president and the secretary of the navy regarding measures to adequately defend the eastern part of North Carolina.

In January, Blackledge had met with Secretary of the Navy Paul Hamilton and discussed the likelihood of stationing gunboats at key locations, specifically Ocracoke Inlet and Beaufort. The secretary assured the congressman that he would send gunboats to the two sites, but by mid-May, however, no such vessels had arrived at either destination. Blackledge, prompted by constituents in his congressional district, wrote to Hamilton on May 21 regarding the status of the proposed deployment of gunboats in eastern North Carolina waters. In his letter, Blackledge inquired whether the gunboats that Hamilton had promised to send to Ocracoke Inlet and Beaufort had indeed been dispatched to those ports. Blackledge advised Hamilton that protection for Ocracoke Inlet was particularly critical since "more than two thirds of the tonnage [of commercial and agricultural exports] of the state" passed through that inlet, and it had "neither fort nor gunboat for its protection." Blackledge felt that Ocracoke would be an especially inviting target, not only to British warships but also to roving privateers, since much of the exports using the inlet was "obliged to lie from a week to 3 weeks on a Road stead open to the Sea and in full view of privateers passing along the Coast . . . without a single gun mounted on a fort or gun boat to defend it." The congressman concluded his correspondence by reminding Hamilton that the port town of Beaufort was itself "open to the sea with an inlet . . . [but had] nothing to protect it."[2]

Blackledge's proactive communication immediately prompted Hamilton to order gunboats to North Carolina. On May 23 the secretary sent an order to Master Commandant Samuel Evans, commander of the Gosport Navy Yard at Norfolk, to "immediately send" five gunboats to Ocracoke "for the purpose of affording protection to our commerce and enforcing the embargo law."[3] On June 2 Evans responded to the secretary, advising him that he had "agreeably to the order . . . dispatched Gunboats Nos. 60, 61, 68 and 146 to Ocracock [sic]." Evans further informed Hamilton that the fifth vessel, gunboat No. 67, had been found "so defective as to require at least a partial repair before she can proceed" to the subject destination. The vessel was at that time undergoing repairs at the Gosport facility, and Evans advised Hamilton that "she will be ready to follow the other four in a few days" if further decay was not discovered.[4] A week later, however, Evans wrote to the secretary that the gunboat was "so rotten in her upper works that it is necessary she should receive a thorough repair. As she is the only boat with sufficient men for her to go to Ocracock . . . her repairs will take up at least a fortnight [fourteen days]. I beg to know whether I shall transfer her men to No. 149 and dispatch her to Ocracock to make up the five ordered there." Evans directed the gunboat commanders whom he had dispatched to Ocracoke to remain there "so long as their provisions will admit." He advised the gunboat commanders that should "you not receive subsequent orders . . . you will report to me . . . your proceedings, as it may be necessary for the Navy Department to know."[5] The four gunboats arrived safely at Ocracoke Inlet on June 5.[6]

Hamilton, having committed to send five gunboats to eastern North Carolina, on June 13 ordered Evans to "transfer the officers and men of gunboat No. 67 to No. 149 and dispatch No. 149 to Ocracock to make the number five."[7] On June 21 Evans dispatched gunboat No. 149 for Ocracoke, but three days later the pilot returned to Norfolk and informed Evans that the gunboat "had only put to sea yesterday," as a "gale from the south" was blowing. Evans immediately wrote to Hamilton that he thought it was "probable" that the gunboat would return to port, owing to the weather. Should the vessel return to Norfolk, Evans was reluctant to "dispatch her again" until he had received further orders from the secretary, inasmuch as a British frigate, the *Belvedere*, was known to be in the Atlantic Ocean immediately off the Virginia Capes. According to Evans, a copy of the declaration of war had been forwarded to the warship's commander, and Evans was confident that the commander of the British warship would not idly allow an American gunboat to pass out into the Atlantic Ocean if he could prevent it.[8] Nonetheless, the gunboat sailed on to Ocracoke.

Moreover, Blackledge, intent on further strengthening naval defenses in eastern North Carolina, in late January had presented to Hamilton for the latter's "consideration" a proposal for the navy to purchase two privately owned vessels at the port of Beaufort. One was a boat of about seventy tons capacity and the other a "little schooner." Blackledge suggested that should Hamilton "be inclined to accept" the vessels, they would be stationed at Beaufort for that town's defense. Obviously, Blackledge intended that the two ships be armed and placed in a state of military readiness by the navy for use in the waters of eastern North Carolina. Hamilton declined the offer, informing Blackledge that "there exists no authority for the Executive to purchase vessels at this time."[9]

On March 8 Blackledge wrote to President Madison and suggested that artillerists be placed aboard gunboats to protect certain North Carolina

Paul Hamilton, President Madison's secretary of the navy since March 1809, deployed gunboats to eastern North Carolina to help strengthen coastal defenses. As the War of 1812 loomed, Hamilton's navy was characterized by navy yards in disrepair and vessels that were "laid up." Zealous economizing on the part of Congress hampered Hamilton's ability to strengthen naval forces. Image courtesy of the Naval Historical Foundation.

towns and communities, specifically Beaufort, Ocracoke, Washington, and New Bern.[10] Each of those locations was within Blackledge's congressional district. As one of the "War Hawk" congressmen, Blackledge owed it to the residents of his district, as well as to all of those persons residing in eastern North Carolina, to push for as much military protection as he could persuade the officials in the nation's capital to provide. Nevertheless, the president did not authorize the augmentation of gunboat crews.

Overall responsibility for the federal government's defense of eastern North Carolina fell severally to three military commanders: Mast. Comm. Samuel Evans and Capt. John H. Dent, both of the United States Navy, and Maj. Gen. Thomas Pinckney of the United States Army. Pinckney and Dent's headquarters were at Charleston, and their respective commands necessitated that the two men closely coordinate with each other on their various military plans and actions. Evans, situated in Norfolk, officially had command of the gunboats he had dispatched to North Carolina pursuant to Secretary Hamilton's directives.

The United States Senate appointed Pinckney, a lifelong resident of South Carolina and a Revolutionary War veteran, as major general in March 1812. Pinckney's command, initially designated as the Southern Department, extended over a vast region covering the entire geographic area of the states of Virginia, North Carolina, South Carolina, and Georgia. On April 29 Secretary of War William Eustis advised Pinckney that it was "desirable" that he should make Charleston or its vicinity his head-quarters.[11] In early June Pinckney relocated from his home in Santee to Charleston and established his headquarters there.[12]

Captain Dent was a career naval officer, having been appointed a midshipman in March 1798 and progressing up the officer ranks until the Senate appointed him captain on December 29, 1811.[13] On March 28, 1812, Secretary of the Navy Hamilton ordered Dent to "take charge" of the Charleston and Wilmington naval stations. By early May, Dent had arrived at Charleston, established his headquarters, and assumed command of the two stations as designated by the secretary.[14] Dent replaced Capt. Hugh G. Campbell, whom the Navy Department transferred to Saint Mary's River, Georgia, to command a naval flotilla at that place.[15]

Samuel Evans, likewise a career naval officer, had been appointed a midshipman in May 1798 and had progressed to the rank of master commandant, a rank he had held since April 1806. He was promoted to captain on July 4, 1812.[16]

While General Pinckney and Captain Dent had taken command at Charleston, they by no means had within their geographic areas of responsibility the military forces and resources capable of defending against British warships and troops. Both commanders faced imposing problems, fundamentally arising from the nation's prior years of employing small army and naval forces. Military and logistical resources were simply not available to these two men to allow them quickly to devise effective defenses, particularly in eastern North Carolina.

To defend and patrol the coastline, ports, sounds, and rivers of eastern North Carolina, Captain Dent had at his disposal only three gunboats at Wilmington—each of them under the immediate command of Sailing Master Thomas N. Gautier. All three vessels were in dire need of repairs, variously requiring new sails, awnings, gun carriages, or structural enhancements. Gautier felt that the Wilmington/Cape Fear location alone

Maj. Gen. Thomas Pinckney, a native of South Carolina, commanded the United States Army's Southern Department (later designated the Sixth Military District) from his headquarters in Charleston. He was chiefly responsible for land defenses in North Carolina, South Carolina, and Georgia. While serving for the duration of the conflict, Pinckney never saw combat. Image courtesy of the Library of Congress.

required "five gun vessels and a heavy Brig."[17] The Department of the Navy had not alerted Dent that gunboats had been deployed from Norfolk to Ocracoke, so he (and Gautier) had no knowledge of that force. The Ocracoke gunboats were acting under orders received from Master Commandant Evans. As a result, in the spring and early summer of 1812, overall naval defenses for eastern North Carolina essentially fell under two naval commanders—Evans and Dent—who had not been directed by the Department of the Navy to coordinate and consult with each other.[18]

General Pinckney, upon assuming command, was consumed first and foremost with defensive measures for Charleston. About mid-May President Madison instructed Secretary of War Eustis to inform the general that "the present critical State of our Relations with Great Britain require[s] that the fortifications on the Sea Board should be put in the best State of Defence, particularly in the Harbours of Savannah & Charleston." Eustis added that it was "desirable" for Pinckney to "concentrate the [army]

Recruits as they are raised and man the different works" along the seaboard.[19] Simultaneously, the secretary—on behalf of the president—requested Gov. William Hawkins to "order into actual service such part of the quota" of North Carolina's detached militia as General Pinckney "may deem necessary for the defence of the fortifications of the Sea Board."[20]

Hawkins, unwaveringly supportive of the Madison administration's war efforts, replied to Eustis on June 3, confirming that he would abide by General Pinckney's militia requisitions once received. He also advised the secretary of North Carolina's continuing and persistent arms dilemma: "No provision has been made by the Legislature of this State to arm Militia. By our Laws they are compelled to arm and equip themselves, but the arms which they procure, in obedience to those laws are not of a description to be useful in the field." The governor added that "the time seems to be fast approaching when it will be indispensably necessary that the Detachment required from this State should have effective arms placed in its possession. I deem it my duty without delay, to adopt such measures as may promise the speedy attainment of that important object." Moreover, Hawkins asked to "be informed of the number and kind of arms, that this State is entitled to, under the Act of Congress passed in 1808 for the purpose of arming and equipping the whole body of the militia of the United States." Hawkins inquired whether the "entitled" number of arms had been transmitted to North Carolina and, if not, when did the War Department expect to forward them.[21]

While overall defense of the coastline was predicated on both navy and army resources, Pinckney was seriously concerned over the assistance he might be able to receive from Captain Dent. On June 16 he wrote to Secretary of War Eustis: "Although the Naval Department does not come within your control . . . the defence of the Sea coast is so intimately connected with an inland naval force that in justification of myself in case any event should render the cooperation of that arm necessary, I think it right to inform you that no reliance can be placed on any immediate assistance from them. On consulting with Captain Dent, I learn that he has under his command here [at Charleston], neither gunboats nor arms, nor a pound of powder."[22] Clearly the naval war assets stationed in the Carolinas in the early summer of 1812 were virtually inconsequential to nonexistent.

Eustis may have discussed the Charleston situation with Secretary of the Navy Hamilton, for on June 20 Hamilton wrote to Dent that "You may be called upon to cooperate with the army & upon the requisition of the commanding officer of the army, you will according to your best skill & judgment cooperate with him, in all objects for the public good."[23]

Dent's compliance with the orders would necessarily be irrelevant, since at that time—in the event that British troops should show themselves at Charleston—Captain Dent commanded a "ghost force" in the port town.

Pinckney was of the opinion that he should visit North Carolina to formulate the defensive measures he thought necessary for the state. On June 6 he wrote to Eustis to advise him that he had written Gov. William Hawkins and requested returns and "necessary information" concerning the status of North Carolina's detached militia. Pinckney proposed to wait at Charleston until he had received an answer from Hawkins, so that "no time may be lost in drawing such of the militia to the support of the posts on the sea board of that state as may be requisite."[24] Hawkins replied to Pinckney on June 10, advising the general that the "quota of Militia required from this State will be raised without delay. The business is now progressing with zeal and activity."[25]

Hawkins had been alerted to the impending call on the state's militia. On May 21 Eustis had informed Hawkins that President Madison had instructed him to request the governor to "order into actual Service such part of the Quota of Militia of North Carolina required by my Letter of April 15th as Genl Pinckney may deem necessary for the defence of fortifications of the Sea Board."[26] Land defenses of eastern North Carolina's port towns would be the responsibility of the state's militia resources, rather than regular army units, which needed to be recruited, organized, equipped, trained, and deployed.

With the declaration of war formally approved by President Madison, a flurry of notices and communications flew out of the nation's capital to military commanders and governors of the states and territories on June 18 and 19. Secretary of War Eustis dispatched to the army's commanding officers at the various locations within the states and territories letters announcing that "War is declared against Great Britain" and instructing the commanders to prepare works and make necessary arrangements for defense.[27] Secretary of the Navy Hamilton informed naval commanders that "war has been declared" between the United States and the United Kingdom of Great Britain and Ireland and that "the President has been authorized to use the whole land & naval force of the United States to carry the same into effect." Hamilton closed his communication by informing the commanders that in "virtue of [the president's] authority, You will consider yourself & all the officers and vessels under your command, as having every Belligerent right of attack, capture & defence. Be upon Your guard."[28] President Madison forwarded to Governor Hawkins the act of

Congress declaring war, copies of the president's war message of June 1 to both houses, and a report of the Committee of Foreign Relations to the House of Representatives.[29]

On June 30 Hawkins issued a proclamation to the citizens of North Carolina declaring that "it is the indispensable duty of every State in the Union with all the means in its power to co-operate with the General Government in carrying on the War with the utmost vigor and activity. I have therefore thought proper to issue this Proclamation hereby requiring and enjoining all officers[,] civil and military[,] in the State of North Carolina according to the duties of their respective stations, to be vigilant in supporting the Country through the contest in which she is at present engaged."[30]

In Bertie County the local militia leaders had assembled their quota of the detached militia—a company consisting of 108 men, including officers. Joseph Hunter Bryan served as captain of the unit, Augustin Pugh as lieutenant, and Lodowick Pruden as ensign. The company was assigned to the artillery service of the state's detached militia.[31] It would now await orders that might come from the state's adjutant general to deploy to a designated locale to meet any exigency that merited action. Otherwise, the company's members carried on with their daily lives, with the war becoming a conversation topic for social gatherings and at the residents' dinner tables.

On July 4 the citizenry of Bertie County gathered in Windsor to celebrate the nation's thirty-seventh Independence Day. The people, assembled at the courthouse, sang patriotic songs and fired the town cannon. They raised their glasses in patriotic toasts, in which they wished the country's "domestic foes a speedy and eternal exit" and expressed the hope that "the army of 1812" might "rival in glory the Army of '76."[32] The people of Bertie were caught up in the excitement of the moment and fully supported the war. Patriotism within the county was at a fever pitch.

The Bertie County detached militia likewise exhibited patriotic zeal and expressed a desire to serve their country. On July 20 Captain Bryan wrote to Governor Hawkins that he had been "instructed by the Volunteer Company which I have the honor to Command and which forms the detachment of Militia from the Bertie regiment to make known to your Excellency their anxious desire to be called into the Service of their Country and beg that if a greater portion of the Militia should be necessary than those already ordered out, that they may be permitted to make themselves useful by immediately repairing to the point where defence is thought necessary."[33] On September 10 Governor Hawkins replied to

Bryan regarding his company's "truly patriotic request." Hawkins wrote: "From men this anxious to serve their Country the utmost efficiency may justly be expected from the operations when [they are] called upon to act in the field."[34] The county's "citizen soldiers" were ready for a call to action.

But the Bertie County detached militia company received no call to march. Instead, the militiamen carried on with their daily lives, keeping abreast of war happenings through articles and accounts presented in the state's newspapers and conversations with their fellow residents at county crossroads and public establishments. Nor was the war forthcoming to North Carolina. The 1812 military campaign was being carried out along the United States-Canada border. The war, should it come to North Carolina and the other southern states, would not come in the foreseeable future. Thus, military and state officials had time to strengthen further North Carolina's coastal defenses.

While the Bertie County detached militia was not called into active service, companies from other counties in the eastern sector of the state were deployed to garrison two forts—Fort Hampton at Beaufort and Fort Johnston near Wilmington. On July 4 General Pinckney wrote to Governor Hawkins and requested that eight companies of North Carolina's detached militia be deployed—four companies to Fort Hampton and four to Fort Johnston. On July 7 Adjutant General Calvin Jones confirmed to the general that four companies of militia (from Beaufort, Craven, Lenoir, and Onslow counties) had been ordered to Fort Hampton and four (from Bladen, Brunswick, Duplin, and New Hanover counties) to Fort Johnston.[35]

While the North Carolina detached militia was ordered to Fort Hampton, Capt. John Nicks of the Third Regiment United States Infantry was commander of the installation that was garrisoned by a detachment from his regiment. Upon learning that four companies of militia were destined to march to the fort, Nicks wrote to Adjutant General Jones: "I have not been officially notified that any troops are to be expected at this place or neighborhood. The United States did not erect the fort on Bogue Bank in order to make it necessary to station a battalion here for its defence. Therefore, I conclude that only one company of the detachment will be stationed at the fort which in addition to the regulars already here are as many and perhaps more than the Public Barracks will quarter and will be sufficient to work the ordnance. I would suggest that the rest be stationed on the commons in the rear of Beaufort because the ground in the vicinity of the fort is inundated almost every high tide."[36] It seems that the army commanders, like the navy commanders, lacked the ability or insight to adequately coordinate with each other on the deployment of military resources.

By August 1812 General Pinckney was progressing in the implementation of his defensive strategy in the southern sector, including North Carolina. Of necessity, the strategy called for utilizing detached militia to man existing coastal fortifications, pending the recruitment and organization of army units, which were slated to replace the citizen soldiers. Pinckney, unsure of how many militiamen he should keep deployed in the non-combat environment, sought guidance from the secretary of war. On August 22 the secretary replied to the general, declaring that "it is extremely difficult to give precise Instructions respecting the number of militia which ought to be kept in Service within the Sphere of your Command. The General Object [of] the President has been to call out & continue in service until the regular Troops could be raised, such Detachments [of militia], as with the Regulars already stationed in them would prove sufficient to repel any assault or attack which might be made upon the several fortified towns . . . on the maritime frontier." The secretary added that from the "Southern States, there is at this time no probability that the Regular Troops will be required for distant operations; and it is desired that the militia should be spared as much as possible, particularly at this season of the year, as our great reliance in case of strong emergencies is in them." Eustis advised Pinckney that "it is presumed" that the reduction of militia in the service of the United States would be "effected gradually" and that army recruits would eventually replace the militia.[37]

By early August the gunboats that the secretary of the navy had specifically ordered to eastern North Carolina had returned to Gosport Navy Yard. The vessels' crews had consumed their stocks of provisions, and, in accordance with Evans's orders, the gunboats returned to Norfolk. Secretary Hamilton, upon learning of this development, on August 11 informed Evans that the "boats from Ocracock so soon as they shall be replenished with stores—must return to their station—their crews must not be reduced."[38] On August 13 Hamilton (who a few days earlier had issued orders transferring Evans from Norfolk to the command of the frigate *Chesapeake*, then lying in Boston harbor), addressed a letter to the "Commanding Officer, Gosport Navy Yard." The secretary iterated that "of the five gunboats stationed at Ocracock, two are to be ordered to the port of Beaufort. The Commanders of all these boats are to be ordered hereafter to procure their supplies through the Navy Agent residing nearest to their respective stations."[39] In short, they were to remain in the waters of eastern North Carolina.

Obviously, Hamilton well understood that he would appear to have reneged on his promise to Congressman Blackledge once the legislator became aware that the gunboats, for which he had diligently lobbied, had departed their station. On August 13 Hamilton wrote to Blackledge that the Ocracoke gunboats "were not ordered by me to return to Norfolk. I have written this day to the Commanding Officer at Norfolk to order them back, if they should have returned and to order two of the five to Beaufort. In [the] future they will remain on their respective station[s], and procure their supplies through the Navy Agent."[40]

Thus, nine months after the "War Congress" convened and two months after the declaration of war was issued, North Carolina's "maritime frontier" remained lightly defended. Two forts, garrisoned primarily by the state's militia, and three deficient gunboats on the Cape Fear River were the only military forces in service. Assuredly, the state's defensive needs appeared to Governor Hawkins, the state's congressional delegation, members of the General Assembly, and citizens in general to be a very low priority to leaders of the general government in the nation's capital. On the other hand, no British combat forces had appeared at any points along the state's coastline. The British, intent on beating back American invasions into Canada, were concentrating their army and naval forces along the northern sector of the United States coast and in the Great Lakes region along the Canadian border. Fortunately for eastern North Carolina residents, military operations in their region were not a component of the British war plans for 1812. Even so, uncertainty over British intentions produced consternation and anxiety, particularly among North Carolina's elected officials charged with protecting and safeguarding the populace.

Despite the scarcity of military assets committed to the state's maritime frontier, one North Carolina congressman—William R. King of the Fifth Congressional District—was of the opinion that at least part of the coastal region was overly defended. In early August, King was visiting the Wilmington area and wrote to Secretary of War Eustis that, in accordance with a conversation he had had with Eustis while still in the nation's capital, he understood

that a portion of the regular troops comprising a part of the new military establishment would be employed in the defence of Fort Johns[t]on and the others exposed points of this state. On my arrival here I learned from Governor Hawkins (with some degree of astonishment) that orders had been issued by Genl Pinckney for the marching of a considerable portion of the militia to be stationed at the Forts; they have since marched. From the natural situation of those places thus ordered to be garrisoned a force vastly inferior to the one now employed would be fully adequate to a complete defence. . . . Against invasion we are protected by nature, very little aid from physical force is necessary. At Fort Johns[t]on where three hundred militia have been ordered in addition to the regular troops already stationed there, it is the general opinion of the military men of this state, as well as the citizens of this place (who are more immediately intrusted in its defence) that fifty or sixty men would be altogether sufficient. . . . Genl Pinckney has not sufficiently appreciated our natural situation.

King, politely requesting the secretary's forbearance, further wrote: "Excuse me for expressing an opinion, but I conceive true policy would dictate that at a time when great variability of opinions prevails, dissatisfaction should not be fomented by the imposition of unnecessary burthens. Rely upon it Sir a much smaller force than is now contemplated by the Genl would render us we believe perfectly secure and general satisfaction would prevail were those men who have volunteered their services to the State be permitted to remain with their families until their services were really warranted."[41] On August 10 Eustis forwarded King's letter to General Pinckney, noting that "All arrangements for the defence of North Carolina being within your Department, the Letter is submitted for your Information."[42]

Unbeknown to Congressman King, General Pinckney was indeed striving to relieve units of North Carolina's detached militia that he had called into service (through Governor Hawkins) immediately after the declaration of war was announced. By the end of August, Pinckney was prepared to discharge portions of the militia then in federal service. On August 27 he wrote to Hawkins that "Since the requisition I had the honor to make to you immediately after the declaration of war to march eight companies of the Militia for the defence of the Sea Coast of the State in which you preside, such progress has been made in the recruiting service, as to render it in my opinion unnecessary to continue the whole of that detachment on duty. I have therefore to request that your Excellency will direct two of the companies ordered to the vicinity of Beaufort and one of those directed to be stationed near the mouth of Cape Fear River to be dismissed."[43]

On the same day, Pinckney wrote to the secretary of war that he was "sorry" that King "has thought the measures of defence adopted for the part of the country in which he resides were more than sufficient. I rather expected that representation of an opposite tendency from various parts of the country would first have reached you." Pinckney, somewhat irritated by Representative King's criticism, particularly after so many North Carolina political leaders had time and again sought increased military resources from the federal government for coastal defense, provided Eustis a detailed justification for his delay in replacing detached militia with regular army troops:

The new levies [recruits] having been sanctioned by you in the conversation alluded to by Mr. King as being intended to garrison the Posts, I take this opportunity of making some remarks concerning them to you. . . .

In conformity of your instruction of the 20th of June which directed that "as far as I might find it advisable I should supply the place of the militia with regular troops." It was my intention immediately to draw some of the recruits to the sea coast for that purpose, but various circumstances had occurred to make the recruiting service unproductive. Brig Genl [William] Polk was designated to superintend the recruiting service in the department composed of the three Southern States and the officers were directed to report themselves to him, this gentleman after some delay declined [the appointment] and it was a considerable time before the recruiting instructions reached the officers who were to act under them; a great portion of the young men of the country had by this time had made their engagements for the summer. . . . The organization of the troops as raised had been confided to the Inspector General [of the War Department], but that office was for a long time vacant. The officer who acted temporarily did not consider himself authorized to appoint assistants and being himself stationed at Head Quarters [War Department, Washington, D.C.], that part of the service was likewise very backward. Being informed however that some of the Officers had begun to collect recruits, I did authorize on the 9th of July [a] special order to Col. [James] Wellborn instructing him to direct the officers under his command to collect and march to Head Quarters at Charleston so many of the recruits as would form a Battalion. To send from the district of Tarborough one company to take post in the neighborhood of Fort Hampton, and one company from the district of Fayette[ville] to take post in the vicinity of Fort Johns[t]on, N.C. . . . To this order Lt. Col. [Andrew] Pickens . . . commanded in the absence of Col. Wellborn. [Brig.] Genl. [Thomas] Flourney whom I had directed on his receiving his commission to replace General Polk in superintending this service, and Col. Wellborn on his return from furlough made strong resistances; they represented in substance that the recruiting service had substantially suffered already from the mere promulgation of the order and they concensused in opinion, separately given, and forwarded on statements made by the officers under their command, that if so many of the recruits should be sent into the lower country, few more would enlist. In consequence of these representations, and finding that the militia already stationed on the sea board had begun to assume some degree of regularity and order, and appeared to be reconciled to their situation, I determined to suspend the order for the removal of the recruits, except two companies for the garrison of the forts in Charleston harbour. . . . General Flourney has been directed to appoint a rendezvous in the upper country of each state as contiguous to the sea board as consistent with health, to which the recruits shall be assembled, for the purpose of being organized and instructed in their duties. In consequence of this arrangement, we have about 250 of the new levies in the harbour of Charleston and near 100 in the healthiest spot which could be found in the vicinity of Savannah; about 30 have also been placed in Fort Johns[t]on, N.C; the remainder will be stationed in the interior until the end of the month of October and most of the militia called out, retained until that period in service, unless after considering the above circumstances you shall direct the recruits to be sooner ordered down, and the militia discharged.

The state of the Recruiting Service in North Carolina which has succeeded better in the middle and lower country than in the corresponding portions of the two Southern States will justify me in immediately dismissing a part of the detachment called for from that state, and I have accordingly requested the Governor to recall three of the companies detached to the service of the U.S. . . . .

On the 4th of July Four companies consisting (if complete) of 256 rank and file, were ordered for the defence of the harbour of Cape Fear, to do duty by detachment in Fort Johns[t]on and to protect the town of Wilmington and the neighboring sea coast. The garrison of Fort Johns[t]on at that time consisted of a subaltern and about 20 privates.[44]

A week later, the issue of detached militia versus regular troops to garrison coastal installations was still attendant with Pinckney when he penned to Eustis: "In North Carolina directions have been given to reinforce Fort Johns[t]on with regulars and with the advance of the recruiting service, we shall progress in the gradual dismition [dismissing] of the militia in that state so that my present expectation is that about the middle of October, we shall have no militia in the service of the three Southern States."[45] The following day a Raleigh newspaper published the news that Governor Hawkins had received information from General Pinckney that such progress had been made in the recruiting service "as to tender it unnecessary to continue in service the whole of the eight companies of militia" that he had requested to be marched to Forts Hampton and Johnston.[46] The mode and constituency of the defense of North Carolina's coast was a sensitive and rabid topic in the summer and early autumn of 1812.

While the issue of land forces seemed to have been resolved, the issue of gunboat deployment was again a primary concern (and complaint) of Rep. William Blackledge in early September. Blackledge had journeyed from Washington, D.C., to Washington, North Carolina, where, on his arrival, he found one of the naval gunboats from Ocracoke. On September 4 he wrote to Secretary of the Navy Hamilton, informing him of the gunboat at Washington and that generally "the boats did not lie at Ocracock . . . where they are wanted, but availing themselves of the latitude of their orders are almost always at Newbern or this place." According to Blackledge, the gunboats routinely left the waters about Ocracoke to sail Pamlico and Albemarle sounds. Blackledge informed Hamilton that the "waters of Roanoke river & Neuse [River] are considered by them [the gunboats' commanders] as the waters of Ocracock because they discharge through that inlet, yet observe no enemy can get into those rivers but through Ocracock Inlet. The use of Gunboats at Ocracock is to prevent an enemy being in that Inlet & to protect the vessels lying in that harbor. It would also be useful in preventing depredations upon the citizens living on Ocracock & Portsmouth Banks, but to lie at Newbern[,] Washington or Edenton they would be of no earthly use." Blackledge noted further that the two gunboats ordered to Beaufort were at that station and would "no doubt occupy their proper Stations at that town which is in sight of the Sea."[47]

With the gunboats periodically vacating the waters of Ocracoke Inlet to sail the inland sounds, the river port towns became more vulnerable to visits by British vessels and roving privateers, moving Governor Hawkins to communicate to Secretary of War Eustis. Hawkins obviously viewed the defense of the inland towns as primarily a responsibility of the War Department. On September 15 Hawkins noted to Eustis that the towns of New Bern and Washington "might possibly experience much injury from the crews of enterprising privateers or those of small vessels of the enemy, who, without difficulty after entering Pamptico [Pamlico] Sound could sail up the rivers on which they are situated and land for the purpose of plundering them. I do not presume that General Pinckney has been inattentive to the situations of those Towns. . . . I am not prepared to urge that they are in eminent danger at present." Nevertheless, Hawkins strongly desired military protection "to guard against an evil" that he believed "timely preparation . . . [could] avert." Eustis, as he had previously done, advised Hawkins that "defence of the southern sea coast" was General Pinckney's responsibility and that the general's judgment regarding "necessary" defensive measures was paramount.[48]

In late September Pinckney was faced with the removal from his department of the only veteran troops under his command. On September 25 Thomas H. Cushing, adjutant general of the War Department, conveyed orders from Secretary Eustis that all of the officers and men of the Second and Third regiments United States Infantry stationed in North Carolina, South Carolina, and Georgia were to be transferred to the Mississippi Territory to join their commands already there. Both regiments had been organized under the act of Congress of April 12, 1808. A detachment of soldiers of the Third Regiment under the command of Capt. John Nicks was stationed at Fort Hampton.[49]

Pinckney was displeased with the War Department's orders. He had primarily employed the relatively few experienced troops within his command, members of the Second and Third regiments, to help train and organize the "New Army" recruits. However, he issued orders to effectuate the transfers and informed the secretary of war of his actions.[50] On October 23 Cushing wrote to Pinckney that "It is much to be regretted that one of the old regiments of Infantry could not have been placed under your command without great inconvenience to the public service. But considering the positions occupied by three of these regiments in the Southwest [Louisiana/Mississippi Territory], the necessity for continuing them there and for employing the remaining four [regiments] in the north, the Secretary was induced . . . to assign the 2nd, 3rd & 7th Regiments" to the Mississippi Territory. Cushing further commented that it had been Secretary Eustis's "intention that the officers & men of these regiments within the Southern States should have been sent to the Mississippi at a much earlier period."[51]

In late October Pinckney ordered Col. James Wellborn to dispatch a detachment from the Tenth Regiment United States Infantry to march to Fort Hampton to relieve Captain Nicks and his command.[52] Then, in early November, Pinckney relieved the detachments of North Carolina militia still on duty at Forts Hampton and Johnston. In addition to Fort Hampton, soldiers from Wellborn's Tenth Regiment would garrison the latter fort.[53]

On November 5 Pinckney wrote to Governor Hawkins that "I am endeavoring to garrison the posts on our Maritime Frontier with the new levies & permitting the Militia to return to their homes, with as little delay as possible; as soon as in pursuance of the orders which I have issued to Col Wellborn of the 10th Regt Infy . . . the detachments of his Regt . . . detached for Forts Hampton and Johnston shall have arrived at those posts. You will please to consider the Troops of the State of No. Carolina now stationed at those posts to be no longer in the service of the United States."[54] The state's citizen soldiers could return to their homes and families and resume their daily livelihoods. Defense of North Carolina's coastal regions now principally rested with the United States Navy and Army, along with the state's detached militia—including Capt. Joseph Hunter Bryan's Bertie County company—"held in readiness to march at a moment's warning."

Governor Hawkins recognized that the federal troops at Forts Hampton and Johnston would not be able to respond effectively to British incursions of any great distances from the two facilities. Hawkins, desiring to prepare the state's militia to deploy as quickly as possible in the event of a British assault or invasion, directed Adj. Gen. Calvin Jones to have the commander of North Carolina's 7,000-man force of detached militia issue orders to select regimental commanders to call their troops into service without further orders from superiors. Jones "required" Maj. Gen. Thomas Brown, overall commander of the state's detached militia, to give orders to Col. Josiah Flowers (of Plymouth), First Regiment Detached Militia, and to Col. Simon Bruton, Second Regiment, to call into service the troops under their commands without further orders from Brown, Hawkins, or Jones. General Brown issued the requested orders, facilitating the deployment of the militia without undue back-and-forth communications.[55]

As 1812 drew to a close, Rep. William Blackledge once again was concerned over the gunboats at Ocracoke Inlet. The commander of the boats had advised Blackledge that "by his orders" the vessels were to remain in the waters of eastern North Carolina for two months and that if he did not receive further orders, then the boats were to return to Norfolk. The vessels had been in the North Carolina waters for about two months, and obviously the commander was on the verge of having the five boats depart and return to Norfolk. To Blackledge this information was incredulous. Therefore, he fired off a letter to Secretary of the Navy Hamilton stating that "I cannot believe you can intend to withdraw them at this time. Of the five now here if more cant be spared two ought to be ordered to proceed to the port of Beaufort, the other three to remain at Ocracock, & one more ought to be spared to go to Swansboro a town 30 miles South of Beaufort."[56] The gunboats did not leave, but their service would soon be terminated by orders from the Navy Department pursuant to an act of Congress.

In March 1812 Congress had passed "An Act concerning the Naval Establishment," which, among other provisions, provided that "as soon as it shall be deemed compatible with the good of the public services, the gun boats now in commission be laid up, and with those not in commission, be distributed in the several harbors of the maritime frontier which are most exposed to attack, to be carefully kept and used as circumstances may require."[57] On February 26, 1813, the new secretary of the navy, William Jones, directed Thomas N. Gautier to "immediately order all the gunboats in the waters of North Carolina to proceed to Wilmington at which place or the most convenient place near Wilmington the whole are to be laid up in ordinary." In essence, the vessels were to be held in reserve, since no British threats were imminent in the area; nevertheless, they were to be maintained and fully equipped and armed for service. The gunboats were to be kept moored low, with sterns facing wharves, buoys, or other appropriate anchorages in the rivers or harbors. Jones further directed Gautier that a sufficient number of crew members was to be retained to take

William Jones replaced Paul Hamilton as secretary of the navy in January 1813. Upon assuming the position, Jones faced a precarious state of affairs in that the American navy was predominantly comprised of gunboats (for protection of ports) rather than seagoing warships. While various North Carolina officials considered gunboats to be appropriate defensive assets for the coast and sounds of North Carolina, Jones—who privately considered gunboats to be a waste of resources—in February 1813 ordered that all such vessels be "laid up" to conserve naval assets. Image courtesy of the Naval Historical Foundation.

care of the boats, but that the "residue of the crews must be paid off & discharged unless Capt. Dent should require them for the two small vessels to be retained in commission at Charleston."[58]

Two days later Jones advised Captain Dent that "All the gunboats of every description & barges at Charleston, or under your command [i.e., Wilmington], must be immediately laid up in ordinary under the care of a master & cook & one seaman for each."[59] On March 15 Dent responded to the secretary that he did not consider the gunboats in North Carolina's coastal waters to be part of his command, since he had received no instructions from the Navy Department to that effect. Furthermore, the gunboat commanders had only occasionally made reports to Dent, and no navy purser (paymaster) under his direction was responsible for paying the crews.[60]

Clearly, the military leaders in Washington were not expecting the British to launch any offensive operations in or along the coastal waters of the southern states. The laying-up of vessels and discharging of significant portions of their crews were cost-saving moves in view of the assumed relatively low risk of invasion or raids. Periodically, residents and military personnel would sight British ships sailing off the coasts of the Carolinas. Nevertheless, although British ships had since October 1812 blockaded the port of Charleston, the coastlines of both Carolinas remained quiet. Even so, Gautier and Dent were both concerned over the "laying up" of gunboats. The Navy Department's philosophy was partially espoused by Secretary Jones in a May 14 letter to Dent. Recognizing that the British clearly employed naval forces superior to their American counterparts, Jones counseled that "the Enemy will, occasionally, visit every part of our Coast is what must be expected, and, whenever it is done with a superior force, we must act on the defensive, giving at the same time, to the force we possess its greatest efficiency . . . you will adhere to the orders of this Department" (in the matter of laying up gunboats).[61]

In Raleigh, Governor Hawkins likewise conceded that the coastal regions of his state could not be totally defended against British raiders. In April he had written to Col. Brickhouse Bell, commander of the Currituck County militia: "You are well aware that the sea-board of our State is so very extensive, that ample protection at every point cannot be afforded to the citizens residing near it. . . . Therefore should the enemy make predatory invasions, the local Militia must immediately give their aid to the Detachment [i.e., detached militia] in repelling them. I feel sensibly for the situation of the people of your County and rely much upon their ability and exertions to drive to their boats those plundering parties by which they expect to be visited."[62]

Then, in mid-May, British war vessels appeared off Beaufort. Congressman Blackledge conveyed the news to Secretary Jones: "[W]hat I have long expected has come to pass—that the British would blockade the ports of this State. We learned today [May 14] that Beaufort is blockaded." Blackledge, highly concerned that the British would land soldiers and marines and conduct raids in the area, reminded Jones that the "two gun boats which were put there under my advice, & removed on consequence of the complaints of the expensiveness of this kind of defence would have afforded ample protection." Blackledge viewed Fort Hampton, with its detachment of soldiers from the Tenth Infantry, as a totally inadequate defense against the British. In his words, "one hundred infantry can take [the fort] with ease."[63]

The arrival of British naval vessels off the coast of North Carolina increased the anxiety of the inhabitants of the coastal region. On May 21 Thomas Singleton, customs collector for the port of Ocracoke, wrote to Secretary Jones that he had been solicited by the inhabitants of Ocracoke, New Bern, Washington, and Edenton to "make application for two Gun Boats to be stationed" at Ocracoke Inlet. Singleton concluded that the two armed boats "would be a sufficient force for the places above mentioned, in as much as their waters lead to this Inlet." Singleton further noted his perception that without gunboats, at least some of the places he mentioned— their banks and customhouses, specifically—were "in great danger" from the enemy, as well as from privateers.[64]

Even the highly influential John Gray Blount of Washington, North Carolina, viewed the highly exposed condition of the seaboard as alarming. Concerned that Ocracoke Inlet was "now wholly unprotected by the sending away the two Gun Boats which were stationed there," he wrote to Governor Hawkins on May 25 and implored him to prevail upon the United States government to order the gunboats back to the inlet.[65] It does not appear that Hawkins wrote to President Madison or Secretary of the Navy Jones. In any case, in June the Navy Department took a more direct role in the defense of eastern North Carolina by removing the region from the command of Captain Dent at Charleston and designating it as a "distinct command" under Thomas N. Gautier at Wilmington. Gautier was to take his orders from, and correspond directly with, the Navy Department in Washington.[66]

The war had now been ongoing for a year, and during that time it had been a faraway conflict for the citizens of eastern North Carolina. State leaders had sought time and time again to prompt the federal government to bolster the coastal defenses. However, North Carolina had no large ports or cities along the coast, such as Norfolk, Baltimore, Philadelphia, New York, and Boston, to entice sizeable British raids. The probability of British raids or actions along the southern sector was remote; the war was not being fought in the South. Furthermore, the conflict had become an expensive affair for the country. Military resources were limited, and financial resources were even more constrained. While North Carolina leaders owed their constituents the best defense they could derive, a year after the declaration of war, the coastline, as well as inland waters and towns, was largely vulnerable to British raids at almost any point. Fortunately, the British had made no moves toward the state.

Within Bertie County, life carried on in a familiar routine for the citizens. The county's detached militia had not been called into service. Very few of the county's young men had volunteered for the regular army. The war, to a large extent, likely seemed to be nothing more than articles in the newspapers and topics of conversation for the average citizen.

Notes

1. Raymond Parker Fouts, *Abstracts from the* Edenton Gazette and North Carolina General Advertiser*, Edenton, North Carolina*, 3 vols. (Cocoa, Fla.: GenRec Books, 1993), 2:141–142 (hereafter cited as Fouts, *Abstracts from the* Edenton Gazette). The *Raleigh Minerva* (weekly) and the *Raleigh Register and North Carolina Gazette* (weekly) both included news of the declaration of war in their editions of June 26.

2. Blackledge to Hamilton, May 21, 1812, Miscellaneous Letters Received by the Secretary of the Navy, 1801–1884 (microfilm, M124), Record Group 45, National Archives, Washington, D.C. (hereafter cited as Secretary of the Navy—Miscellaneous Letters Received).

3. Hamilton to Evans, May 23, 1812, Letters Sent by the Secretary of the Navy to Commandants and Navy Agents, 1808–1865 (microfilm, M441), Record Group 45, National Archives (hereafter cited as Secretary of the Navy—Commandant Letters).

4. Evans to Hamilton, June 2, 1812, Letters Received by the Secretary of the Navy from Commanders, 1804–1886 (microfilm, M147), Record Group 45, National Archives (hereafter cited as Letters from Commanders to the Secretary of the Navy).

5. Evans to Hamilton, June 9, 1812, Letters from Commanders to the Secretary of the Navy.

6. Evans to Hamilton, June 26, 1812, Letters from Commanders to the Secretary of the Navy. Evans informed Hamilton: "I have this day received a letter from Mr. [Lewis B.] Page the Senior Sailing Master of the four Boats that first sailed for Ocracoke. He informs me they have all arrived safe after a passage of three days."

7. Hamilton to Evans, June 13, 1812, Secretary of the Navy—Commandant Letters.

8. Evans to Hamilton, June 24, 1812, Letters from Commanders to the Secretary of the Navy.

9. Blackledge to Hamilton, January 26, 1812, Secretary of the Navy—Miscellaneous Letters Received; Hamilton to Blackledge, January 29, 1812, Miscellaneous Letters Sent by the Secretary of the Navy ("General Letter Books"), 1798–1886, (microfilm, M209), Record Group 45, National Archives (hereafter cited as "General Letters" Sent by the Secretary of the Navy).

10. Blackledge to Madison, March 8, 1812, in J. C. A. Stagg et al., eds., *The Papers of James Madison: Presidential Series*, 6 vols. to date (Charlottesville: University of Virginia Press, 1999), 4:234–235 (hereafter cited as *James Madison Presidential Papers*).

11. Pinckney to Eustis, April 11, 1812, and Eustis to Pinckney, April 29, 1812, Letters Received by the Office of the Adjutant General, 1805–1821 (microfilm, M566), Record Group 94, National Archives (hereafter cited as Adjutant General—Letters Received). Pinckney was born in South Carolina in 1750 and served with distinction in the American Revolution. See David S. Heidler and Jeanne T. Heidler, eds., *Encyclopedia of the War of 1812* (Annapolis: Naval Institute Press, 1997), 417-418.

12. Pinckney to Eustis, June 3, 1812, Letters Received by the Secretary of War, Main Series, 1801–1870 (microfilm, M221), Record Group 107, National Archives (hereafter cited as Secretary of War—Letters Received).

13. Officers of the Continental and U.S. Navy and Marine Corps, 1775–1900, Naval Historical Center, Washington, D.C., http://www.history.navy.mil/books/callahan/reg-usn-d.htm.

14. Hamilton to Capt. John H. Dent, March 28, 1812, Letters Sent by the Secretary of the Navy to Officers, 1798–1868 (microfilm, M149), Record Group 45, National Archives (hereafter cited as Secretary of the Navy—Letters to Officers); Dent to Hamilton, May 4, 1812, Letters Received by the Secretary of the Navy from Captains ("Captains' Letters"), 1805–1861; 1866–1885 (microfilm, M125), Record Group 45, National Archives (hereafter cited as Secretary of the Navy—Captains' Letters).

15. Hamilton to Campbell (& others), June 19, 1812, Secretary of the Navy—Letters to Officers.

16. Officers of the Continental and U.S. Navy and Marine Corps, 1775–1900, Naval Historical Center, Washington, D.C., http://www.history.navy.mil/books/callahan/reg-usn-e.htm.

17. Gautier to Secretary of the Navy Paul Hamilton, March 16, 1812, Letters Received by the Secretary of the Navy from Commissioned Officers Below the Rank of Commander and from Warrant Officers ("Officers Letters") 1802–1884 (microfilm, M148), Record Group 45, National Archives (hereafter cited as Secretary of the Navy—Officers Letters); Dent to Hamilton, May 4, 1812, and Gautier to Dent, April 22, 1814, Secretary of the Navy—Captains' Letters.

18. Gautier continued to report officially as a subordinate officer to Captain Dent until June 1813. During the whole of that time, Gautier continued to receive orders from the Secretary of the Navy. In June 1813 the Department of the Navy established North Carolina as a "distinct command, corresponding directly with, and amenable only to" the Department of the Navy. Sec. of the Navy William Jones to Capt. John H. Dent, June 29, 1813, Secretary of the Navy—Letters to Officers.

19. Eustis to Pinckney, May 21, 1812, Adjutant General—Letters Received.

20. Eustis to Hawkins, May 21, 1812, William Hawkins, Governors Letter Books, State Archives, Office of Archives and History (hereafter cited as Hawkins Letter Books).

21. Hawkins to Eustis, June 3, 1812, Hawkins Letter Books; Secretary of War—Letters Received.

22. Pinckney to Eustis, June 16, 1812, Secretary of War—Letters Received.

23. Hamilton to Dent, June 20, 1812, Secretary of the Navy—Letters to Officers.

24. Pinckney to Eustis, June 6, 1812, Secretary of War—Letters Received. Having recently been informed by Eustis that the defense of Norfolk was being directed by the War Department, Pinckney also wrote: "I am happy to find that you have provided for the defence of Norfolk, which I believe to be the only place of importance on the sea coast of Virginia the whole of the state however below the blue ridge, including the city of Richmond itself is on account of the excellence of its internal navigation so much exposed to predatory incursion, that after I shall have

done what is in my power for the defence of the three southern states [North Carolina, South Carolina, and Georgia] I shall think it necessary to proceed to the state of Virginia to make the necessary dispositions for the troops in that quarter, unless I shall previously have received information from you that my presence will be unnecessary."

25. Hawkins to Pinckney, June 10, 1812, Hawkins Letter Books.

26. Eustis to Hawkins, May 21, 1812, Hawkins Letter Books.

27. Eustis to Gens. Henry Dearborn, Thomas Pinckney, William Hull, James Winchester, Joseph Bloomfield, and James Wilkinson, Col. Constant Freeman, Lt. Cols. John R. Fenwick and Daniel Bissell, and Gov. Daniel D. Tompkins (of New York), June 18, 1812, Letters Sent by the Secretary of War Relating to Military Affairs, 1800–1889 (microfilm, M6), Record Group 107, National Archives (hereafter cited as Secretary of War—Letters Sent). As of the date of this letter, seventeen regiments of infantry were authorized by previous acts of Congress. The regular army consisted of about 10,000 men, half of whom were new recruits.

28. Hamilton to Capts. John Shaw, H. G. Campbell, and John H. Dent and Sailing Master Thomas N. Gautier, June 19, 1812, Secretary of the Navy—Letters to Officers; Navy Department General Orders and Circulars, 1798–1862 (microfilm, M977), Record Group 45, National Archives.

29. Madison to Hawkins, June 19, 1812, Hawkins Letter Books.

30. Proclamation by Gov. William Hawkins, June 30, 1812, Hawkins Letter Books.

31. *Muster Rolls of the Soldiers of the War of 1812 Detached from the Militia of North Carolina, in 1812 and 1814* (Raleigh: Ch. C. Raboteau, 1851; Winston-Salem: Barber Printing Company, 1926), 63, 65 (hereafter cited as *Muster Rolls of North Carolina's Detached Militia*). Five companies comprised the artillery component of North Carolina's quota of the 1812 detached militia. The other companies were from Wake, Edgecombe, Carteret, and Brunswick counties.

32. Fouts, *Abstracts from the* Edenton Gazette, 2:143.

33. Bryan to Hawkins, July 20, 1812, William Hawkins, Governors Papers, State Archives (hereafter cited as Hawkins Governors Papers); Hawkins Letter Books.

34. Hawkins to Bryan, September 10, 1812, Hawkins Letter Books.

35. Sarah McCulloh Lemmon, *North Carolina and the War of 1812* (Raleigh: State Department of Archives and History, 1971), 33; Pinckney to Eustis, August 27, 1812, Secretary of War—Letters Received; Jones to Pinckney, July 8, 1812, Adjutant General Militia Returns, Orders of Officers, 1811–1813 (AG-2), Records of the Adjutant General's Office, State Archives, Office of Archives and History (hereafter cited as Adjutant General Militia Returns and Orders); Hawkins to Pinckney, July 9, 1812, Hawkins Letter Books; Hawkins to Jones, July 9, 1812, Adjutant General Militia Returns and Orders. Hawkins wrote to Jones: "I have been requested by Major General Pinckney to order into service eight companies of the detachment from this state to defend the sea coast—four to be stationed at Fort Hampton and four at Fort Johnston. I have this day instructed Maj. General [Thomas] Brown [Second Division, North Carolina Militia] to detach four companies of artillery or infantry from the vicinity of Wilmington to be stationed at the latter

place. I have now to request you to issue the necessary orders to cause the same number to be called into service and stationed at the former place." Jones issued the necessary orders to the designated militia commanders on July 10 and 11, 1812. Jones to Brig. Gen. Croom, July 10, 1812; Jones to Colonel, Beaufort County, July 11, 1812; Jones to Colonel, Craven County Regiment, July 11, 1812; Jones to Commandant, Onslow County Regiment, July 11, 1812; Gen. Jones to Brig. Gen. Smith, July 12, 1812; and Jones to Major [Nathan] Tisdale, July 12, 1812, Adjutant General Militia Returns and Orders.

36. Capt. John Nicks to Adj. Gen. Calvin Jones, July 27, 1812, Adjutant General Militia Returns and Orders.

37. Eustis to Pinckney, August 22, 1812, Secretary of War—Letters Sent.

38. Hamilton to Evans, August 11, 1812, Secretary of the Navy—Letters to Officers.

39. Hamilton to Commanding Officer, Gosport Navy Yard, August 13, 1812, and Hamilton to Evans, August 7, 1812, Secretary of the Navy—Commandant Letters. Hamilton ordered Capt. John Cassin to proceed from Washington City and assume command of the Gosport Navy Yard, thus replacing Captain Evans. Cassin arrived at Gosport on August 23 and assumed command of the station, as well as the gunboats assigned to the North Carolina waters at Ocracoke and Beaufort. At that time, overall command of naval and army/militia forces for eastern North Carolina still fell to three commanders—Cassin, Dent, and Pinckney. Secretary of Navy to Capt. John Cassin, August 10, 1812, Secretary of the Navy—Commandant Letters; Cassin to Hamilton, August 25, 1812, Secretary of the Navy—Captains' Letters.

40. Hamilton to Blackledge, August 13, 1812, "General Letters" Sent by the Secretary of the Navy.

41. King to Eustis, August 3, 1812, Secretary of War—Letters Received.

42. Eustis to Pinckney, August 10, 1812, Secretary of War—Letters Sent.

43. Pinckney to Hawkins, August 27, 1812, Hawkins Letter Books.

44. Pinckney to Eustis, August 27, 1812, Secretary of War—Letters Received. President Madison appointed William Polk, a staunch Federalist from Mecklenburg County, a brigadier general on March 25, 1812. Polk declined the appointment. William Mecklenburg Polk, *Leonidas Polk, Bishop and General* (New York: Longmans, Green and Co., 1893), 34; William S. Powell, ed. *Dictionary of North Carolina Biography*, s.v. "William Polk."

45. Pinckney to Eustis, September 3, 1812, Secretary of War—Letters Received. Hawkins acknowledged to Pinckney on September 12 that he had received the general's letter requesting that three companies of North Carolina detached militia at Forts Hampton and Johnston be discharged. Hawkins to Pinckney, September 12, 1812, Hawkins Letter Books.

46. *Raleigh Register and North Carolina Gazette*, September 4, 1812.

47. Blackledge to Hamilton, September 4, 1812, Secretary of the Navy—Miscellaneous Letters Received.

48. Hawkins to Eustis, September 15, 1812, Secretary of War—Letters Received; Eustis to Hawkins, September 18, 1812, Secretary of War—Letters Sent.

49. Francis B. Heitman, *Historical Register and Dictionary of the United States Army*, 2 vols. (Washington: Government Printing Office, 1903), 1:83–86; Cushing to Pinckney, September 25, 1812, Letters Sent by the Office of the Adjutant General, Main Series, 1800–1890 (microfilm, M565), Record Group 94, National Archives (hereafter cited as Adjutant General—Letters Sent).

50. Pinckney to Eustis, October 6, 1812, Secretary of War—Letters Received.

51. Cushing to Pinckney, October 23, 1812, Adjutant General—Letters Sent.

52. Headquarters, Southern Department, Charleston, S.C., Orders, October 30, 1812, Southern Department General Orders Received & Orders Issued, June 1812–February 1813, Vol. 2, Record Group 98, National Archives (hereafter cited as Southern Department Orders).

53. General Orders, Southern Department, November 4, 1812, Southern Department Orders.

54. Pinckney to Hawkins, November 5, 1812, Hawkins Letter Books.

55. Hawkins to Calvin Jones, November 4, 1812, Adjutant General Militia Returns and Orders; Jones to Hawkins, November 5, 1812, Hawkins Governors Papers; Flowers to Adj. Gen. Robert Williams, July 14, 1813, Adjutant General Militia Returns and Orders.

56. Blackledge to Hamilton, undated (received by the Navy Department in December 1812), Secretary of the Navy—Miscellaneous Letters Received.

57. *United States Statutes at Large* 2 (1845): 699.

58. William Jones to Gautier, February 26, 1813, Secretary of the Navy—Letters to Officers. Paul Hamilton resigned as navy secretary on December 29, 1812. Amid criticism for "errors and mismanagement," as well as accusations of alcoholism, Hamilton resigned his position, which President Madison accepted. William Jones, a Philadelphia merchant and sea captain, was offered the post on January 3, 1813. He was much more qualified for the position than his predecessor. Donald B. Hickey, *The War of 1812: A Forgotten Conflict* (Champaign: University of Illinois Press, 1989), 106; Edward K. Eckert, "William Jones: Mr. Madison's Secretary of the Navy," *The Pennsylvania Magazine of History and Biography*, Vol. 96, no. 2 (April 1972): 167–182.

59. Jones to Dent, February 28, 1813, Secretary of the Navy—Letters to Officers.

60. Dent to Jones, March 15, 1813, Secretary of the Navy—Captains' Letters.

61. Jones to Dent, May 14, 1813, Secretary of the Navy—Letters to Officers.

62. Hawkins to Bell, April 14, 1813, Hawkins Letter Books.

63. Blackledge to Jones, May 14, 1813, Secretary of the Navy—Miscellaneous Letters Received.

64. Singleton to Jones, May 21, 1813, Secretary of the Navy—Miscellaneous Letters Received.

65. Blount to Hawkins, May 25, 1813, in David T. Morgan, ed., *The John Gray Blount Papers*, 3 vols. (Raleigh: North Carolina Department of Cultural Resources, 1982), 4:196–198.

66. Jones to Dent, June 29, 1813, Secretary of the Navy—Letters to Officers.

CHAPTER 3

Slow to Enlist

In the early summer of 1812, recently commissioned army officers spread out across the nation to recruit young men for the new regiments authorized by Congress in January and June 1812.[1] The War Department established six recruiting departments and forty-eight recruiting districts within the states and territories to oversee and manage the recruiting service related to the additional infantry regiments. North Carolina, South Carolina, and Georgia comprised Recruiting Department Number 2, with its headquarters at Columbia, South Carolina. The War Department appointed Col. James Wellborn of the Tenth Regiment United States Infantry to superintend the recruiting business within the department. War Department officials divided the state of North Carolina into three recruiting districts, with principal rendezvous established at Salisbury, Fayetteville, and Tarboro.[2] Recruits who enlisted within a specific district were transferred to that district's rendezvous site, where they were to be clothed, organized into companies, armed, and initially trained and drilled.

Officers for the Tenth Regiment United States Infantry set up recruiting stations at various communities in North Carolina and Virginia to encourage men to enlist.[3] Three residents from the northeastern region of the state—Jesse Copeland of Perquimans County, Joseph Bryant of Halifax County, and William Speller Rhodes of Bertie County—received and accepted officer appointments in the Tenth Regiment. Copeland and Bryant received captain commissions and the command of companies, while Rhodes was appointed a first lieutenant and assigned as a subordinate officer to Captain Bryant.[4] Copeland and Bryant generally recruited men from the northeastern part of the state and, more specifically, from their home areas.

Lieutenant Rhodes, as a member of Bryant's recruiting contingent, apparently experienced extremely poor recruiting results in his home community. He enlisted only one Bertie County native—William Avis—age twenty-two, who signed up at Windsor on August 11, 1812. Detailed War Department records do not exist to document the amount of effort that Rhodes may have invested in recruiting in the locales he visited. While enlistment registers clearly indicate that he failed to enlist any meaningful number of recruits, he most likely did not dedicate any significant time to the "recruiting service." Rhodes was afflicted with "flux," a disorder in which large quantities of fluids are discharged from the body. His chronic condition forced him to resign his commission in late April 1813, after having served less than a year.[5]

A majority of Bertie County citizens strongly supported the pro-war Republican Party and the Madison administration's war measures. Such support, often accompanied by openly exhibited patriotic, anti-British zeal, would suggest that the county's young men would have enlisted in the United States Army in significant numbers. But within Bertie County there was no patriotic surge of young men rushing to enlist in the army. When the war began, only two county residents (other than Lieutenant Rhodes)—William Brogden and Charney Cale—were serving in the army. Both men were members of the Third Regiment United States Infantry, a regiment that had been raised in 1808 in North Carolina and South Carolina and at the time of the declaration of war was serving in the Mississippi Territory. On June 26, the day after news of the declaration of war reached Bertie County, twenty-one-year-old county native Caleb Garrett enlisted in the Tenth Regiment at Edenton; Captain Copeland enlisted Garrett.[6]

During July and August, six and eleven county residents, respectively, enlisted in the Tenth Regiment to serve in Captains Bryant and Copeland's companies. Three of those men were rejected for undisclosed reasons. One additional county resident, William Hodder, enlisted in the same regiment in September, the last Bertie County resident to enlist in the army in 1812.[7]

Bertie County's political leaders and influential citizens had vocally and publicly espoused support for President Madison and the nation's move to war with Great Britain. Although the nation's leaders and military commanders had made strong calls for army volunteers, Bertie County men obviously were reluctant to enlist. The county's overall support for the war had not translated into an outpouring of enlistments in the army. Several factors seemed to influence the low number of enlistments. First, no active efforts were made by army commanders to recruit within the county until 1814, and no recruiting office was established in Windsor. Second, Bertie County men did not travel the forty-plus miles to Tarboro, the nearest recruiting rendezvous, to join the army. Those few men who enlisted during 1812 did so primarily at Edenton, where Capt. Jesse Copeland had established a recruiting office.[8] Third, army pay was low, only five dollars a month for a private at the start of the war—grossly insufficient enticement for men to leave their farms and families to traipse off to war and endure the

Table 1

Bertie County Enlistees in the Tenth Regiment
United States Infantry in 1812

Month/No. of Enlistees	Names
June/1	Caleb Garrett
July/6	John M. Brickell, Cader Hale, Zadock Haste, James Hoggard, Joseph Lawrence, Hardy White
August/11	William Avis, Josiah Brantly, David Douglas, Elias Hawkins, Nathaniel Holloman, Asa Powell, Miles Rawlings, William Wilkinson, Jasper Buck (rejected), Rian Cale (rejected), Williamson Lawrence (rejected)
September/1	William Hodder

Note: Information recorded in the registers for the War of 1812 period did not include place of residence for enlistees but rather place of birth. For that reason the author reviewed all registers covering the war period initially to identify those men whose place of birth was Bertie County. Many entries contain incomplete information, including place of birth, place of enlistment, enlisting officer, and company/regiment. Therefore, the comprehensiveness of the roster of Bertie County soldiers identified by the author is of necessity based on the available information entered in the registers. The author also sought to identify and document other pertinent information, such as 1810 Bertie County census entries and pension files, in order to confirm the residences of identified soldiers. Such information was not comprehensive, however, and collaborating data was not located for every identified soldier.

associated hardships of army life.[9] Fourth, a precedent had previously been set that men in the eastern part of the state did not rush to enlist in the army. In June 1809 Col. Edward Pasteur of New Bern, former adjutant general of the North Carolina militia and commander of the recently authorized Third Regiment United States Infantry, had spent almost a year recruiting for his command. The recruiting service had progressed so slowly in the eastern sector of the state, however, that he was "induced" to terminate efforts in that region. He reassigned all of his officers to the state's Piedmont region, where results proved much better.[10] In a related matter, in May 1812 Reading Sheppard of Pitt County declined an appointment as a captain in the infantry, advising Secretary of War Eustis that "I think it will be hard to raise a company in this District."[11]

Another factor—the lack of British warriors in the proximity of North Carolina—may likely have resulted in the predominant view among the male population that service in the army was not imperative to repel invaders and marauders. The citizens did not witness the British war machine—they were not directly threatened by the king's soldiers, as all was quiet and peaceful in the Albemarle Sound region.

Additionally, the United States government was largely unprepared to handle in an efficient manner significant numbers of recruits in the summer and fall of 1812. In the rush to implement the recruiting service, the War Department had not effectuated a responsive supply and logistical network. Many newly enlisted soldiers who assembled at recruiting rendezvous did not receive the clothing, equipment, tents, arms, and other necessities to which they were entitled. Obviously, news of the conditions at the sites quickly circulated within the adjoining communities and regions, negatively influencing the propensity of some residents to sign up for military service.

In early September, Congressman William Blackledge visited the recruiting rendezvous in Tarboro. Arriving on the fifth, he found about 200 recruits under the command of Lt. Col. Benajah White of the Tenth Regiment. Although there were enough young men gathered to form the equivalent of two military companies, they had neither arms nor clothing. For the most part, there was a significant assemblage of young men at the site who desired to serve in a military organization that was unprepared for them. Blackledge was told that the recruits' clothing was at Fayetteville and that an officer had been "dispatched there to hurry them [the clothes] on" to Tarboro. Blackledge wasted no time in formulating a letter to Secretary of War Eustis, in which he "repeat[ed] a warning," which he had previously conveyed to Eustis, not to "suffer to[o] large a body of men to remain at any rendezvous in this State long, and particularly not to remain without arms [and clothing]." According to the congressman, to do so gave "rise to complaints of neglect & inattention" by the residents, which were "difficult to combat." [12]

Blackledge's communication focused the secretary's attention on problems evident at the North Carolina recruiting centers, particularly the Tarboro situation. Eustis directed Adj. Gen. Thomas H. Cushing to alert Maj. Gen. Thomas Pinckney of the problems. On September 29 Cushing wrote Pinckney: "I am directed by the Secretary of War to inform you that the recruits at the different rendezvous & Stations in North Carolina, and particularly at Tarboro, are represented to be in a miserable state as to clothing, discipline, etc." Cushing added that Secretary Eustis desired

Pinckney to appoint an officer to be a deputy inspector general for the Southern Department and to "order him immediately to North Carolina to visit & inspect the recruits there." Finally, Cushing directed Pinckney to call on Hanson Kelly, deputy commissary of purchases at Wilmington, "to purchase such clothing as may be necessary" for the recruits' "comfortable accommodation."[13]

Shortly thereafter, Lieutenant Colonel White wrote to Secretary Eustis that Thomas H. Blount, the collector for the port of Washington, North Carolina, held a variety of tents, camp kettles, and other military stores that he had lately secured from the confiscated cargo of a merchant vessel. White requested Eustis to order Blount to provide the tents and other military stores to the Tarboro rendezvous, inasmuch as the troops there were "entirely destitute of those articles and suffer very much for them." According to White, about 250 privates and noncommissioned officers were assembled at Tarboro.[14] On October 21 Eustis directed Blount to deliver the tents and other camp equipage belonging to the Department of War to White at Tarboro.[15] At that time, sixteen Bertie County residents had enlisted in the Tenth Regiment, and likely all, or at least a portion of them, would have been assigned to the Tarboro rendezvous.

The federal government's capability to provide any semblance of adequate supplies and stores for the recruits at the station was challenged. In late October Congressman Blackledge again stopped in Tarboro on his way back to the nation's capital. To his chagrin and dismay, conditions for the soldiers were still deplorable. On November 4, having arrived back in the nation's capital, Blackledge again notified Eustis that of the more than 200 soldiers at the Tarboro recruiting station, "only about 110 of them had received their summer cloathing, [and] that no part of their winter cloathing had been received except about 80 blankets." The congressman noted that the troops "have not a tent, an article of Camp Equipage, arms or ammunition." He further stated that the "complaints made of this post, are rather of the want of everything but provisions. . . . [the complaints] have rendered a suspicion, that you have not been kept apprized regularly by the officer whose duty it was to do it of all the number of troops at this post. Whether you have or not, you can see from the Statement . . . and if you have not the thing should be made known [to] your Department." To exacerbate the situation even more, Blackledge reported that about sixty troops were sick and that Capt. John G. Blount (of the Eighteenth Regiment United States Infantry) had "every possible attention paid to the sick, and did all in his power to make things ware [wear] the best possible appearance."[16] It is very likely that the Tarboro site also lacked crucial medical supplies, since in early September the surgeon of the Tenth Regiment assigned to that station reported that the troops there were "destitute of medical & hospital supplies."[17]

Secretary Eustis obviously received Blackledge's poignant letter the day it was written, since on that same day Eustis penned another directive to Collector Thomas H. Blount at the port of Washington. He ordered Blount: "You will . . . deliver to Colonel White of the US Army all [of] the Camp Equipage rec[eive]d from the wreck of the Brig Hannah in August last, belonging to this Department."[18] Clearly the War Department's logistical system was not meeting the early wartime demands of the army, at least not in eastern North Carolina.

Throughout the war, army officers in North Carolina chronically complained to the War Department that their troops were not adequately supplied with critical items, particularly clothing. As early as June 1812, Colonel Wellborn notified the War Department that recruits in his department looked "naked for the want of arms & cloathing." In late September Secretary Eustis notified Callender Irvine, commissary general of the army (headquartered at Philadelphia, Pennsylvania), that the troops in North Carolina were "destitute of clothing" and instructed Irvine to advise Hanson Kelly, deputy commissary at Wilmington, as to what arrangements Irvine had made "for supplying the troops in that Quarter . . . on that subject." With the onset of cold weather and the arrival of the winter of 1812–1813, the critical need for clothing for the North Carolina soldiers had not been remedied. Wellborn, in a number of communications written to superior officers in December, complained that the soldiers of the Tenth Regiment were "compelled to march naked" and that his troops at the Salisbury rendezvous were "destitute of almost every article of cloathing and [had] not blankets and no tents." In February 1813 he wrote to the inspector general at Pinckney's headquarters in Charleston that his recruits' lack of adequate winter clothing had negatively influenced his officers' recruiting efforts. He noted: "our nakedness in so inclement a season has had a tendency to through [throw] a damp on the young men of the Country who [are] Inclined to join us."[19]

During the nine-month period from September 8, 1812, to June 12, 1813, no Bertie County men enlisted in the United States Army. From July through December 1813 only six county residents joined the army, yielding a total of only twenty-six county men—or roughly 2.5 percent of the military-age men—to enlist and serve in the army during the first year and a half of the war. Bertie County men were indeed slow to enlist in the military.[20]

Table 2

Bertie County Enlistees in the United States Army
(Various Regiments) in 1813

Month/No. of Enlistees	Names
July/1	Joseph Johnson
September/2	Milbourn Farmer, John Sowell
October/3	John Crumwell, Whitmel Baker, Lewis Sheahon

Note: The author calculated the estimated enlistment rate of Bertie County men by dividing the number of enlistees (26) by the approximate number (1,000) of military-age men in the 1810 federal census of Bertie County, as noted in the first chapter.

While Wellborn and his officers faced assorted impediments in recruiting North Carolina men, by the fall of 1812 they had enlisted a sufficient number of men in the state and Virginia to reportedly come close to completing the Tenth Regiment. On October 30, 1812, a Raleigh newspaper reported that the regiment was "nearly complete," with four companies in Virginia and six companies in North Carolina.[21]

In late October General Pinckney directed Wellborn to immediately order a detachment from his regiment to march to Fort Hampton and relieve Capt. John Nicks and his men of the Third Regiment, which the War Department had transferred to the Mississippi Territory. Pinckney further ordered Wellborn to send a company of men to Fort Johnston, near Wilmington, to relieve the North Carolina militia and some officers and men of the Eighteenth Regiment, then serving there.[22] Wellborn assigned Capt. Joseph Bryant and his company to Fort Hampton and Capt. Jesse Copeland and his company to Fort Johnston.[23] The majority of Bertie County men (eleven in number) who had enlisted in the Tenth Regiment were serving in Bryant's company and thus were assigned to Fort Hampton. Only five county men were members of Copeland's company and would have been stationed at Fort Johnston.[24] (All Bertie County men who had enlisted in the army at this time were members of those two companies.)

In January 1813 the War Department discontinued the recruiting rendezvous at Tarboro and Fayetteville as part of its realignment of recruiting districts across the states and territories. The department designated North Carolina as a distinct recruiting district with its principal rendezvous at Salisbury. Colonel Wellborn was designated superintendent of the North

Carolina district.[25] Thereafter, recruiting activities under Wellborn's oversight were concentrated primarily in the Piedmont region of the state. During 1813 no army officers visited Bertie County to recruit.

Bryant and Copeland's companies, including the Bertie County members, performed garrison duty at Forts Hampton and Johnston, watching the coastline for British war vessels while drilling and training. Copeland's men reportedly were well provisioned and cared for at Fort Johnston. On March 13 Copeland wrote a letter to the editor of the *Edenton Gazette* in which he stated that the fort "shows like the brilliant spirit of war. Everything is in a complete state for action and our movements are like clock work. . . . my men are well clothed and fed and are in good health and high spirits[;] they have just received their pay and money appears as plenty as dirt[;] there is at this time about $12,000 among them."[26]

The service and experience of Captain Bryant's company at Beaufort were in drastic contrast to that of Copeland's unit. The service rendered by Bryant's company was characterized by the same degree of neglect from the War Department that had occurred in the early stages of the regimental recruiting efforts. On June 2, 1813, Captain Bryant wrote to Col. Francis H. Huger, adjutant general of the Sixth Military District (General Pinckney's command, formerly the Southern Department), that "I am sorry to say, we have been much neglected at this place. I have not received cartridge boxes yet, or scarcely any thing else. Some of my men I enlisted twelve months past, have not even received a hat, since they enlisted [in] the service or any thing like soldiers clothing, more than shirts, socks & trowsers, which they have worn out; their last pay was received 31st December 1812. They are now naked and moneyless. I have a fine set of young men & good soldiers."[27]

Soon both companies were to depart eastern North Carolina for the war front along the New York-Canada border. On June 1 the War Department issued orders to General Pinckney transferring Bryant and Copeland's companies to Sackets Harbor on Lake Ontario. The department also ordered the rest of Wellborn's Tenth Regiment to march to Norfolk en route to the same destination and directed Bryant and Copeland to "march their companies . . . by the most eligible route . . . to join that regiment . . . this day ordered from Norfolk to repair to Sackett's Harbour."[28]

The War Department's orders did not reach General Pinckney's headquarters until June 26. In the meantime Pinckney had ordered parts of Bryant and Copeland's companies to march to Charleston, while the general ordered Captain Bryant to personally report to Colonel Wellborn at Salisbury. Captain Copeland had begun marching from Fort Johnston to Charleston with his men. On the 26th Col. Francis Huger, adjutant general for the Sixth Military District, wrote to the War Department that he would write by that day's mail to halt Copeland and order him to Norfolk. Huger added that Colonel Wellborn would be directed to order Bryant to "collect his company and proceed to Norfolk."[29] It seemed that Captains Bryant and Copeland's companies, with their constituents of Bertie County men, would now see service in an active theater of the war.[30]

The War Department's transferring orders reached Captain Bryant on June 19. Two and one-half weeks later he responded to Asst. Adj. Gen. Charles K. Gardner that he would "make every execution in my power to obey," but, that "my men being nearly naked [from the lack of clothing provided by the War Department]," he had been forced to send an officer "in pursuit of clothing and contingent money." He further advised Gardner that once he had acquired clothing and money, "nothing . . . will prevent my immediate march but the want of some company to relieve me, as there is no company here except my own." At the time, Bryant's company was incompletely manned, with one officer (besides himself) and fifty-six privates. He advised the adjutant general that there were a sufficient number of men (recruits) at Raleigh and Louisburg belonging to the Tenth Regiment to complete his regiment, and that he would "be glad to take them on with me." Gardner apparently did not authorize the augmentation of Bryant's company with the noted recruits.[31]

Bryant also appealed to Colonel Huger for a company to be dispatched to Fort Hampton to relieve him and his men so that he could march his command "with the least possible delay to join my regiment now on its way to Sackett's Harbor." He further noted that he wished his company, "if possible," to be "made complete, since he was about to encounter a long march."[32] To replace Bryant's company, on July 3 General Pinckney requested Gov. William Hawkins to "provide temporarily" a militia company until relieved by regular troops. Simultaneously, Colonel Huger wrote to Colonel Wellborn, directing that "any disposable forces" that the latter officer had were to replace Bryant and Copeland's companies.[33]

By late September Bryant and Copeland's companies, along with the rest of the Tenth Regiment, had arrived at their New York destination. However, the War Department had ordered Colonel Wellborn to remain in North Carolina and continue to superintend recruiting activities.[34]

Ninth Military District General Hospital, Burlington
Vt. December 13th 1814.

It is hereby Certified that William Avis a private in the company of Capt George Vashons, in 10th Regiment U. States Infantry is incapable of performing the duty of soldier by reason of a wound in the hand while he was actually in the service of said and in the line of his duty.

By satisfactory evidence and accurate examination it appears that on the tenth of July in the 1814 being engaged at a place called Champlain in the State of New York; he received a wound in the hand; and he is thereby not only incapacitated for military duty but in the opinion of the undersigned is one half disabled from obtaining his subsistence by manual labor.

Edw.d Purcell
Actg Hospt Surg.

William Avis, a Bertie County resident, enlisted at Windsor on August 11, 1812, in the Tenth Regiment United States Infantry. He was wounded at Champlain, New York, on July 10, 1814, and subsequently discharged from service due to disability resulting from the wound. Above, a copy of Private Avis's disability discharge document reflects that he had been wounded to such an extent to disable him from military service, and he was honorably discharged on December 14, 1814. Document from pension file for William Avis, Federal Pension Application Files, Record Group 15, National Archives, Washington, D.C.

+ 2705.

Nº 1 ✓

By Colin Buckner, Major, Commanding the 20th Regiment, U. S. Infantry at Norfolk.

BE IT KNOWN,

That William Harris a private in Captain Charles Gee's Company in the 20th Regiment United States Infantry, having served during the war the time for which the said Wm Harris was enlisted; he is hereby Honorably discharged from the service of the United States; and that he is entitled to mileage for one hundred & eight miles, it being the distance from this place to Windsor N.C. his place of residence; and to prevent any ill use that might be made of this discharge, by its falling into the hands of any other person, here follows a description of the said Wm Harris viz: Thirty one years of age, dark hair, blue eyes, dark complexion, five feet four inches high, by occupation a Seaman born in Bertie Coty N. Carolina & Enlisted 25th March 1814

" Registered,"

Charles Gee Capt

Given under my Hand at Norfolk, this 25th day of March. 1815.

Colin Buckner Major 20 Infy

Bertie County resident William Harris served in Capt. Charles Gee's company, Twentieth Regiment United States Infantry, at Norfolk, Virginia. He was discharged at Norfolk in March 1815, following the close of the war. Document from pension file for William Harris, Federal Pension Application Files, Record Group 15, National Archives.

On July 20, 1813, Colonel Wellborn, writing from Salisbury, advised Asst. Adj. Gen. Charles K. Gardner that he had received orders from Major General Pinckney to go to Columbia to take charge of the recruiting district. Wellborn complained that "It appears I am not yet to take command of the [Tenth] regiment raised principally by my own exertions." He further grumbled that officers who had entered the army at lower ranks than he had been promoted to outrank him. He wrote: "I did not expect that those who entered the service as Lieut. Colonels would be first promoted and then to rank me, it would be improper for me to state my impression on this subject and I would be equally so to state my feelings."[35]

In late November both Capts. Joseph Bryant and Jesse Copeland died of non-combat-related causes on consecutive days.[36] The Tenth Regiment would continue to serve in the northern New York region throughout the remainder of the war. Only one Bertie County member of the regiment, Pvt. William Avis, suffered a battle casualty during the regiment's deployment. He was wounded in one of his hands on July 10, 1814, at Champlain, New York. On December 13, 1814, Dr. Edward Purcell, acting hospital surgeon for the Ninth Military District General Hospital at Burlington, Vermont, deemed Private Avis "incapacitated for military duty" as a result of a "lame hand." Avis was discharged by reason of disability the following day.[37]

In early 1814 two officers of the Twentieth Regiment United States Infantry (a unit authorized by Congress in June 1812 and raised primarily in Virginia) visited the Albemarle Sound region to recruit. In late January Capt. Charles Gee and Lt. John H. Howard, both stationed at Norfolk, arrived in Windsor and enlisted their first Bertie County recruits for the Twentieth Regiment. Although the officers enlisted only three men (Hardy Todd, Jesse Thompson, and Westley Moore), Gee soon returned to Windsor and experienced somewhat more success. From February 12 through 21, Captain Gee enlisted a dozen men in the town. About mid-March he once again "came to town" and enlisted five additional county men. During the period January–March 1814, twenty-three county men enlisted in the regiment, the largest influx of recruits from Bertie County to join any regiment during a three-month period during the war. Additionally, during that period nine additional county residents enlisted in other regiments, including the Thirty-fifth, the Thirty-ninth, and the Forty-third Regiments United States Infantry.[38] While the early 1814 enlistment rates were greater than those experienced in 1812 and

Table 3

Bertie County Enlistees in the United States Army during the War of 1812, by Regiment (Includes Rejected Recruits)

Branch and Unit	1812	1813	1814	Totals
Infantry				
Tenth Regiment	19		1	20
Eighteenth Regiment		1	2	3
Twentieth Regiment		1	29	30
Twenty-fourth Regiment			2	2
Thirty-fifth Regiment		2	12	14
Thirty-ninth Regiment			2	2
Forty-third Regiment			7	7
Artillery				
Unidentified Regiment	1		1	2
Rifles				
Unidentified Regiment			1	1
Second Regiment		1		1
Fifth Regiment			1	1
Other				
Unidentified		1		1
Totals	20	6	58	84

Note: Registers of Enlistments. Appendix 2 presents brief service histories of the Bertie County men whom the author identified as having enlisted in the army. The author identified eighty-seven men who enlisted and/or served in the army during the period of the war. Eighty-four men enlisted (including recruits who signed up to serve but were rejected) during the period, while three men (Charney Cale and William Brogden of the Third Regiment United States Infantry and William Speller Rhodes of the Tenth Regiment United States Infantry) were members of the army before war was declared. The majority of the county men who enlisted were 25 years old or younger. Of the eighty enlistees for whom age data was captured in the Registers of Enlistments, sixty-seven (almost 84 percent) were aged 25 or younger. Hardy Todd enlisted at the age of 40; he was the oldest county man to serve in the army during the war. Todd deserted in September 1814, only to return to his unit in late February 1815—after the war had concluded. He was tried by court-martial for desertion, found guilty, and dishonorably discharged from the army in March 1815. Todd held the distinction of being Bertie County's oldest soldier and, also, the only one to receive a dishonorable discharge.

1813, there was still no rush by military-age residents of Bertie County to sign up for the army.

The county residents who enlisted in the Twentieth and Thirty-fifth Regiments were assigned to companies stationed in the Norfolk area. There they kept a constant vigil for British warships and invaders from the Atlantic Ocean and the Chesapeake Bay. However, throughout the remainder of the war until the Treaty of Ghent was ratified in February 1815, no British invasion took place at Norfolk.

From late January 1814 through mid-June 1814, seven Bertie County men crossed the Roanoke River to Plymouth, where they enlisted in Capt. Henry Garrett's company of the Forty-third Regiment United States Infantry. Those men were all eventually assigned to Fort Hampton under the command of Garrett, a Plymouth native, and saw no combat. Five of the men were discharged at the fort in August 1815, their terms of enlistment (to serve during the war) having expired. One man deserted in late July 1815, while the seventh soldier was discharged at Fort Hampton in November 1815.[39]

During the whole of 1814, a total of fifty-eight Bertie County men joined the army, enlisting in ten different units. The majority of the recruits joined the Twentieth and Thirty-fifth Regiments. During the war, only eighty-four county residents enlisted in the army—less than 10 percent of the county's estimated military-age population.

Since the army regiments in which Bertie County men served experienced virtually no combat, no Bertie County men were killed in action during the war. Pvt. William Avis (Tenth Regiment) was the county's only battle casualty. Eight county residents died of disease and illness. During the war, fifteen Bertie County soldiers deserted from their regiments, of whom ten men never returned to duty. Thirteen county soldiers were discharged prior to the end of the conflict (one of those men reenlisted). In total, only fifty-five Bertie County residents were still serving in the army in February 1815 when news of peace spread across the country.[40]

Notes

1. *United States Statutes at Large* 2 (1845): 669–671, 764. The act of January 11, 1812, authorized the raising of 10 regiments of infantry, 2 regiments of artillery, and 1 regiment of light dragoons. Under this and previous acts, a total of 17 infantry regiments had been authorized. The act of June 26, 1812, stipulated that the infantry component of the United States Army was to consist of 25 regiments. For brief histories of the various regiments, see Francis B. Heitman, *Historical Register and Dictionary of the United States Army*, 2 vols. (Washington, D.C.: Government Printing Office, 1903).

2. General Orders, Adjutant General's Office, War Department, July 4, 1812, General Orders and Circulars of the War Department and Headquarters of the Army, 1809–1860 (microfilm, M1094), Record Group 94, National Archives (hereafter cited as War Department General Orders and Circulars); *Raleigh Register and North Carolina Gazette,* May 22, 1812; Wellborn to Adj. Gen. Thomas H. Cushing, May 23, 1812, Letters Received by the Office of the Adjutant General, 1805–1821 (microfilm, M566), Record Group 94, National Archives (hereafter cited as Adjutant General—Letters Received).

3. Officers of the Tenth Regiment were authorized to enlist men at a number of locations in North Carolina and Virginia in 1812, including (but not limited to): North Carolina—Bertie County, Buncombe County, Chowan County, Guilford County, Halifax County, Mecklenburg County, Perquimans County, Rockingham County, Rowan County, Salem, Salisbury, Stokes County, Surry County, Wake County, and Wilkes County; Virginia—Franklin, Pittsylvania County, Princess Anne County, and Prince Edward County. The author identified these locations by reviewing and noting available information in Registers of Enlistments in the United States Army, 1798–1914 (microfilm, M233), Record Group 94, National Archives (hereafter cited as Registers of Enlistments).

4. Copeland to Eustis, March 30, 1812; Bryant to Eustis, April 8, 1812; and Rhodes to Eustis, May 17, 1812, Adjutant General—Letters Received.

5. Charles K. Gardner, *A Dictionary of All Officers Who Have Been Commissioned or Have Been Approved in the Army of the United States, 1789–1853* (New York: G. P. Putnam and Company, 1853), s.v. "Rhodes, William S." (hereafter cited as Gardner, *Dictionary of Army Officers*); Registers of Enlistments, William Avis entry; Wellborn to Asst. Adj. Gen. Charles K. Gardner, April 10, 1813, Adjutant General—Letters Received.

6. Registers of Enlistments, William Brogden, Charney Cale, and Caleb Garrett entries; Gardner, *Dictionary of Army Officers*, s.v. "Copeland, Jesse"; Copeland to Eustis, March 30, 1812, Adjutant General—Letters Received.

7. Registers of Enlistments, entries for identified soldiers.

8. The author thoroughly reviewed the Registers of Enlistments in attempting to identify places of enlistment for those recruits who, according to the registers, had been born in Bertie County. He identified only one county resident, William Avis of the Tenth Regiment United States Infantry, who enlisted at Windsor during the years 1812–1813. Clearly, no recruiting office was established at Windsor. Similarly, the

author was able to identify no county residents who enlisted at Tarboro during those two years.

9. Donald R. Hickey, *The War of 1812: A Short History* (Urbana: University of Illinois Press, 1995), 21.

10. Pasteur to Sec. of War Henry Dearborn, June 13, 1809, Letters Received by the Secretary of War, Main Series, 1801–1870 (microfilm, M221), Record Group 107, National Archives (hereafter cited as Secretary of War—Letters Received).

11. Sheppard to Eustis, May 5, 1812, Adjutant General—Letters Received.

12. Blackledge to Eustis, September 5, 1812, Secretary of War—Letters Received.

13. Cushing to Pinckney, September 29, 1812, Letters Sent by the Office of the Adjutant General, Main Series, 1800–1890 (microfilm, M565), Record Group 94, National Archives (hereafter cited as Adjutant General—Letters Sent).

14. Lt. Col. Benajah White to Eustis, October 13, 1812, Secretary of War—Letters Received.

15. Eustis to Collector [Thomas H. Blount], Port of Washington, N.C., October 21, 1812, Letters Sent by the Secretary of War Relating to Military Affairs, 1800–1889 (microfilm, M6), Record Group 107, National Archives (hereafter cited as Secretary of War—Letters Sent).

16. Blackledge to Eustis, Nov. 4, 1812, Secretary of War—Letters Received.

17. Eustis to Hanson Kelly, September 2, 1812, Secretary of War—Letters Sent.

18. Eustis to Thomas Blount, November 4, 1812, Secretary of War—Letters Sent.

19. Wellborn to Col. A. Smith [Smyth], undated (but about late May or early June 1812), Adjutant General—Letters Received; Eustis to Callender Irvine, September 29, 1812, Secretary of War—Letters Sent; Wellborn to William R. Boots, December 16 and 27, 1812, Adjutant General—Letters Received; Wellborn to Cushing, February 13, 1813, Adjutant General—Letters Received.

20. Registers of Enlistments.

21. *Raleigh Register and North Carolina Gazette*, October 30, 1812.

22. General Orders, October 30, 1812, Southern Department General Orders Received & Orders Issued, June 1812–February 1813, Vol. 2, Record Group 98, National Archives.

23. The author found no direct orders from Colonel Wellborn to Captains Bryant and Copeland assigning them and their companies to Forts Hampton and Johnston respectively. Nevertheless, the author ascertained that such orders were indeed issued, inasmuch as various records clearly document that those commanders and their units served at the two locations.

24. Registers of Enlistments. The members of Bryant's company were: William Avis, Josiah Brantly, John M. Brickell, David Douglas, Elias Hawkins, William Hodder, James Hoggard, Nathaniel Holloman, Asa Powell, William Speller Rhodes, and William Wilkinson. The members of Copeland's company were: Caleb Garrett, Zadock Haste, Joseph Lawrence, Miles Rawlings, and Hardy White.

25. General Orders, War Department, January 15, 1813, General Orders and Circulars of the War Department and Headquarters of the Army, 1809–1860 (microfilm, M1094), Record Group 94, National Archives (hereafter cited as War Department General Orders and Circulars).

26. Raymond Parker Fouts, *Abstracts from the* Edenton Gazette and North Carolina General Advertiser*, Edenton, North Carolina*, 3 vols. (Cocoa, Fla.: GenRec Books, 1993), 3:33; *New Bedford* (Mass.) *Mercury*, June 18, 1813.

27. Bryant to Huger, June 2, 1813, Adjutant General—Letters Received.

28. General Orders, Adjutant General's Office, War Department, June 1, 1813, War Department General Orders and Circulars.

29. Huger to Adjutant and Inspector General, War Department, June 26, 1813, Adjutant General—Letters Received. On March 19, 1813, the War Department reorganized the wartime military establishment into nine military districts across the states and territories. The War Department designated the geographic region of North Carolina, South Carolina, and Georgia, previously known as the "Southern Department" and commanded by General Pinckney, as "Military District No. 6." The district's headquarters remained at Charleston, and Pinckney continued to command from that location (except when he traveled to other sectors of his command and temporarily relocated his headquarters). General Orders, War Department, March 19, 1813, War Department General Orders and Circulars.

30. While Captains Bryant and Copeland's companies were ordered to proceed to Sackets Harbor, only a dozen Bertie County men were members of those units. Lt. William Speller Rhodes (Bryant's company) had previously resigned, and three men—Zadock Haste, Joseph Lawrence, and Hardy White (all of Copeland's company)—had deserted. One other Bertie County resident, Cader Hale of Capt. Thomas N. Nelson's company, likewise accompanied the Tenth Regiment to New York. Registers of Enlistments, entries for identified individuals.

31. Bryant to Gardner, July 6, 1813, Adjutant General—Letters Received. The author found no documentation or other evidence that Gardner ordered any troops to be transferred to Bryant's company to "fill out the ranks." Gardner was appointed assistant adjutant general on March 18, 1813, and served under Adjutant and Inspector General Abimael Y. Nicoll. See Col. William H. Powell, U.S. Army, *List of Officers in the Army of the United States from 1779 to 1900* (New York: L. R. Hamersly & Co., 1900), 65.

32. Bryant to Huger, July 5, 1813, Adjutant General—Letters Received.

33. Pinckney to Hawkins, July 3, 1813, William Hawkins, Governors Letter Books, State Archives, Office of Archives and History; Huger to Wellborn, July 3, 1813, Sixth Military District, Letters Sent, March 1813–June 1815, Entry 33, Record Group 98, National Archives, 1:80.

34. A Norwich, Connecticut, newspaper reported on September 22 that "last Wednesday [the fifteenth] a detachment of . . . troops under the command of Capt. Copeland, embarked at this place for New London." *Norwich* (Conn.) *Courier*, September 22, 1813.

35. Wellborn to Gardner, July 20, 1813, Adjutant General—Letters Received. During the whole of the war, the War Department never placed Wellborn in command of his regiment "in the field." He continuously served in a largely administrative capacity, superintending recruiting activities under the purview of General Pinckney.

36. Gardner, *Dictionary of Army Officers*, s.v. "Bryant, Joseph," and "Copeland, Jesse." On December 29, 1813, the *Evening Post* (New York) reported the deaths of Captains Bryant and Copeland and that both officers were buried at Plattsburg with military honors. They most likely died from disease/illness stemming from the harsh northern climate.

37. Registers of Enlistments, entry for William Avis.

38. Registers of Enlistments, entries for William Boyce, Shadrack Britt, Jarvis Butler, Jonathan Cook, Jesse Eason, Moses Freeman, John S. Holley, Hardy Hunter, Ryan Jernigan, Ephraim Kanady, William King, Westley Moore, Ebenezer Reddick, Asa Redditt, William Revels, Josiah Simons, Moses Spivey, Solomon Stone, Jesse Thompson, Hardy Todd, Nimrod West, James Williams, and Parker Williams, all members of the Twentieth Regiment United States Infantry. Entries for John Brantley and Cyrus Carr, Thirty-fifth Regiment United States Infantry. Entries for William Butler and Henry Meazles, Thirty-ninth Regiment United States Infantry. Entries for John D. Barber, Solomon Craft, and Frederick Rogers, Forty-third Regiment United States Infantry. Entry for William M. Brickell, United States Artillery.

39. Registers of Enlistments, entries for John D. Barber, Allen Bentley, Thomas Burnham, Solomon Craft, Frederick Rogers, Kenneth Barber, and King White. Kenneth Barber deserted on July 27, 1815, apparently from Fort Hampton. King White was discharged on November 5, 1815.

40. The author developed statistics on Bertie County's army soldiers from information derived from Registers of Enlistments. Regarding military deserters, in July 1815 the War Department—at the direction of President Madison—publicly announced that "all deserters from the army of the United States, during the late war, may peaceably and safely return to their homes without being subject to punishment or trial on account of such desertion." *Raleigh Register and North Carolina Gazette*, July 21, 1815.

CHAPTER 4

Anxiety and Excitement in the East

June 1813 found Bertie County and the rest of northeastern North Carolina relatively quiet and tranquil, but residents in the region were anxious about the possibility of visits by British war vessels and troops. British forces had moved closer to the area. In mid-June British forces had entered the Chesapeake Bay, and on June 20 British men-of-war appeared in Norfolk harbor, approximately 100 miles from Bertie County. Two days later troops from the warships came ashore on the Virginia mainland and assaulted Craney Island. The island, which guarded the mouth of the Elizabeth River and the key component of Norfolk's defense, was garrisoned by Virginia militia units under the command of Brig. Gen. Robert B. Taylor. Taylor's forces, together with gunboats under the command of Capt. John Cassin, as well as marines and sailors from the frigate *Constellation* (which was "bottled-up" in the harbor by the British blockade), repulsed the British. On June 23 British troops landed at Newport News and captured Hampton two days later, committing a number of outrages against the civilian population of the village. Next the British raided up the James River past Smithfield before returning to their vessels. The vessels then moved into Chesapeake Bay and its tributaries to raid and plunder, but they soon returned to Lynnhaven Bay (Norfolk) and anchored.[1] The warships were now within striking distance of North Carolina's coast and waterways.

On June 28 British raiders landed in the extreme northern sector of Currituck County and reportedly did "considerable damage," prompting Maj. Caleb Etheridge of Currituck County to call out two companies of the county's militia. The militiamen were, however, "short of arms, Scarce of ammunition and [had] no provisions" except that which they obtained by "harsh means." Major Etheridge wrote to Col. Josiah Flowers at Plymouth, commander of the First Regiment North Carolina Militia (Detached), immediately seeking arms, ammunition, and supplies, "Supposing it [Flowers's] duty to furnish or cause to be furnished such supplies as are necessary."[2]

Flowers, who had available none of the items the major sought, in turn wrote immediately to Joseph H. Bryan at Windsor. In May Gov. William Hawkins had appointed Bryan to the position of quartermaster general for

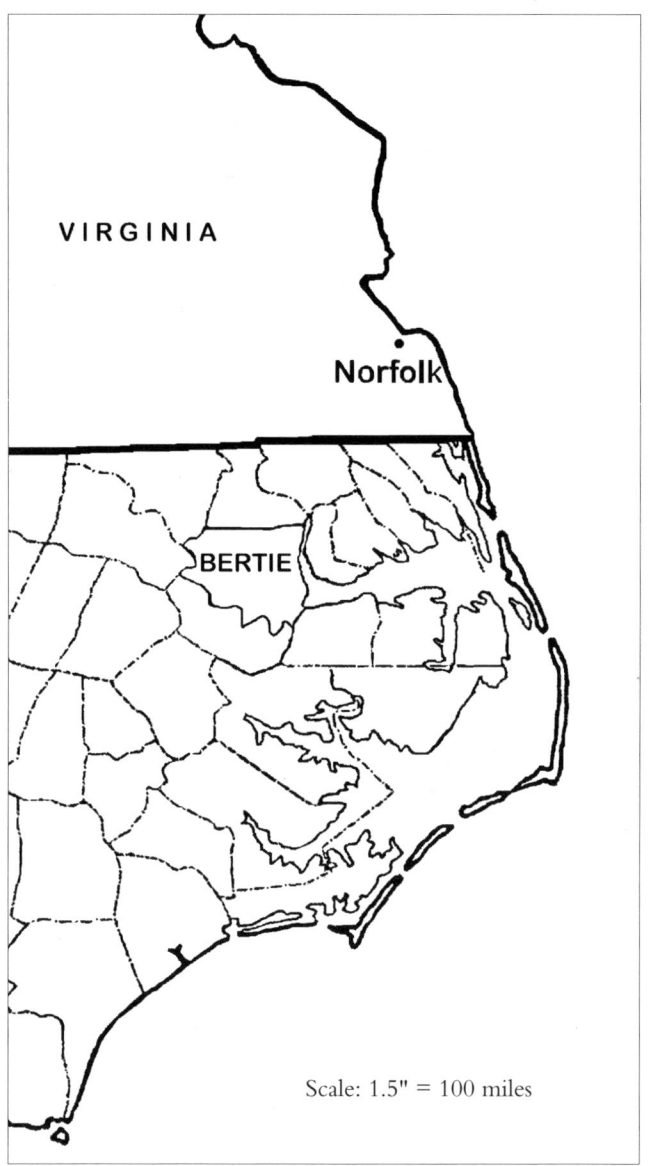

VIRGINIA

Norfolk

BERTIE

Scale: 1.5" = 100 miles

By the early summer of 1813, British warships and military forces were stationed in the waters around Norfolk, Virginia, where they were employed in conducting raids. The British forces were within easy striking distance of northeastern North Carolina, thereby causing a degree of alarm among residents of the area. Bertie County is approximately one hundred miles from Norfolk. Map prepared by Susan Trimble.

the state's detached militia.[3] In that capacity General Bryan was responsible for overseeing and managing the supply system for the state's detached militia. But Bryan, like other officers in charge of militia (and army) units in eastern North Carolina, faced dire challenges in executing his logistical functions. Even though Bryan was the chief quartermaster officer in the state, he likewise had none of the items sought by Flowers on behalf of Major Etheridge. He responded to the colonel that

none of those articles are placed at my disposal nor have I instructions to furnish any. I do not know whether the detachment are in Service by direction of State authorities or by direction of the General Government. If by the latter the contractor for supplies at Norfolk would be the proper person to supply the men with their rations. I shall immediately dispatch an inquiry to his Excellency the Governor with a view to making such arrangements as the nature of the case may require. [I]n the mean time I should recommend . . . to Maj'r Etheridge to purchase such articles of necessity as his immediate wants may require for which he no doubt will be remunerated. Whenever I hear from his Excellency, I will communicate the result.[4]

Bryan quickly prepared a letter to the governor and sent it to Raleigh by an express rider. Enclosing copies of Flowers's letter to him and his reply to Flowers, Bryan noted: "believing as I do that a speedy supply of the articles required are absolutely and indispensably necessary I have hired an express to bear this to you with a view that you may give me such instructions as you deem necessary by next Friday's mail. It is unnecessary I presume to mention to your Excellency that if I am to act efficiently in the Quarter Masters Department it is necessary I should have some general instructions authorizing me in cases of necessity like the present to use my efforts to furnish the requisite supplies."[5]

Three days later Hawkins responded that another individual had advised him earlier of the British raid in Currituck County. The governor noted that upon receipt of that information, he issued orders through the state's adjutant general to each of the colonels of Camden, Chowan, Currituck, Gates, Pasquotank, and Perquimans counties to deliver upon application of Colonel Flowers or either of the field officers of the First Regiment the arms that had been furnished to them by the state "to be used by such portion of the Detachment as may be called into service to repel the enemy."[6]

Hawkins also asserted that, regarding munitions of war, he had no legal authority to use state funds to purchase such items, since the "last General Assembly expressed their determination by a vote, not to place it in the power of the Executive to apply any of the public monies towards the procurement of them." Hawkins, fully aware of the dire need of munitions for North Carolina's detached militia, informed Bryan that "a few weeks past," he had determined "to purchase them upon my own responsibility, should wants render it indispensably necessary, and since my determination to do so I have been able to procure a supply." He added that should he have the opportunity to acquire "a quantity" of lead and powder in Raleigh, he would "certainly purchase it in the want of the General Government neglecting to furnish a supply which has been promised" (and which he still expected to receive). The governor concluded that "For the present, the troops must rely upon their own resources, and those of the persons whom they are called out to defend, for a supply of ammunition & as well as for subsistence. Should you, however, as Quarter-Master General to the Detachment cause them to be furnished with such supplies as they cannot dispense with, the General Government must unquestionably . . . pay off your accounts, as they have no officer in that section of the Country to furnish them."[7] Unfortunately, Hawkins was apparently unaware of the War Department's regulations that prohibited state officials and/or militia officers from purchasing munitions, supplies, provisions, and other items on behalf of the federal government without explicit authority from an army officer with specific purview over such transactions.[8]

During June a number of North Carolina's elected officials—senators, representatives, and the governor—sent a flurry of letters to the secretary of war and the secretary of the navy, once again seeking additional military resources to defend the state's coastal region. On June 11 Governor Hawkins wrote to North Carolina's two senators—David Stone (of Bertie County) and James Turner—enclosing memorials and letters from residents of New Bern, Beaufort, and Wilmington expressing grave concerns of the inadequate defenses provided for those locales. Hawkins desired that the senators convey the concerns to the secretary of the navy. Two days later, Stone and Turner, along with Reps. William Gaston and William H. Murfree, and a Mr. William Kinney, jointly wrote to Sec. William Jones that the towns situated on the waters connected with Pamlico Sound were "in danger of visits from the enemy." The writers advised Jones that the communities could be guarded "at a small expense" with one or two naval vessels armed with from ten to sixteen guns and manned with a force of seventy to one hundred men stationed at the swash at Ocracoke Inlet. They sought the secretary's "early attention" to their plea "in order to relieve the anxiety" that was felt by residents in some of the towns along the referenced tributaries.[9]

Rep. William R. King likewise wrote to Jones, calling the secretary's attention to the "exposed situation of the Sea Coast of North Carolina."

While King acknowledged the inadequate defenses employed along the whole coast of the state, he specifically directed his comments to the town of Wilmington (situated within his congressional district). King was extremely concerned over the deactivation of the gunboats at the Wilmington naval station. Without gunboats on patrol, Wilmington and the Cape Fear River were "altogether destitute of any protection," except what was "afforded by a sandy mound called a Fort." (Here King refers sarcastically to Fort Johnston.) According to King, Wilmington could not defend itself against "the most inferior force," and two banking establishments were thusly exposed to raiding parties. In his view, "a small naval force" comprised of gunboats alone (owing to the shallowness of the waters around Wilmington) was sufficient for the port town's protection. He concluded: "I hope you will take this subject under consideration; and oblige me with an answer." [10]

On June 14 Jones replied to King, Stone, Turner, Gaston, and Murfree that "three Gun Boats will immediately be ordered into Service for the protection of the waters of North Carolina, two of which will be stationed at Ocracoke and one at Beaufort." [11] On June 22 Jones ordered Sailing Master Thomas N. Gautier, commander of the Wilmington station, to "prepare for immediate service, six of the Gun Boats under your command and . . . recruit . . . petty officers and men and ordinary seamen for each boat." He also directed Gautier to retain three of the gunboats at Wilmington and dispatch two to Ocracoke Inlet and one to Beaufort. Jones advised Gautier that his command would extend over the entire force (the six vessels) to which he would give orders. He then informed the officer that he was to act under the immediate orders of the Department of the Navy and communicate directly with the department's headquarters in the nation's capital. Jones further noted, "I expect of you the utmost vigilance and attention, as well as [to] protect the waters and coast assigned to your command." [12] The gunboats that earlier in the war had been dispatched to the waters of North Carolina, only to be ordered to be laid up in ordinary, were now to be rushed back into service and crews recruited to man them.

Also on June 22, Senator Stone wrote to Governor Hawkins that Secretary Jones had promised to post five gunboats on the North Carolina coast—two to be stationed on the Cape Fear River, one at Beaufort, and two at Ocracoke Inlet. Stone confided in the governor that he was "not entirely satisfied" with the defensive arrangements made for the state by the central government, since regular army troops who had voluntarily enlisted in North Carolina had been transferred out of the state to protect "Sister States." [13]

Six days later Stone sent a letter to Secretary of War John Armstrong asserting that, with the British navy effectively blocking trade in and along the Chesapeake Bay, the importance of Ocracoke Inlet to North Carolina "and at this time to all states" had increased. The senator advised the secretary that the trade of New Bern, Washington, Plymouth, Edenton, and "the now more important trade of Elizabeth City[,] . . . at this time more valuable" than normal (because of the blockade of Norfolk and the conduit of commerce from that port to Elizabeth City by way of the Dismal Swamp Canal), were exposed to interruption. Stone inquired of Armstrong if he would "have the goodness to consider whether a company of militia may not be employed to assist in the protection of . . . [Ocracoke] Inlet."[14]

Armstrong conceded to Stone's request. On July 4 Stone advised Governor Hawkins that Armstrong had informed him that he had issued an order for a company of militia to be stationed at or near Ocracoke.[15] Five days later the secretary wrote to Hawkins, directing him to "put four companies of the drafted militia of North Carolina into active service as follows, one at Ocracock, one at Beaufort, & two at Wilmington."[16]

John Armstrong, a veteran of the Revolutionary War, succeeded William Eustis as secretary of war in January 1813. He oversaw the restructuring of the United States Army into nine military districts and sought to strengthen American defenses with more regular troops (as opposed to militia forces). Nevertheless, Armstrong found that the regular forces could not recruit enough men to eliminate the need for militia. North Carolina officials regularly implored Armstrong to augment the state's land forces, but with limited success. Armstrong resigned as secretary of war in September 1814 as a direct result of the British raid and destruction of the nation's capital in August 1814. Image courtesy of the Library of Congress.

On June 30 Congressman Murfree wrote to Secretary Jones to advise him that defense of the North Carolina coast was needed in Currituck County near the Virginia line "from the plundering incursions of the enemy." According to the congressman, 110 militiamen were "stationed on the beach at Currituck Inlet" but were "useless for want of means of transportation [to meet the enemy]." Murfree added that 130 to 140 families were potentially exposed to the British raiders, whose ships were along the coast in the vicinity "almost every day." In Murfree's opinion, the stationing in Currituck Sound of a "gun boat of the smallest size or even a large barge mounting one nine-pounder [cannon] with half the number of men now on the beach, would afford ample means of defence against the small craft which can pass [through] the inlet." [17]

Every eastern North Carolina congressman had appealed to "Washington" for additional military forces in their districts and protection for their constituents and their property. The availability of military assets, particularly naval vessels, to the central government, was severely limited, however, and the leaders in Washington were understandably slow in diverting such resources to eastern North Carolina.

Although North Carolina's elected officials, particularly those from the eastern section of the state, had for more than a year pleaded continually with federal authorities to station more military forces along the coast, certain residents were justifiably apprehensive that such forces would not be in place if and when British forces showed themselves. The highly influential John Gray Blount of Washington, North Carolina, on June 17 wrote to Capt. James Taylor of the United States Navy (and formerly the collector at Ocracoke) that he feared "much mischief will be done . . . before any arrangement can be made to protect" Ocracoke. Blount had received unconfirmed intelligence from William Blackledge (then a former congressman, having been replaced by William Gaston) that the British had recently boarded a Spanish vessel in the Atlantic Ocean and that the Spaniards had obtained information that a squadron of British ships was preparing to sail to Ocracoke. [18]

Indeed, British forces were then only a few days from launching a raid at Ocracoke. British admiral Sir John B. Warren, commander of his majesty's naval forces in the Chesapeake Bay, had decided to follow up his attacks on Craney Island and Hampton with a raid on the North Carolina coast. Warren designated Rear Adm. George Cockburn to lead the expedition, ordering him to destroy American shipping at Ocracoke. To carry out the raid, Warren dispatched from his Chesapeake Bay force seven vessels and

500 ground troops under the command of Lt. Col. Charles Napier (who likewise had commanded elements of the landing forces at Craney Island and Hampton). The British force arrived off Ocracoke Bar after dark on July 11 and dropped anchor.

Cockburn and Napier decided to launch their raid "at once" to prevent the Americans from "collecting any Force from the Neighborhood, or exerting additional Means of Defence in consequence of our appearance." Cockburn directed that preparations be made to disembark the troops in the darkness of the night, although the weather was "not so favorable" as the admiral wished for such a maneuver. At two o'clock in the morning of the twelfth, the British landing forces moved toward the shore, but because of the distance to be covered and a heavy "swell" that was running, it was "considerably" after daylight before the initial parties made their way ashore. Cockburn reported to Warren that, because of the unfavorable conditions, the Americans "had some little Time to prepare for Defence."

British gunners opened fired on two privateers—a brig (the *Anaconda*) and a schooner (the *Atlas*)—which hoisted American colors and fired on the approaching British boats. Both vessels soon conceded to the British—the crew of the *Anaconda* abandoned the brig, and the *Atlas* struck its colors. British troops immediately boarded the vessels and took possession of them, they being the only armed vessels in the harbor. A number of neutral merchant ships in the area set sail to avoid the British forces. According to Cockburn, the British vessels were unable to overtake any of the merchant boats because they became grounded on shoals and "the American Vessels having been much favored by the Breeze." The merchant ships fled inland and delivered news of the British attack to the inland port towns.

Napier divided his troops into two divisions and successfully landed on Ocracoke and Portsmouth islands. The British faced no opposition—no army or militia units were present in the area; neither were any American gunboats patrolling at the inlet or even within the adjacent waterways. Despite the many appeals from state leaders to the central government, not one military asset was stationed at Ocracoke Inlet when Cockburn and Napier's forces arrived. John Gray Blount's fear of British military forces landing at Ocracoke Inlet before proper defenses were established had come to pass. The residents of both islands immediately submitted to the mercy of the British troops. Having secured their positions on both islands, the British began raiding and plundering the island communities, driving live-stock and fowl to their ships, and gathering other provisions and personal belongings of the residents.[19]

Between February and July 1813, Adm. George Cockburn commanded British naval forces that constantly threatened American interests and raided communities around Chesapeake Bay. In July Cockburn commanded naval forces that had been detached from the Chesapeake Bay fleet; those men, in conjunction with army troops under Lt. Col. Charles Napier, raided the port of Ocracoke. While Cockburn and Napier's forces were at Ocracoke only a few days, their presence and actions created a state of alarm in eastern North Carolina. Image courtesy of the Library of Congress.

Late in the day on July 12, a vessel that had fled from Ocracoke that morning reached New Bern, and its crew members spread the news of the British invasion. Over the next couple of days, accounts of the British attack and raid on Ocracoke and Portsmouth islands began arriving in the various communities of eastern North Carolina. Excitement and panic ensued as the residents and militia commanders envisioned the British forces continuing to advance inland and similarly raiding port towns. The predominant view among the inhabitants was that the British were intending to "sweep" through the sounds and rivers of eastern North Carolina. On July 14 Josiah Collins Jr. of Edenton, who had learned of the raid while in Washington, North Carolina, delivered the distressing news to Col. Josiah Flowers at Plymouth. Flowers immediately called out five companies of militia to go to Ocracoke "to repel the enemy and guard the exposed Frontier coast." Flowers issued his orders pursuant to a discretionary order given to him in October 1812 by Maj. Gen. Thomas Brown, commanding officer of the North Carolina detached militia.[20]

Flowers sent a dispatch to Maj. John McCotter of the First Regiment North Carolina Militia (Detached) at Edenton, announcing that the British "have come over Ocracock Bar in considerable force . . . and have done considerable damage." In consideration of a potential raid on the town, McCotter naturally was concerned over its exposed situation and the need for additional defensive measures there.[21]

Flowers also directed a dispatch to Quartermaster Gen. Joseph H. Bryan at Windsor, seeking arms and munitions. As had been the case in late June, when Flowers had made a similar appeal, Bryan still had no arms or munitions at his disposal. On this occasion, however, with British troops on North Carolina soil, Flowers's request appeared "so pressing" to Bryan that he concluded that it was his duty "to endeavor . . . every exertion to procure supplies of powder & lead in the neighboring towns." Bryan quickly discovered that no sufficient quantities of either item could be acquired in northeastern North Carolina and that the militia detachments were useless without ammunition. He thus felt "justified" in traveling to Norfolk in the hope of obtaining such supplies from the army. Arriving in Norfolk, Bryan applied to Brig. Gen. Robert B. Taylor, commanding officer of the Fifth Military District, to draw a supply of powder and lead from the magazine at that place. Unfortunately, General Taylor informed Bryan that he "had not a pound of powder to spare." Nonetheless, Taylor allowed Bryan to draw 1,000 pounds of lead. Bryan also obtained a quantity of gun flints and cartridge paper. Having no funds to remit for the acquisitions, Bryan purchased them on sixty days' credit, payable on September 18. He then hired a wagoner to transport the items to Edenton and deliver them to the commanding officer (Maj. John McCotter) at that location.[22]

On July 15 Lt. Col. Duncan McDonald of the Chowan County militia advised Governor Hawkins that he anticipated a visit to Edenton from the British. McDonald felt that it was "so practicable for them to invade us in our present unprepared situation." He further presumed that towns such as Edenton, in which branches of the state bank were situated, were the most likely locations for the British to strike. Therefore, he "deemed it necessary to order out the Militia" belonging to Chowan County to place the town in the best state of preparation that the short notice he had received and the means within his power would permit. McDonald informed the governor that ammunition was scarce in the area and that he had sent express messengers to the adjoining towns for all the munitions that could be procured. He was "sorry to state," however, that "very little was obtained." Therefore, he sent an express rider to Norfolk for a supply that he hoped would reach Edenton the following evening.[23] (McDonald appeared to be unaware that General Bryan had gone to Norfolk for the same purpose for which McDonald had dispatched a rider.)

At New Bern, Col. Nathan Tisdale of the North Carolina militia called out the Craven County militia, believing the British were about to attack the town. Tisdale sent an urgent message to Governor Hawkins for assistance as frantic preparations were made to bolster the town's defenses. Upon learning of the situation through Tisdale's correspondence, Governor Hawkins went with a troop of cavalry to New Bern to lend assistance and command the state's militia forces there in the event of a British attack. The governor would not return to Raleigh until about mid-August.[24]

Farther south, concerns were prevalent that Fort Hampton would be taken, "there being only forty men to defend that post." Around Wilmington, Brig. Gen. William W. Jones, commanding officer of the Third Brigade of North Carolina militia, ordered 500 militiamen "in the neighborhood" to report to Fort Johnston, where only about 70 soldiers were stationed for its defense. Like the other communities in the eastern sector of the state, the inhabitants viewed Wilmington as being in a "defenceless situation."[25]

In Pasquotank County, Col. Thomas Banks received news of the invasion at three o'clock in the morning on the fifteenth in an express letter from Major McCotter. Banks immediately dispatched requests to several of the county's militia captains to assemble in Elizabeth City "without delay" with their equipment. By that afternoon upward of 200 men with arms had assembled in the village, but most of the troops carried shotguns but no ammunition. Banks was forced to seek some arms and ammunition from a privateer schooner then lying in the harbor at Elizabeth City. Brig. Gen. Jeremiah Brite, commander of the First Brigade North Carolina Militia, authorized the requisition from the vessel.[26]

On July 16 Maj. John Wilroy of the Camden County militia offered "a number of [militia]men" who were stationed at the Camden courthouse to augment Banks's militia force. According to Wilroy, he had been informed of a "great probability" that the British were "about to effect a landing at Elizabeth [City]." He requested Colonel Banks to write back immediately, stating whether such a landing seemed imminent and if any assistance was wanted from Camden County.[27] The entire eastern sector of North Carolina was in a state of nervousness and excitement. Commanders of militia units in every coastal and inland port town in the sector believed that the British were likely to enter their communities.

While militia commanders and others rushed to build up defenses in the various villages and mobilize militia units throughout the eastern part of the state, Cockburn and Napier's forces remained at Ocracoke and Portsmouth for four days, carrying out their plundering. The officers learned that there were no vessels "of any size nor other object" worthy of their attention at Washington or New Bern. Therefore, rather than sailing inland, on the sixteenth the British forces re-embarked on their ships and sailed back toward the Chesapeake Bay. On July 19, after arriving back in the bay, Cockburn expressed to Admiral Warren his belief that the British blockade of the Chesapeake had been materially, if not entirely, frustrated because the ports of Beaufort and Ocracoke had not been similarly blockaded. Cockburn noted that there was "easy inland navigation from Norfolk to Elizabeth Town [Elizabeth City]" through the canal and that goods were then transported in small craft to Ocracoke and Beaufort. He recommended to his superior officer that both locations should be strictly blockaded.[28] Not until September 1 did Warren issue orders to his naval commanders and proclaim that "all the outlets from the Albemarle and Pamptico sounds, connected to inland navigation with the port of Norfolk, and ports of Beaufort and Ocracoke, North Carolina, Cape Fear river . . . [would be] in a state of strict and rigour[ou]s blockade."[29]

The slow means of communication (i.e., written correspondence, delivered principally by riders on horseback) greatly hampered efficient and timely communications for military purposes during the early nineteenth century. On July 18, one week after the British arrived at Ocracoke and two days after they had departed (and the presumed threats to the state's inland port towns no longer existed), Adj. Gen. Robert Williams directed Col. Thomas Worley, commander of the Bertie County militia, to "forthwith . . . order into actual service, the Detachment of Militia in your Regiment." The county's detached militia company was to "proceed without delay to Edenton," and the commanding officer of the detachment was to report to the commanding officer of that place.[30] Additionally, Williams ordered the detached militia companies from Gates, Hertford, Northampton, Pasquotank, and Perquimans counties to report similarly to Edenton.[31]

Capt. Augustin Pugh commanded the Bertie County company (artillery service) of detached militia. Earlier in the year Governor Hawkins had appointed Capt. Joseph Hunter Bryan, its former commander, quartermaster general for the state's detached militia. On July 19 the company, seventy-nine members strong (including Peggy Whitehead, who served as cook), arrived in Edenton, where Pugh reported to Maj. John McCotter. The company, along with the others that Williams had ordered to Edenton, remained there for six days, training and drilling, at the direction of Colonel Flowers. At that time, no British warriors were on North Carolina soil, so on July 25 Flowers discharged the companies from service and allowed the men to return to their homes.[32]

Throughout the remainder of the war, British forces failed to launch another incursion into North Carolina. They had landed at Ocracoke and Portsmouth unopposed by any army, militia, or naval forces (except the two privateer vessels). On August 7 Secretary of the Navy William Jones conveyed his assessment of the British incursion to Sailing Master Gautier. Jones noted that "the enemy was attracted to Ocracock only by the valuable objects and property there." In Jones's view there was no strategic purpose for the British raid, since they, "as might have been expected," withdrew as soon as their object of raiding and pillaging was attained. Jones apparently was pleased that no naval gunboats had been at Ocracoke Inlet, since "such was . . . [the British] force that if the whole flotilla of the station had been there, it would probably have fallen." Jones fully recognized that the American naval forces along the coast could not match the corresponding forces of the British. "Such is the extent of exposure of our Coast and Harbours, and such the powerful maritime means of the enemy, that we cannot expect to oppose an equal force, at every point, which he may assail."[33]

The departure of the British from Ocracoke naturally led to a subsiding of anxiety and excitement among the residents of eastern North Carolina. In Raleigh, however, the success and ease of the British raid had heightened concerns among the state's leaders as to the ability of militia units to respond to incursions from an enemy promptly and adequately. Therefore, in August Adjutant General Williams issued a series of orders to the generals commanding divisions and brigades in the eastern sector of the state, as well as to the commandants of militia in thirty-one eastern counties, that in the event of an enemy raid or threatened incursion they were to report with their units to pre-designated locations—all perceived feasible targets of the British. The orders, issued on August 21, stated:

When an invasion of the enemy shall hereafter take place in your section of this State, or when you may entertain a well grounded belief, that an invasion is about to take place, in either case you are hereby required to march Forthwith such number of troops, within your command, as in your judgment that occasion may require, to the town of [_____], and there report yourself to the commanding officer who may be at that station without further orders. All the arms and munitions of war within your command are also to be conveyed to that station. It is to be understood however by you, that any orders which you may receive from either of your general officers [i.e. division or brigade commanders] are to have their effect.

Table 4

Locations to Which Militia Detachments Were to Report in the Event of British Invasion or Raid

Pre-designated Location	Number of Detachments to Report
Edenton	7
Elizabeth City	4
Washington	6
New Bern	5
Beaufort	1
Wilmington	6
Swansboro	1
Smithville	1
Total	31

Note: Data was compiled from Adjutant General Militia Returns and Orders, August 21, 1813.

The Bertie County detached militia company was designated to report to Edenton, as were companies from Chowan, Gates, Hertford, Northampton, Tyrrell, and Washington counties.[34]

By August 1813 another issue had arisen, creating additional consternation, particularly in Bertie County and other communities of the northeast region of the state. The pro-Republican constituents of Bertie County and other communities in the region had become thoroughly disgusted with United States senator David Stone. Stone, a Bertie County native and Republican, was a former state legislator and former governor of the state. In December 1812 the Republican-dominated North Carolina General Assembly had appointed him to fill the Senate seat of Jesse Franklin, who declined to seek reelection. Stone's six-year term commenced on March 4, 1813.[35]

The 1813 session of Congress was primarily concerned with war matters. Originally elected as a war man, Stone had not consistently voted to support the Madison administration's war measures. His votes and antiwar position in the Senate soon met with strong disapproval across North Carolina. He was not in accord with the Republican-espoused war policies of the Madison administration. He voted against bills involving direct taxes, the embargo, the prohibition of illegal trade, and the confirmation of Albert Gallatin as an envoy to peace negotiations under the mediation of the emperor of Russia.[36]

Only five months after Stone took his seat in the Senate, his fellow Republicans in Bertie County desired to see him removed from office. On August 12 a number of county citizens met at a theater in Windsor to "take into consideration, and to express their opinion in a public manner of, the conduct of . . . David Stone." Rev. Richard Poindexter was unanimously called to chair the meeting, and James W. Warburton was appointed secretary. Poindexter spoke to those in attendance and explained that the meeting's purpose was to investigate the conduct of "Public Men, in order to perpetuate entire the pure Principles of a Republican Form of Government." Other citizens addressed the assembly and expressed "indignation at the conduct" of Senator Stone and his "Apostasy from the Republican Principles on which he was elected." Those who attended the meeting appointed a committee to draw up resolutions to reflect the essence of the opinions expressed, and that body created the two following resolutions:

Resolved, that this meeting view with sentiments of indignant disapprobation, the conduct of David Stone, Esq. a Senator in Congress from this State, in the side he has lately taken in opposition to the dearest interests of our Country—to the positive stand which he formerly took in favour of a vigorous prosecution of the War—and to the Republican Principles, on the faith of which he was elected.

Resolved, that as his votes in Congress on Gallatin's nomination, the various Tax Bills, and the Embargo, are so inconsistent with the principles which he professed previous to his appointment, we view them as the emanations of a sacrifice on the alter of Ambition or Corruption.[37]

During the ensuing two months, additional anti-Stone meetings were held in Camden, Currituck, and Hertford counties.[38]

When the 1813 session of the North Carolina General Assembly convened on November 15, a major piece of business for the legislators was discussion and consideration of Stone's actions in the United States Senate. While a number of hard-line legislators stood by Stone and supported him,

David Stone, a resident of Bertie County and a former North Carolina governor, assumed Jesse Franklin's seat in the United States Senate in March 1813. Stone served primarily as a liaison between Gov. William Hawkins and the secretaries of war and the navy in seeking to bolster North Carolina's coastal defenses. However, his inclination not to support all of President Madison's war measures prompted his North Carolina constituents and certain officials to call for his removal from office. Stone eventually resigned in November 1814. Image courtesy of the State Archives.

the legislators voted to censure him. The lawmakers felt that Stone's votes in Congress reflected a lack of support for "those who are fighting our battles" and who "should receive the support confiding in which they enlisted under our banners." The legislators resolved that "Stone hath disappointed the reasonable expectations and incurred disapprobation of this General Assembly." Bertie County's three assemblymen—George Outlaw, Timothy Walton, and Whitmell H. Pugh—were hard against Stone. Many persons across the state called for his immediate resignation from the Senate.[39]

Senator Stone, however, did not resign his seat until almost a year later. On November 21, 1814, he was at his home (Hope) in Windsor when he wrote to Governor Hawkins and formally resigned from the United States Senate. In referencing his votes against various war measures of the Madison administration, Stone asserted to Hawkins that "I determined neither to incur responsibility for measures adopted against my judgment; nor longer to engage myself in the disagreeable task of opposing those Legislative provisions by a majority thought necessary for conducting an arduous war."[40]

In the late summer of 1813, British naval vessels stationed off the coast of North Carolina implemented Admiral Warren's orders to blockade the state's ports. The British blockade, coupled with the congressionally mandated trade embargo approved earlier in the year, greatly hampered residents' abilities to market their goods and commodities. In Currituck County some persons apparently decided to trade with British forces cruising off the coast. Soon rumors began circulating within the region that certain county residents were trading with the British.[41] The rumors reached the army command at Norfolk. On August 25 Brigadier General Taylor, commanding at Norfolk, sent Robert E. Steed, a War Department secret agent, to the county to seek evidence of the purported illegal trading. Steed took with him John L. Lovett, a Virginia magistrate, and within a few days the two men were in Currituck County talking with certain people and gaining information. Steed and Lovett learned that the "enemy was well supplied with fresh provisions out of Currituck" and that a number of residents "believed" that Deputy Collector Malachi Jones, Maj. Caleb Etheridge, Capt. Thomas Williams, and Capt. Thomas Bray were "at the head of the illegal trade." Steed and Lovett also heard rumors that Malachi Jones had frequently cleared vessels to sail to Baltimore allegedly loaded with shingles, when it was "well known that the same vessels were loaded with livestock, with only shingles on deck." The subject vessels were purportedly "only absent four or five days, and then returned empty, which was impossible for any vessel to go to Baltimore and back [in such short periods]." Residents further informed Steed and Lovett that British licenses had been sold to county militia captains of certain merchant vessels and that Major Etheridge was part owner of one or two of the ships. Steed prepared an affidavit relating to the "gained information" and submitted it to Governor Hawkins.[42]

On October 5 Adj. Gen. Robert Williams forwarded to Capt. Augustin Pugh a September 14 letter from Maj. Gen. Thomas Pinckney to Governor Hawkins and Steed's affidavit. The general stated that should the governor "be of opinion in consequence of the information" of the purported treasonable activities in Currituck County that "troops might with propriety be stationed at Currituck Inlet," then the state's detached militia might be employed at the inlet. Accordingly, Williams ordered Pugh, upon receipt of the communication, "Forthwith to march with all the Detached Militia under your command to Currituck Inlet and there to remain in the service of the United States. That you endeavor with all means in your power to stop all supplies conveying to, or other communications made to the enemy. That you select the most advantageous position at or near the Currituck Inlet for this purpose. That after you arrive at the place of destination you immediately make report to me of the names and numbers of the officers and soldiers under your command." [43]

Simultaneously with his orders to Captain Pugh, Williams forwarded the Steed affidavit and the Pinckney-Hawkins letter to Lt. Col. Brickhouse Bell of the Currituck County militia and ordered Bell to "procure sufficient testimony . . . before two or more Justices of the Peace within the county." Williams stated that should the justices "deem such [testimonial] evidence sufficient," then Bell was to use his "authority in having arrested by proper warrants" all persons "concerned in such treasonable practices." [44]

On October 8, a Raleigh newspaper reported the overall results of Steed and Lovett's information-gathering effort: "the Governor has received information that certain of our citizens of Currituck County, heretofore of respectable standing, have been concerned in the treasonable practice of supplying the enemy with live stock and other provisions." The paper did not mention that Captain Pugh's Bertie County company had been ordered to deploy to Currituck Inlet to curtail the illegal activities. [45]

For unknown reasons Williams's orders did not reach Captain Pugh in Windsor for ten days. Pugh received the orders on the morning of October 15. He immediately sent word to the members of his company to rendezvous in Windsor on the twenty-fourth prepared and equipped to deploy to Currituck County. In addition, he wrote to Quartermaster General Bryan, requesting him to furnish at Windsor the necessary camp equipage for his company and the proper means of conveying baggage and other equipment to the place of destination by the twenty-fourth. [46]

Bryan replied on the eighteenth, informing Pugh:

it is not of my power to furnish you with camp equipage, cartridge Boxes, or anything else. You will therefore have to rely on your own resources for supplies of such articles as the service may require. Each man should prepare himself with a cartridge Box of some sort, and should take with him from home, at least provisions for a week. Any and every aid that I can give you, will be cheerfully done, but I have no instructions to act in any way toward the troops now called out, and to take the responsibility on myself, would be over acting the part assigned me. . . . those who gave you your orders could have ordered me if they had thought it necessary; in pressing cases, such as invasion of the Country I should not hesitate to act without orders, but in the present instance there could be no excuse for it. [47]

Captain Pugh and his men now confronted the same chronic issue that so many North Carolina detached militia companies had faced: when they were ordered into active service, they did not have, and could not obtain from the officials who were charged with the requisite logistical responsibilities, the equipment, provisions, and supplies absolutely necessary for them to fulfill their missions. On October 20 Pugh wrote to Adjutant General Williams, forwarding Bryan's response and noting that the inability for him to acquire the essential items would produce "unnecessary hardships which those under my command will be obliged to undergo." Pugh also advised Williams that "It may make some delay in my marching but I shall not fail to use my best endeavors to march with as much dispatch as possible, and report myself agreeable to your order."[48] Pugh and his Bertie County militiamen were destitute patriots, devoid of absolutely essential items for active military service and unable to procure them.

Pugh and his men were delayed three days in departing Bertie County. On October 27 the members of his company assembled in Windsor, where they were formerly mustered, and soon departed the town for Currituck County. Only 66 men (including Pugh and the other officers) were mustered on that day. Of the 79 men who had deployed to Edenton in July, 51 were likewise present and deployed to Currituck Inlet. Pugh and his command reached the inlet on November 2.[49]

Williams replied to Pugh on November 3, advising him that the United States contractor at Fort Hampton had been instructed "by express order" to supply the Bertie County detached militiamen with all provisions necessary for "soldiering." In condescending language, Williams pointed out to Pugh that "It is the first duty of officers, and particularly those who are immediately associated with the service to pay every attention to the wants and comfort of their men. That the sick should be particularly attended to. In the relative duties of an army, the rule of 'doing as we would be done by' applies as well as in civil life."[50] It is unclear what prompted Williams to incorporate this verbiage in his communication.

A month later Adjutant General Williams advised Pugh that if he had not previously done so, he was to immediately report to Major General Pinckney at Charleston, S.C., "stating the number of men under your command, and also the supplies and medical aid which you may stand in need of. This is done so that the men under your command . . . may obtain all such things necessary for armies and which you and the Soldiers under your command may want."[51] Indeed, Pugh and his men were suffering from want of necessary items that had not been furnished to them in the five weeks they had been in service at Currituck Inlet. On December 6 Brig. Gen. Jeremiah Brite (Pugh's brigade commander) and Col. Brickhouse Bell advised Williams that Captain Pugh had requested them to inform the adjutant general that he and his company were still without camp equipage. Pugh and his men, without necessary camp equipment (including tents), had moved off the sandbar at Currituck Inlet and relocated at the county courthouse, "the weather being so severely cold, that [they] could not quarter" at the inlet. Both Brite and Bell were of the opinion that Pugh's company's service was "quite unnecessary through the winter," as there was no enemy on the coast, nor any "elicit [sic] trade carrying on by the inhabitants of Currituck County." The officers concluded their letter by stating that there had been but one effort made to supply the enemy with provisions and that the deputy collector (unnamed) who resided near Currituck Inlet had prevented the attempt.[52]

By the end of December, Captain Pugh was growing quite weary of service along the Atlantic seaboard during a cold, damp season. On the twenty-eighth he penned a letter to Williams, the tone of which clearly reflected a degree of irritation. He declared that he had written "many letters" to Williams but was "much astonished" that he had not received an answer to one of them. In a chastising and sarcastic manner, he conveyed to the adjutant general that since he arrived in Currituck County, he had not received "the scratch of [Williams's] pen in answer to one of them. . . . I alone must wait in suspense until swift rolling time [death] the sure informer of all secrets shall give me notice." Pugh seemed to be upset with Williams for his directive of early December requiring him to report to General Pinckney the number of men under his command and the supplies and other items he required. He asserted that when he first arrived at Currituck Inlet, he reported to Williams the number of men who arrived with him and that he had also conveyed to Pinckney similar data and the supplies and medical equipment that he and his men needed.[53] His appeals had not resulted in action by his superior officers.

As might have been expected, Pugh's letter raised the ire of the adjutant general. On January 18, 1814, Williams tersely fired back. First, he stated that he had provided answers "to all things proper for this office to answer." Second, he took Pugh to task for being unfamiliar with his duties and military protocol: "It is presumed that when any person is appointed to a military office, that the person appointed understands the duties attached thereto but if he does not his ignorance is his own misfortune." Third, Williams laid out the procedures and protocol that Pugh should have followed to obtain supplies once his Bertie County company went into active United States service:

On the 5th day of October 1813 an order was issued to you requiring you to march with all the detached militia under your command to Currituck Inlet, and there to remain in the service of the United States. Whenever you acted under this order, you were then in the service of the United States and to the United States officers alone you are to look for supplies and if these supplies are not furnished, the fault is not in the State Government Officers. Notwithstanding this, an order was issued from this office to the United States contractor of supplies at Fort Hampton to give you and the men under your command all supplies necessary, and this was done untill you had time to report yourself to the United States officers. On the 3rd day of November last I wrote to you a letter stating the words following: "Your letter of the 20th ultimo is received and an immediate answer has been given to it. The contractor who supplies the troops stationed at Fort Hampton at the town of Beaufort in Carteret County has been directed by express order to supply your troops with every provisions necessary for the soldiery. The name of this person is not known to us but if he should fail to comply with that order immediately, it is requested that you will report the fact to this office when military procedures shall be awarded against him. In case this person should fail to comply with this order Major Joseph H. Bryan of Bertie County has been requested to attend to your wants." You have never reported to this office the fact whether this Contractor did or did not comply with this order, and the presumption was from thence almost conclusive that he did comply with the order.[54]

On January 30, 1814, Governor Hawkins wrote to Pugh that, on the basis of representations made to him, he had determined to permit the members of Pugh's company to return to their homes. "You will, therefore as soon as convenient march them to the County of Bertie and dismiss them with instructions to hold themselves in readiness until the 10th day of April next, to march against the enemy should the State be invaded. Your returns upon dismissing will as heretofore be forwarded to Maj. Genl Pinckney and to the Adjutant General of this State. The General Government will doubtless in the course of a Short time send a paymaster to the County of Bertie to pay off the Officers and Men." The governor concluded that it "has frequently given me much pain to learn that the supplies allowed by Act of Congress have not been furnished the company and the cause of this neglect is yet inexplicable to me. Whilst the faithful discharge of their duties as Citizens altho experiencing this want of attention on the part of the Officers of the General Government bespeaks them [as] real patriots, it also gives them just claim to their Country's gratitude."[55]

On February 13 Pugh's Bertie County company was discharged from United States service at Currituck Courthouse. Sixty-nine men were present when discharged. During its tenure in Currituck County, eight men joined the company, and one man was discharged during the unit's service. Four men deserted. The members returned to their homes in Bertie County, having served less than four months. Captain Pugh marched his command back to Windsor, where the men were "dismissed" to await "further orders." When the men returned home, the federal government had not given them one cent of pay for their service.[56] Pugh's company was not again called into service during the remainder of the war. Obtaining their pay would become a contentious issue between the North Carolina and United States governments. The men would not receive their pay until almost a year after the war ended. The state of North Carolina, not the federal government, eventually paid them.

As the spring of 1814 approached, Governor Hawkins continued to endeavor to provide the best defense for the coastal region he could, given the limited resources available to him. In March he sent a circular letter to the Committees of Safety of Edenton, New Bern, Washington, and Wilmington, noting that the season of the year was approaching "when we may reasonably expect a visit from the Enemy to the sea-board of this State." He wished "to make every arrangement and to adopt every measure to place each of our valuable towns in a State of preparation to meet the events, apportioned to the means placed at my disposal." Hawkins advised the committees that he had:

made application to the President of the United States, through our Senators in Congress for the residue of arms to which this State is entitled or such portion thereof as can be forwarded under the Act of Congress of 1808 for arming the whole body of the Militia of the United States. If they are obtained I will cause a portion of them to be deposited in our Sea-port Towns. But for the present we must rely upon the muskets and bayonets we now have in the hands of the Militia and such guns as each man can furnish himself with. The sum appropriated by the last General Assembly for procuring arms and munitions of war, will not be more than sufficient to purchase the latter. Some powder and lead has already been obtained and more is expected. A portion of it will shortly be forwarded to your Town. I have not yet been able to appoint contractors to furnish rations of provisions at the Several Towns. . . . I feel authorized to request you, in the event of troops being called to the defence of it [your town] to employ some person to furnish them rations, whose accounts shall be paid by the State upon his abstracts duly authenticated. And further to cause munitions of war to be procured in case an attack should be about to be made before those articles are furnished by my agents for which payments shall immediately be made by the State.[57]

Senator David Stone, after a face-to-face meeting with Secretary of War John Armstrong in April 1814, concluded that North Carolina and its officials were not held in high regard by President Madison's administration. Thus, in Stone's view, the defense of his home state's coastal areas had suffered. On April 12 Stone wrote to Hawkins that "It is with extreme regret and mortification I perceive that neither the people nor the Executive of North Carolina appears to hold the same place in the care and confidence of the President of the United States as are conferred upon those of other portions of the Union. So far is North Carolina from having any Son standing high enough in the confidence of the President to be entrusted with the defence of our own Sea Board." The senator was extremely concerned that North Carolina's defense was "committed" to General Pinckney, who "neither knows any thing of what may be necessary for our defence, nor can be informed of the occasions which may require his interposition in season for any effectual or useful preparation." Stone felt that it "would be far more convenient for the functionaries" of North Carolina to correspond directly with the secretary of war and receive orders and instructions from him, rather than for war department orders and communications directly affecting North Carolina to be sent to Pinckney, who in turn had to relay them to officials in Raleigh.[58]

Fortunately, British forces did not again return to invade North Carolina. British vessels cruised the ocean off the state's coast, enforcing the blockade. The federal government committed to erecting several fortifications known as "Martello towers" at key locations along the state's seaboard. The squadron of a half-dozen gunboats continued to ply the waters around Ocracoke, Beaufort, and Wilmington, but they did not confront any British warships. For the most part, life returned to a degree of normality for the residents of the eastern region, and they did not again experience the level of anxiety and excitement that consumed them in the summer of 1813 when British "boots" were on North Carolina soil.

Notes

1. David S. Heidler and Jeanne T. Heidler, *The War of 1812* (Westport, Conn.: Greenwood Press, 2002), 130.

2. Flowers to QM Gen. Joseph H. Bryan, June 28, 1813, William Hawkins, Governors Papers, State Archives, Office of Archives and History, Raleigh (hereafter cited as Hawkins Governors Papers). Colonel Flowers's regiment included companies detached from the militia regiments of Camden, Chowan, Currituck, Gates, Hertford, Pasquotank, Perquimans, Tyrrell, and Washington counties. See *Muster Rolls of the Soldiers of the War of 1812 Detached from the Militia of North Carolina, in 1812 and 1814* (Raleigh: Ch. C. Raboteau, 1851; Winston-Salem: Barber Printing Company, 1926), 3–9.

3. Hawkins to Bryan, May 24, 1813, and Bryan to Hawkins, May 26, 1813, William Hawkins, Governors Letter Books, State Archives, Office of Archives and History (hereafter cited as Hawkins Letter Books).

4. Bryan to Flowers, June 28, 1813, Hawkins Governors Papers.

5. Bryan to Hawkins, June 28, 1813, Hawkins Governors Papers.

6. Hawkins to Bryan, July 1, 1813, Hawkins Letter Books. Adj. Gen. Robert Williams immediately issued the orders as directed by Governor Hawkins. The subject orders went to the commanders of militia regiments in Camden, Chowan, Currituck, Gates, Pasquotank, and Perquimans counties. Williams to Commandants of Militia Regiments (cited counties), undated (between June 28 and July 2, 1813), Adjutant General Militia Returns, Orders of Officers, 1811–1813 (AG-2), Records of the Adjutant General's Office, State Archives, Office of Archives and History (hereafter cited as Adjutant General Militia Returns and Orders).

7. Hawkins to Bryan, July 1, 1813, Hawkins Letter Books; Flowers to Hawkins, June 28, 1813, Hawkins Governors Papers.

8. War Department regulations stipulated that "militia detachments in the service of the United States must be made under the requisition of some officer of the United States regularly authorized to make such requisition on the executive authority of the State or the Territory, from which the detachments shall be drawn." Once called out, militia units were to be inspected and mustered by an officer of the army, who was required to immediately complete a muster and inspection report and submit it to the War Department. After being properly called out, mustered, and inspected by army officers with requisite authorities for such functions, the militia units were considered to be in the service of the United States government. At that point, the United States government assumed responsibility for supplying, equipping, paying, and providing medical care to the militia. The federal government, however, did not furnish clothing/uniforms to the militia. Militia called into service by state and territorial governors—without being called up, inspected, and mustered by authorized army officers—were not considered to be in the service of the general government. In such cases, the federal government assumed no responsibility for the expenses incurred by militia called into service solely on the authority of a state or territorial governor, including expenses for

supplies, munitions, equipment, and other items purchased by such units. Such was the case with Governor Hawkins calling out certain militia companies (including Capt. Augustin Pugh's company) in eastern North Carolina in the summer of 1813. General Orders, War Department, March 19, 1813, General Orders and Circulars of the War Department and Headquarters of the Army, 1809–1860 (microfilm, M1094), Record Group 94, National Archives, Washington, D.C.; Sec. of War John Armstrong to Maj. Gen. Thomas Pinckney, April 8, 1813, Letters Sent by the Secretary of War Relating to Military Affairs, 1800–1889 (microfilm, M6), Record Group 107, National Archives (hereafter cited as Secretary of War—Letters Sent).

9. Hawkins to Stone and Turner, June 11, 1813, Hawkins Letter Books; Stone and Turner, Gaston, Murfree, and Kinney to Jones, June 13, 1813, Miscellaneous Letters Received by the Secretary of the Navy, 1801–1884 (microfilm, M124), Record Group 45, National Archives (hereafter cited as Secretary of the Navy—Miscellaneous Letters Received).

10. King to Jones, undated (but ca. June 12, 1813), Secretary of the Navy—Miscellaneous Letters Received.

11. Jones to King, June 14, 1813, Jones to Gaston, Turner, and others in Congress from North Carolina, June 14, 1813, Miscellaneous Letters Sent by the Secretary of the Navy ("General Letter Books"), 1798–1886, (microfilm, M209), Record Group 45, National Archives.

12. Jones to Gautier, June 22, 1813, Letters Sent by the Secretary of the Navy to Officers, 1798–1868 (microfilm, M149), Record Group 45, National Archives (hereafter cited as Secretary of the Navy—Letters to Officers).

13. Stone to Hawkins, June 22, 1813, Hawkins Letter Books. Stone specifically noted in his letter that North Carolina soldiers had been sent to New Orleans, Savannah, Charleston, and Norfolk.

14. Stone to Armstrong, June 28, 1813, Letters Received by the Secretary of War, Unregistered Series, 1789–1861 (microfilm, M222), Record Group 107 (hereafter cited as Secretary of War—Letters Received [unregistered]).

15. Stone to Hawkins, July 4, 1813, Hawkins Letter Books.

16. Armstrong to Hawkins, July 9, 1813, Secretary of War—Letters Sent.

17. Murfree to Jones, June 30, 1813, Secretary of the Navy—Miscellaneous Letters Received.

18. Blount to Taylor, June 17, 1813, Secretary of War—Letters Received (unregistered).

19. Cockburn to Adm. Sir John B. Warren, July 12, 1813, in William S. Dudley and Michael J. Crawford, eds., *The Naval War of 1812: A Documentary History* (Washington, D.C.: Naval Historical Center, Department of the Navy, 1985), 2:184–186 (hereafter cited as Dudley and Crawford, *The Naval War of 1812*); David S. Heidler and Jeanne T. Heidler, eds., *Encyclopedia of the War of 1812* (Annapolis: Naval Institute Press, 1997), 367.

20. Flowers to Williams, July 14, 1813, Adjutant General Militia Returns and Orders; Flowers to [Lt.] Col. Duncan McDonald, July 16, 1813, Hawkins Letter Books.

21. McCotter to Charles Price, July 14, 1813, Hawkins Letter Books.

22. Bryan to Hawkins, July 20, 1813, Hawkins Governors Papers.

23. McDonald to Hawkins, July 15, 1813, Hawkins Letter Books.

24. Morgan, *The John Gray Blount Papers,* 4:206–207; Hawkins to Sec. of War John Armstrong, August 20, 1813, Secretary of War—Letters Received.

25. Hanson Kelly, Deputy Commissary, Wilmington, to Armstrong, July 19, 1813, Secretary of War—Letters Received.

26. Banks to Hawkins, July 19, 1813, Hawkins Letter Books; Brig. Gen. Jeremiah Brite to Dr. William Martin and William Gregory, July 15, 1813, Hawkins Letter Books.

27. Wilroy to Banks, July 16, 1813, Hawkins Letter Books.

28. Cockburn to Warren, July 19, 1813, in Dudley and Crawford, *The Naval War of 1812,* 2:365–366.

29. *Raleigh Minerva,* October 15, 1813.

30. Williams to Lt. Col. Commandant, Bertie County Regiment, July 18, 1813, Adjutant General Militia Returns and Orders.

31. Williams to Lt. Col. Commandants, regiments for Chowan, Gates, Hertford, Northampton, Pasquotank, and Perquimans counties, July 18, 1813, Adjutant General Militia Returns and Orders.

32. Compiled Service Records of First Regiment (McCotter's) North Carolina Militia (Detached), Record Group 94, National Archives (hereafter cited as Compiled Service Records, with appropriate unit designation); Maj. J. J. Creecy to Williams, July 31, 1813, Adjutant General Militia Returns and Orders; Flowers to Williams, July 21, 1813, Adjutant General Militia Returns and Orders. The author reviewed all compiled service records for members of Captain Pugh's company, as well as the associated company caption cards, to identify the members who deployed to Edenton, to ascertain the dates of deployment and develop statistics, and so forth. Peggy Whitehead, wife of Pvt. Joseph Whitehead (of the company), served as company cook during its time in Edenton. While her name appears on the company's muster rolls for the period, she did not receive any pay (since women were not explicitly authorized by North Carolina law to serve in the militia).

33. Jones to Gautier, August 7, 1813, Secretary of the Navy—Letters to Officers.

34. Williams to Maj. Gens. William Croom, Thomas Brown, Thomas Wynns, Calvin Jones; Brig. Gens. Jeremiah Brite, Jeremiah Slade, Hardee Smith, Thomas Holliday, William W. Jones; and commandants for Beaufort, Bertie, Bladen, Brunswick, Camden, Carteret, Chowan, Columbus, Craven, Cumberland, Currituck, Duplin, Edgecombe, Gates, Green, Hertford, Hyde, Johnston, Lenoir, Martin, Nash, New Hanover, Northampton, Onslow, Pasquotank, Perquimans, Pitt, Sampson, Tyrrell, Washington, and Wayne counties, August 21, 1813, Adjutant General Militia Returns and Orders.

35. Hawkins to Stone, December 12, 1812, Hawkins Letter Books.

36. Melanie Johnson Taylor, "David Stone: A Political Biography" (master's thesis, East Carolina University, 1968), 84–87 (hereafter cited as Taylor, "David Stone"); Sarah McCulloh Lemmon, "Dissent in North Carolina during the War of 1812," *North Carolina Historical Review* 44 (April 1972): 111.

37. *Raleigh Register and North Carolina Gazette*, August 27, 1813.

38. *Raleigh Register and North Carolina Gazette*, September 24, October 8, 22, 1813.

39. Samuel A. Ashe, Stephen B. Weeks, and Charles L. Van Noppen, eds., *Biographical History of North Carolina*, 8 vols. (Greensboro: Charles L. Van Noppen, 1905–1917), 4:422–426.

40. Taylor, "David Stone," 117–118.

41. Lemmon, "Dissent in North Carolina during the War of 1812," 108.

42. Affidavit by Robert E. Steed, August 30, 1813, enclosed with Williams to Lt. Col. Brickhouse Bell, October 5, 1813, Adjutant General Militia Returns and Orders.

43. Williams to Pugh , October 5, 1813, with enclosures (A) Robert E. Steed Affidavit, August 30, 1813, and (B) Maj. Gen. Thomas Pinckney to Gov. William Hawkins, September 14, 1813, Adjutant General Militia Returns and Orders.

44. Williams to Bell, October 5, 1813, Adjutant General Militia Returns and Orders.

45. *Raleigh Register and North Carolina Gazette*, October 8, 1813.

46. Pugh to Williams, October 20, 1813, Adjutant General Militia Returns and Orders.

47. Bryan to Pugh, October 18, 1813, Adjutant General Militia Returns and Orders.

48. Pugh to Williams, October 20, 1813, Adjutant General Militia Returns and Orders.

49. Compiled Service Records of First Regiment (McCotter's) North Carolina Militia (Detached), Pugh's company; Pugh to Sec. of War John Armstrong, March 11, 1814, Compiled Service Record of Capt. Augustin Pugh.

50. Williams to Pugh, November 3, 1813, Adjutant General Militia Returns and Orders. Also on the third, Williams sent an order to the contractor at Fort Hampton to furnish Captain Pugh's company at Currituck Inlet "with all and every provisions necessary to the soldiering." Williams to the Contractor furnishing the troops at Fort Hampton, Beaufort, Carteret County, November 3, 1813, Adjutant General Militia Returns and Orders.

51. Williams to Pugh, December 4, 1813, Adjutant General Militia Returns, Orders to Officers, 1813–1817 (AG-6), Records of the Adjutant General's Office, State Archives (hereafter cited as Adjutant General Militia Returns and Orders, 1813–1817).

52. Brite and Bell to Williams, December 6, 1813, Adjutant General Militia Returns and Orders, 1813–1817.

53. Pugh to Williams, December 28, 1813, Adjutant General Militia Returns and Orders, 1813–1817.

54. Williams to Pugh, January 18, 1814, Adjutant General Militia Returns and Orders, 1813–1817.

55. Hawkins to Pugh, January 30, 1814, Hawkins Letter Books.

56. Compiled Service Records of First Regiment (McCotter's) North Carolina Militia (Detached), Pugh's company; Pugh to Armstrong, March 11, 1814, Compiled Service Record of Capt. Augustin Pugh. The members of Captain Pugh's company were paid in early February 1816.

57. Hawkins, circular letter to the Committees of Safety of Newbern, Edenton, Washington, and Wilmington, March 12, 1814, Hawkins Letter Books.

58. Stone to Hawkins, April 12, 1814, Hawkins Letter Books.

CHAPTER 5

Suffering and Dying at Norfolk

During much of 1813 British warships maintained an ever tightening blockade along the East Coast of the United States, and an enemy squadron roamed around the Chesapeake Bay. Raiding parties landed at will, burned several villages in Maryland, and prowled the Potomac River southeast of the nation's capital. The British sailed out of the bay, but by the spring of 1814 a strong squadron was back, harassing communities and residents along the shores as it pleased. Then in May sensational news arrived from Europe—Napoleon had fallen. His defeat released thousands of battle-hardened British veterans for service on new fronts—presumably across the Atlantic to engage the Americans. Reports circulated that the British military had one objective—"unconditional submission" of the United States. The *London Times* had reported that "there is no public feeling in this country stronger than that of indignation against the Americans." Thus, the summer of 1814 found the youthful American republic threatened with national extinction. Its people were polarized by dissension over the war, its treasury was empty, its economy was in ruins, its coasts were blockaded and defenseless, its army was bogged down on the northern borders, its navy was bottled up in harbors, and the most powerful nation in the world seemed on the verge of delivering a *coup de grace* blow against it.[1]

In the early morning of August 16, persons along the western shore near the mouth of the Chesapeake Bay spotted almost two dozen British vessels—warships and transports—entering the bay. By mid-morning, express riders were scurrying for Norfolk to inform the military commanders that a formidable British force was coming. The ships did not veer toward Norfolk harbor, however, but instead sailed north out of sight up the bay. Riders were dispatched to hurry to Washington to pass along the alarming news of the approaching squadron.[2] Now, in the third year of hostilities, the fighting seemingly was shifting from the Canadian border to the "doorsteps" of the nation's capital.

Two days later the lead British ships anchored in the Patuxent River off Benedict, Maryland. The following morning at dawn, thousands of British troops began coming ashore at Benedict. By late in the day on Saturday, the twentieth, the command was organized and marching north from the town. Secretary of State James Monroe had left Washington and traveled to

James Monroe played a crucial role in the War of 1812, serving as secretary of state and secretary of war. He helped fashion the Madison administration's war policies. He assumed the role of acting secretary of war following John Armstrong's resignation in September 1814. Subsequently, Monroe was appointed secretary and filled the position throughout the remainder of the war. Image courtesy of the White House Historical Association.

Nottingham, Maryland (a community in the path of the British), to "scout" for himself. From the village he sent a message back to officials in the capital—"The enemy are in full march for Washington." Panic ensued. People in the nation's capital piled into their carriages and buggies and began streaming out of the city.[3]

On August 24 the British forces reached Bladensburg, Maryland, on the outskirts of Washington, where they quickly repulsed American forces, predominantly militia, that had assembled there. Late in the day the British marched defiantly into Washington, where they burned public buildings, including the Capitol, the White House, and the Library of Congress, and pillaged the city. They departed on the following day and retraced their route back to their ships, aboard which they re-embarked on August 30.[4]

The British next moved on Baltimore, where the flotilla arrived on September 11. On the following two days land and naval forces assailed

North Point and Fort McHenry, but, unable to breach the American defenses, the British prudently abandoned the effort and withdrew back into the Chesapeake Bay.[5]

In Norfolk Brig. Gen. Moses Porter, then commander of the army and militia forces in the area, was gravely concerned that the British forces would next set a course for an assault on his position. Porter had about 5,000 troops (mostly Virginia militia) under his command, of whom 1,300 were reported on sick rolls.[6] When the British squadron entered the bay, Porter called upon the militia commanders of the neighboring communities for 2,000 additional troops. He informed Secretary of War John Armstrong that he would discharge the additional troops "as soon as the plans of the enemy are developed" but that he had "no doubt" that an attack would be made on Norfolk once the British had completed their operations up the bay. He inquired as to whether or not Armstrong concurred "in the belief that an attack shall be expected" at Norfolk; if so, he asked the secretary to compare his means of defending Norfolk with the force of the enemy and to determine what "augmentation" should be made to his defenses. Porter, in the meantime, endeavored to strengthen his post and prepare "to receive and repel" the enemy.[7]

On September 1 Acting Secretary of War (and Secretary of State) James Monroe, having returned to the nation's capital after vacating it in the face of the British attack, wrote to General Porter and Gov. James Barbour of Virginia that "the Enemy have embarked on board their vessels in the Patuxent [River] and will as I presume in execution of their desolating system, proceed immediately to some other of our principal Towns. Norfolk is known to be one in which they have fixed their attention. Baltimore and Richmond are others against which they will move. . . . Be on you[r] guard prepared at every point, and in all circumstances, to repel the invaders."[8]

On September 4 Governor Barbour—unaware that Secretary Armstrong had departed Washington and that President James Madison had named Secretary of State James Monroe to serve simultaneously as acting secretary of war—wrote to Armstrong to inform him that General Porter had requested 1,500 more Virginia militiamen to be sent to Norfolk to bolster its defenses. Barbour, needing his Virginia militia units to defend Richmond—and considering that to this date in the conflict Virginia had sent tens of thousands of its citizen soldiers to defend its coastline and communities—suggested that Porter's requisition should be made from North Carolina. Barbour noted that North Carolina's commercial interests were "intimately connected with Norfolk," justifying an appeal to Gov. William Hawkins for troops to reinforce Porter's command. Monroe concurred with Barbour.[9]

On September 5 Porter informed Monroe that he was making "every exertion in preparing for the worst." He noted that his troops were "unusually unhealthy" and that the sick report "increases daily," which he feared would continue at "an alarming degree." Porter was considering asking Barbour for even more militia.[10]

The following day Monroe warned Governor Hawkins that the "Enemy are descending the Chesapeake and as there is a strong ground to believe they may make an attempt at Norfolk." He requested Hawkins to order 1,500 members of the North Carolina detached militia to Norfolk and to have the detachment "move with all possible expedition" and report to General Porter. Four days later Col. James Bankhead, Porter's adjutant general, suggested to Hawkins that "it would be extremely desirable to have the troops which are ordered from North Carolina to this post armed and equipped and . . . that as little delay as possible may take place in complying with the requisition." Monroe's letter arrived at Hawkins's office on the eleventh.[11]

Porter likewise wrote to Hawkins and requested that the North Carolina militia detachment to be sent to Norfolk be armed, inasmuch as there was a "grave scarcity" of military arms in Norfolk. However, Porter was highly skeptical that the troops would be so equipped, since he had learned that the state was "almost entirely destitute of arms."[12]

By the middle of September, letters and orders were flying into and out of Raleigh as state officials labored to comply with the War Department's request to send the equivalent of one and one-half regiments of militiamen to Norfolk. On the fifteenth, Beverly Daniel, aide-de-camp to Governor Hawkins, sent a communication to the commandants of militia in Bertie, Camden, Chowan, Edgecombe, Franklin, Gates, Granville, Halifax, Hertford, Johnston, Martin, Nash, Northampton, Pasquotank, Perquimans, Tyrrell, Wake, and Warren counties. The communiqué directed the commanders to order the detached companies within their counties to "march with all possible dispatch to aid in the defence of Norfolk" and ordered the designated detachments to rendezvous "as soon as practicable" at Gates Court House, where they were to be organized and marched to Norfolk.[13]

Governor Hawkins directed Brig. Gen. Jeremiah Slade of Martin County, commander of the Fifth Brigade of the North Carolina militia, to

In early September 1814, Virginia governor James Barbour encouraged the War Department to appeal to Governor Hawkins for North Carolina militia to augment forces defending Norfolk. Subsequently, two regiments of North Carolina militia were sent to Norfolk. A company of Bertie County troops was part of the first regiment detached to Norfolk in October 1814. Image courtesy of the Library of Congress.

proceed to Gates Court House on or before September 30. There Slade was to organize the troops into "fifteen complete companies" and to constitute a regiment (about 1,000 men) and a battalion (about 500 men). As soon as the troops were properly organized, Slade was to send them to Norfolk under the command of a colonel who was to report to General Porter. Hawkins enumerated the officers to be assigned to the detachment: Lt. Cols. Duncan McDonald of Chowan, Andrew Joyner of Martin, and Maurice Smith of Granville, and Majs. James Clarke of Edgecombe, John C. Green of Warren, and Joseph F. Dickinson of Hertford. The governor advised Slade that Lieutenant Colonel McDonald was expected to command the regiment, since he outranked (in terms of time in grade) the other two men of his same rank. Hawkins further granted Slade the discretionary latitude to appoint officers, enclosing blank commissions for that purpose. While the governor authorized General Slade to organize the troops, he was unable to offer him command of the detachment, since it was "short of the number of troops necessary to constitute the command of an officer of [Slade's] rank." Hawkins regretted that circumstance.[14]

While state officials stipulated that the North Carolina militia destined for Norfolk was to arrive at Gates Court House by September 30, General Porter—aware that the British were descending the Chesapeake Bay and fully expecting an attack on his post—desperately desired that the requested militia detachment be sent to Norfolk sooner. Colonel Bankhead, on behalf of Porter, advised Hawkins on the seventeenth that the "importance of having the re-enforcement required from North Carolina, at an early period, will be the General's justification for urging your Excellency to order the Troops to proceed with the utmost expedition." [15] While Bankhead's correspondence was en route to Raleigh, Adj. Gen. Robert Williams wrote to Porter that the 1,500 men to aid in the defense of Norfolk "will rendezvous at Gates Court House . . . on the 30th of the present month, from whence they will proceed in the most direct route" to Norfolk "as soon as their organization shall have been effectuated." Williams added that it was "much to be regretted that the want of arms in this State, precludes the possibility of arming the above detachment as requested by you. The commanding officer of the detachment [General Slade] has been informed that the men would be furnished with arms, etc. on their arrival at Norfolk." [16] Porter, upon learning that the North Carolina detachment was not armed, confided to Acting Secretary of War Monroe that he was "apprehensive [that] I shall be compelled to order them to return [to North Carolina]." The war had now been ongoing for more than two years, and yet troops designated to defend such a critical location—a major harbor and headquarters for the Fifth Military District—still did not have adequate arms (or other essential equipment). [17]

Within Bertie County, militia commanders set about organizing the detached company to march to Gates Court House. Capt. Jonathan H. Jacocks was to command the detachment. On September 24 militiamen gathered in Windsor to designate the members of the company. The commanders first sought volunteers to fill out the company's ranks. Failing to obtain enough volunteers to constitute the company, the officers next "drafted" men, selecting one individual out of every eight until a full complement of troops was attained. [18]

With September 30 quickly approaching and the ongoing influx of hundreds of militiamen into the little village of Gates Court House, Hawkins sent additional instructions to General Slade. Hawkins noted that it was his understanding that the troops to be sent to Norfolk would be required to fulfill a six-month tour of duty. The British forces that had pillaged Washington and assaulted Baltimore were still descending

Chesapeake Bay in their warships, prompting Acting Secretary of War Monroe to request additional militia from North Carolina in anticipation of an "immediate attack on Norfolk." To this call, Hawkins had directed the detached militia companies from Chatham, Orange, and Person counties (in addition to the fifteen companies ordered there earlier) to march immediately to Gates Court House. Hawkins advised Slade that the additional companies were expected to arrive at the rendezvous site by October 5. He recommended that Slade organize the initial fifteen companies bound for Gates Court House into the regiment and battalion necessary to fulfill the 1,500-man request made by General Porter. Command of the regiment was still to fall to Lt. Col. Duncan McDonald. Command of the 500-man battalion was to be tendered to Lt. Col. Maurice Smith. Hawkins also informed Slade that he had ordered Maj. Gen. Calvin Jones, the new quartermaster general for the state's detached militia, to repair to Gates Court House to procure the necessary means of transportation for the troops to travel to Norfolk. (The North Carolina General Assembly had promoted Joseph Hunter Bryan, the former quartermaster general for the detached militia, to major general and appointed him to the command of the First Division of the state's militia.) Hawkins ended his communication to Slade by authorizing him to make "deviations in some degree from the instructions" he had received, if he found it necessary to do so.[19]

On September 29 Captain Jacocks and his company of Bertie County militia marched away from Windsor destined for Gates Court House, more than forty miles away. By sundown on the following day, Jacocks and his company had not arrived at the rendezvous site. On the twenty-first, Maj. Gen. Calvin Jones informed Governor Hawkins that all of the regimental officers and an estimated 1,200 troops were in the area around Gates Court House. The Bertie company had still not arrived, and according to Jones, Jacocks and his troops were expected to arrive later that day (and did so).[20]

The little village was overrun with militiamen and was a "beehive" of activity. The troops sought shelter in dwelling houses, outhouses, barns, the courthouse and jail, under porches and piazzas, and in field encampments and adjoining woods. A representative for Jarvis and Brown of New Bern, the contractor designated to provide provisions to the troops, had been in town for some days and had supplied beef, bacon, and cornmeal rations but provided no soap, vinegar, or candles—articles considered by the troops as of "almost indispensable necessity." A Dr. Stephen Davis established a temporary medical facility to care for any troops that might require assistance; fortunately the large majority of the men were healthy. Field officers were busy organizing the troops in preparation to march to Norfolk, assigning officers, and preparing muster rolls. General Jones hired wagoners from the area to transport equipment and baggage for the troops to Norfolk.[21]

On October 3 four companies of McDonald's regiment—designated the First Regiment North Carolina Militia (Detached)—departed Gates Court House under the command of Maj. John C. Green and "took up the line of march" for Norfolk. The following day four more companies left, and finally, on the fifth, the last two companies—including one comprised predominantly of Bertie County men—marched away from Gates County.[22]

General Slade, under the authority and latitude granted to him by Governor Hawkins, did not maintain the original composition of Captain Jacocks's Bertie County company—nor Jacocks as an officer in the regiment. He dismissed Jacocks, who immediately returned home to Windsor. Slade assembled a company of troops from Bertie (82 men), Hertford (19), and several other counties. He appointed Capt. James Iredell, a highly influential lawyer from Chowan County, to command the company. He commissioned Gavin Hogg (a Bertie County lawyer who arrived at the rendezvous as a private in Jacocks's company), William M. Darlett of Bertie County, and Lemuel Creecy of Wake County as lieutenants.[23]

The highly influential and affluent Jacocks—a key member of Bertie County's Republican contingent and devout pro-war advocate—was incensed that General Slade had summarily dismissed him. Furthermore, his pride and "sensibility" had been "wounded." Back at his home on October 10, he composed a lengthy letter to Governor Hawkins in which he expressed his utmost displeasure with Slade's actions. He wrote:

In conformity to your orders to the Col[onel] of this County [Thomas Worley], that number of detached Militia, which your requisition demanded, (amounting to a full Company) having been furnish[ed] by the legal authority of the Col[onel]. I was placed in command, and in obedience to the further instructions of your Excellency, marched them to Gates Courthouse. Soon after my arrival at that place having reported myself and company to Genl Slade, I was forthwith dismissed from the service, without even the formality of an interview, or any reasons being assigned in justification of such a procedure.

What contributed much to the aggravation of what I conceive, an unwarranted extension of his authority, was that every subordinate officer attached to my company, was in a like manner displaced, & their stations filled by the promotion of privates from the same, and other companies.

I Sir am not the only person whose sensibility hath been wounded & whose rights have been abused, but a number of other officers, as respectable in point of numbers as they are irreproachable in character, have been treated with equal indignity.

If my request does not transcend the limits of propriety, you will confer on me not only a special obligation, but contribute much to the relief of my insulted feelings by furnishing me, with such information . . . of Genl Slade's conduct, with regard particularly to his dismissal of Officers, legally commissioned, and his promotion of others, who were not only privates, but many of whom, were not recognized as a part of the requisition from the State, but had repaired to Gates Court House, the place of general rendezvous, in pursuit of Military preferment. That Genl Slade has made a sacrifice, of the feelings and rights of others for the gratification of his own political prejudices, his conduct in this instance will undubitably attest, a conduct the unprecedented oppression of which, has not only given myself and many other officers sufficient cause of remonstrance and complaint, but seems very justly to have subjected him to the censure and indignation of a much exasperated community.

If, Sir, Genl Slade has acted in obedience to your instructions, and in conformity to those laws which should regulate his conduct as an officer invested with superior authority, without selecting his political opponent as the object of his resentment, I will cheerfully submit to the grievance even without a measuring however great may be the sacrifice of my personal feelings, but thinking my allegation to be a just one, I appeal to you as the only medium, through which I can obtain redress, to assist me in bringing him before the tribunal to which wanton and unprovoked conduct is certainly amenable.

. . . Not to speak of my own case, Sir, there are not only instances of Officers, who had held commissions for several years, & whose intellectual acquirements and blameless conduct should have been a sufficient recommendation; but who regardless of pecuniary expenditures & personal fatigue, had equipped themselves, and volunteered their services in defence of their country & were contemporaneously rejected and their places filled by privates from the ranks, which they had commanded.

Such, Sir, is an imperfect but correct representation of the conduct and oppression of Genl Slade of which I complain & as I wish to proceed coolly & dispassionately in the investigation thereof, as my only means of redress; I appeal to you for aid, in promoting furtherance of these views, whose motives of accomplishment, are not actuated from any selfish or revengeful considerations, but such as I conceive to be inseparably connected with my own honor & reputation.[24]

General Slade had acted in concert with the authority the governor had granted him. In reporting to Hawkins following his organization of McDonald's regiment, Slade declared: "In Officering the detachment I have not confined myself to the officers in commission but have selected from the best materials within my control & have commissioned those who had none."[25] Hawkins, apparently satisfied with Slade's actions, did not respond to Jacocks's appeal.[26]

Gen. Calvin Jones left Gates Court House on October 4 and arrived the following day in Norfolk, where he immediately conferred with General Porter. Porter informed Jones that McDonald's regiment would be assigned to a location known as Moorings Rope Walk, situated about a mile from the town. According to Porter, the site was a large field, a healthy environment nearly surrounded by water, which would aid in maintaining proper discipline and order of the camp. Porter also informed Jones that the North Carolina troops were "to be trained and then put on Garrison duty or kept in readiness to be removed to exposed or threatened points." Porter added that he had been able through "great exertions" to collect and repair about a thousand stands of arms fit for service. Porter hoped soon to be able to arm the entire North Carolina detachment.[27]

The uncertainty over whether Porter would be able to procure sufficient arms for the North Carolina regiment and the tardiness of communications between Norfolk, Raleigh, and Gates Court House prompted state officials to recall the troops that had left that place and order them to return to the town. When Porter requested that North Carolina troops be sent to his command, he informed Governor Hawkins that such troops should be armed, since there was "a scarcity of arms" in Norfolk. North Carolina was unable to furnish sufficient arms for the detachment, however. Neither could the War Department immediately send arms to Porter. Therefore, on October 3 Hawkins directed Slade to have the troops remain at Gates Court House pending clarification of the arms issue. Also on the third, Adjutant General Williams wrote to Porter informing him that the North Carolina militia had been ordered "to be stationed at Gates Court House where they will remain until it shall be ascertained whether you will be able to furnish them arms and still find it necessary to call them to that point." General Slade or Lieutenant Colonel McDonald had been instructed to communicate directly with Porter regarding that matter.[28]

Slade, immediately upon receipt of Hawkins's letter, dispatched an express rider after the companies that were marching to Norfolk, with orders for them to return to the rendezvous location. Slade also wrote to Porter, advising him that "a regiment was organized and ready to march to Norfolk if he should require it" but that "the troops were stationed at Gates Court House and would await his determination." He also wrote to Gen. Calvin Jones, who was then at Norfolk, "to provide for the return of the troops."[29]

By October 4 General Porter had been "fortunate in procuring more arms than anticipated" and had determined that he would "be able to equip nearly or quite all of the Carolina requisition upon their arrival." He then wrote separate letters to Hawkins and Williams, requesting that the North Carolina troops be marched to Norfolk. After receiving Slade's letter informing him that the North Carolina troops had been stopped on their march to Norfolk, Porter replied to Slade: "I regret extremely to learn that the N.C. troops have been stopped on their March to the defence of this place, under the erroneous impression that they were not wanted or could not be armed. In my letter to his Excellency Governor Hawkins of the 4th inst, I mentioned my having been fortunate enough to procure nearly or quite a sufficient number of arms; and as the circumstances under which I made the requisition for troops continue to be equally urgent, I cannot but lament their detention, more particularly without having been consulted on the subject . . . therefore I trust that you will be ready to order the troops under your command to this place with the least possible delay."[30] Slade then ordered the Carolina troops on to Norfolk.

On the eighth, with all ten companies of McDonald's detached regiment en route to Norfolk or having arrived there, Slade penned a letter to Hawkins, summarizing the steps and actions he had taken. He explained that he formed three companies from the troops of five counties—Bertie, Halifax, Hertford, Martin, and Northampton—and appointed Capt. James Iredell to command one of them (of which Bertie County men comprised about 73 percent of its members). There being no United States officers at the courthouse authorized to inspect and muster the regiment (per War Department regulations), Slade appointed Maj. Joseph F. Dickinson to perform that duty. The major inspected the regiment by companies, signed a muster roll, and forwarded it to the War Department. Dickinson likewise prepared an inspection return and muster roll with a description list. Slade sent a copy of each document to Adjutant General Williams, along with a roster of the officers whom he placed in command of the troops. Slade formed three companies consisting of the troops from Camden, Chowan, Pasquotank, Perquimans, Tyrrell, and Washington counties and placed the units under the command of captains from those locales. He ordered those companies to return to their respective homes and to hold themselves in readiness to march should they be needed for the defense of the Albemarle Sound region. He ordered the balance of the troops who had arrived at Gates Court House (i.e., companies from Chatham, Orange, and Person counties) to return to their homes in accordance with Hawkins's orders dated October 3.[31]

The initially deployed companies of the North Carolina regiment marched into Norfolk on October 7. General Jones remarked that the appearance of the North Carolina militia "on their entrance into Norfolk . . . did them considerable credit." The troops then encamped at Moorings Rope Walk. Jones, who had inspected the site, felt it was "the best encampment for health & convenience . . . about Norfolk." At the time, workers were repairing a bridge that united the peninsula (on which the Rope Walk was situated) with the town. The following day Jones accompanied Generals Porter and Taylor to the major facilities in the Norfolk defenses—

Craney Island and Forts Norfolk and Nelson. They next rode the whole of the lines of defense in the area, leading Jones to conclude: "The strength of this place is very formidable and is daily increasing." Jones then departed Norfolk and returned to North Carolina, leaving McDonald's North Carolina troops in a "healthy" environment and within a secure command. All seemed well for North Carolina's citizen soldiers.[32]

On October 10 General Slade composed his last communication from Gates County to Governor Hawkins. He declared that the "marching and counter marching" of the militia had "produced some difficulty," but it was "now over and the troops composing the 1st Regiment are either quartered in Norfolk or on their march to that place." Slade advised Hawkins that he was going to depart Gates Court House the following day and return to his home in Martin County. He had fulfilled his duties relative to the regiment raised to aid in the defense of Norfolk.[33]

Colonel McDonald's regiment had no sooner arrived in Norfolk than it appeared to Secretary of War Monroe that the size of Porter's command might well be decreased. The British naval and land forces that had attacked the nation's capital and Baltimore had not descended to the Norfolk area, and many British warships had left the Chesapeake Bay altogether. General Porter had reported to Monroe that "forty of the enemy's vessels have gone to sea," but unsubstantiated reports indicated that "about as many more still remain in the bay." Monroe then advised Porter that if he deemed it safe to reduce his present militia force, it would be proper to make the reduction by dismissing units of the Virginia militia first, since they had been "longest in the service."[34]

But the ever cautious Porter did not feel confident in reducing the size of his force by discharging militia units. On October 15 he apprised the secretary that on the previous day "the whole of the enemy's squadron," except two frigates, had gone to sea "bearing Southwardly." Porter had learned from a British deserter that the departing fleet intended to sail to Bermuda (a British colony) and, according to other information, obtain reinforcements. Porter was highly skeptical of the reports, thinking that it was possible that "the old squadron may have gone out [to sea] to meet the new one and surprise us by an unexpected return." Porter concluded that "Altho' many of the enemy's vessels have gone to sea since the affair at Baltimore, yet we have good reasons for believing that all their troops were with the squadron last here. The number and size of the vessels [still in the bay] justify the opinion."[35]

Only two days later, Porter's opinion had changed, however. He informed Monroe that "By the departure of the enemy the time has arrived, when according to your instructions, I may proceed to make a reduction in my command." He had decided to discharge all but four regiments of the Virginia militia then stationed at Norfolk. The resulting reduced command would consist of about 6,000 troops, including Colonel McDonald's North Carolina militia regiment and regular army forces at the post. Porter, anticipating that Monroe would envision that the 6,000-man retained force was still "too large," stated that he would be "be pleased to know your wishes upon the subject; but . . . the ulterior object of the enemy for the campaign is not yet developed, & I know no place which unites more advantages for winter quarters to the foe, than Norfolk." He added that as the

term of service of a great proportion of the Va. militia retained, will expire in a short time, I submit to you whether it would be not better, to supply their places by a requisition upon North Carolina. This will relieve Va. in part from the immense pressure of the war which has operated on her almost ever since its declaration, and judging by the Carolina Regt [Colonel McDonald's] here in service, they are extremely willing to participate in the danger and exposure of the times. Should you determine upon [a] call [on] North Carolina for an additional requisition, it is desirable that I should know it, as soon as your engagements will admit. I shall be happy to receive your commands.[36]

It now seemed that more North Carolina militiamen would be sent to southeastern Virginia to relieve the burden of constant deployments on that state's militia forces and to join their North Carolina comrades in maintaining a constant vigil for sea-based British warriors.

On October 17, ten days after the initial arrival of companies in McDonald's regiment at Norfolk, the regiment held its first formal muster. Within the short time the unit had been at the post, almost 10 percent of the members of Captain Iredell's company were reported as sick—a rate more than twice that for the rest of the regiment at the day's muster.[37] The cold, damp months of winter had not arrived, yet a significant number of the men in the predominantly Bertie County company were not feeling well. The men were apparently suffering from a lack of adequate clothing, for on October 22 General Porter reported to Governor Hawkins that the "North Carolina Regiment is a fine one, but it is to be regretted, that the privates cannot be furnished with warmer clothes as they are almost all clad in summer apparel. They are this day moving into their winter quarters."[38] Apparently, the cool autumn nights and lack of stout shelter had put some of the troops "under the weather."

The inability of the North Carolina and federal governments to adequately supply and care for all troops called into United States service was once again looming as more detrimental than British bullets, shells, and bayonets. News of the regiment's need for clothing had quickly reached Raleigh, prompting citizens of the city to subscribe "handsomely for the relief of the detached militia now serving at Norfolk, who are suffering for the want of clothing."[39]

In the meantime, General Porter had requested that another regiment of detached militia from North Carolina be sent to his command. On October 25 Secretary of War Monroe wrote Governor Hawkins that since the state of Virginia presently had "in the field over seven thousand men for the protection of this place [Washington, D.C.] and Baltimore, in addition to the very large force at Richmond and Norfolk . . . I have thought it proper to give orders to Brigadier General Porter, who has command of the 5th Military District, to call for such portions of the detailed militia from your state as shall make your quota at Norfolk two thousand men and to keep them up at that number. . . . I take the liberty to advise you of this arrangement, that when the respective calls are made you may be prepared to furnish the men from such parts of the State as may be most convenient and least bothersome to the men themselves."[40] Simultaneously Monroe authorized Porter to make the call on Hawkins for another 1,000-man regiment of North Carolina militia. Four days later Col. James Bankhead sent the request to Raleigh; it reached Adjutant General Williams on November 9.[41]

November 10 was extremely busy and involved for Williams. He issued general orders to the militia commanders of Caswell, Chatham, Guilford, Orange, Person, Randolph, Rockingham, Stokes, Surry, and Wilkes counties to have their detached militia companies rendezvous at Hillsborough on November 28 in order to be organized into a regiment and marched to Norfolk. "As soon as the organization may be effected you are required to march immediately the regiment . . . the most direct way to Norfolk and report to Brig Gen Porter of the United States Army, commanding at that place." He wrote to Col. Richard Atkinson of Person County and appointed him to organize the regiment at Hillsborough and then command and march it to Norfolk. He wrote to the United States contractors for North Carolina, Jarvis and Brown at New Bern, requesting them to provide the requisite provisions and supplies at Hillsborough for the troops slated to report there. As a contingency in case those men could not or would not provide such provisions and supplies, he wrote to John

Street, a United States contractor at Hillsborough, to ascertain if he was able to supply the troops. Williams wrote to Colonel Bankhead at Norfolk, advising him that orders had been issued calling for the troops to be sent to Norfolk to rendezvous on November 28 at Hillsborough, where they would be organized and immediately marched to Norfolk. Williams projected that "in all probability" it would be "about the 15th of December before the regiment can arrive at Norfolk." Further, he submitted a copy of his general orders to a Raleigh newspaper for publication in the paper's edition on the following day.[42]

In Norfolk, Colonel McDonald's regiment had settled into the daily routine suffered by units stationed at posts at which they primarily drilled and trained in anticipation of the arrival of enemy forces. Every morning the troops were "roused between daylight and sunrise by the reveille . . . breaking upon the stillness of the morning." From nine until eleven o'clock the officers drilled their individual companies, and from three o'clock until sunset the regiment exercised as a unit. Their duty had quickly become rather "routine," with the regiment's officers living "quite comfortably" in log huts, while the privates and noncommissioned officers took shelter in tents.[43]

General Porter endeavored to have rudimentary huts constructed for the troops within his command, since cold weather had arrived and the militia, particularly, were "thinly clad." In October Secretary Monroe had authorized huts to be built, but the quartermaster general at Norfolk did not have the necessary funds or the means for the construction. By early November work on the huts reportedly had "progressed considerably" but had been curtailed since the carpenters had depleted the supply of boards and, again, the quartermaster's department for the post was void of funds for the effort. By late November, Porter regretted to inform Monroe that "measles and other plagues" among the troops were daily causing an increase in the sick and number of deaths. However, he hoped to find at least partial relief by moving troops into huts, which were again being constructed.[44]

On November 19 Colonel Bankhead, on behalf of General Porter, wrote to Adjutant General Williams that it "would have been much more gratifying" to General Porter if the required North Carolina force (Colonel Atkinson's regiment) could reach Norfolk before the end of November rather than the projected date of December 15. Virginia militia units, whose terms of service had expired, were being discharged. According to Bankhead, without the reinforcement from North Carolina the Norfolk post would be inadequately defended in case of an attack. He requested that Atkinson's troops be ordered to repair to Norfolk at an earlier period.[45]

Bankhead's appeal did not move Williams or Governor Hawkins to amend their orders to Atkinson or the county commanders of the troops assigned to rendezvous at Hillsborough. On November 28 Colonel Atkinson organized more than 1,050 militiamen who had assembled at the village into a regiment of ten companies, designated as the Fifth Regiment North Carolina Militia (Detached). By December 15 the regiment had arrived at Norfolk.[46]

While Atkinson's regiment was early-on en route to Norfolk, the suffering of McDonald's regiment due to the inadequate clothing, blankets, and other items was being considered and discussed by North Carolina's legislators. On December 1, the legislators formally recognized that the "part of the Militia of this State, now in the service of the United States from their poverty and other causes, are without Blankets and winter cloathing suitable to the vigour of the approaching season." To help resolve the shortage of such crucial items, they authorized the governor to draw up to $10,000 from state funds to be used at his direction for the purchase of shoes, blankets, and winter clothing for the said militiamen who were without these articles.[47]

The winter season had arrived, and the damp, cold weather experienced by the Norfolk region at such times of the year could be brutal on men without adequate clothing, shoes, shelter, and other essential items (blankets, fuel, and so on). Suffering transmuted into dying as the "camp plague" ravaged the regiment. By December 1 five Bertie County members of Iredell's company—Jethro Sowell, James Mizell, John Boyce, William Brown, and James Williams—had died.[48]

Throughout December the rates of sickness and death intensified within the regiment. By late December/early January, 79 members of McDonald's regiment (about 8 percent of the regiment's original strength) had died of disease and illness. Of that number, 8 were Bertie County residents, including Miles Gillam and Cullen Sholars, who both died on Christmas Day. Timothy Mizell of Bertie County died on December 16. At the start of the New Year, more than 20 percent (184 men) of the regiment were reported on sick rolls. Twenty-three Bertie County men (more than 28 percent of their company's strength at the time) were included in that number.[49]

Members of Colonel McDonald's regiment were suffering and dying at distressing rates. A month had passed since the North Carolina legislature had authorized the state's governor (now William Miller, whom the

General Assembly had elected during its 1814 session) to expend up to $10,000 to clothe and provide for the troops. Nevertheless, the state government failed to provide one piece of clothing or any other essential item of comfort or shelter to the destitute troops. Sickness, suffering, and death among the troops continued to increase. Even so, to the absolute credit of the North Carolina "patriots," they continued to persevere. Relatively few of the troops deserted. By early January only twelve members of the regiment had been reported as permanently deserting. Only one Bertie County resident, Thomas Harrell, had deserted and not returned. While seven other Bertie County men had deserted, they all had returned. Four men (Joshua Harrell, Stephen Howell, Bowen Driver, and James Williford) had departed camp without leave in late October. At least two of those men—Harrell and Howell—traveled to their homes to assist their families, who were struggling in providing for themselves. Three men—Josiah Bird, Zacheus Champion, and David White—deserted on December 22, but all three returned to their company on December 26. In mid-January they all suffered courts-martial. It is likely that they traveled to their homes for Christmas, since it was disclosed during Champion's trial that he had gone a "distance of one hundred miles" during his absence, and Bertie County is approximately one hundred miles from Norfolk.[50]

Governor Miller, rather than acting expeditiously to relieve the suffering of the troops from his home state, seemed to be more focused on military protocol and offering a brigadier general from the state's militia the command of the North Carolina troops at Norfolk. On January 11, 1815, he wrote to Secretary of War Monroe that there were "two complete Regiments of the detached Militia of this State in the service of the United States at Norfolk, Va. I should be glad to be informed as soon as convenient whether the services of a Brigadier General from North Carolina are now requisite."[51]

Col. Richard Atkinson's regiment had been at Norfolk for only three and one-half weeks when on January 9 he held a formal muster of his troops. By that time seven members of his unit had died, and ten had deserted. On that day, 152 members (almost 15 percent) of his regiment were reported on sick rolls.[52] Norfolk was indeed a very unhealthy environment for the hundreds of men assembled together.

On January 10 Miller dispatched a letter to Col. Constant Freeman, commanding officer at Norfolk (General Porter having resigned in December 1814), requesting that he obtain from Colonels McDonald and Atkinson an accounting of the specific items needed by the members of their regiments.[53] It had been forty days since North Carolina legislators

William Miller succeeded William Hawkins as governor of North Carolina during the latter days of the War of 1812. New to the governorship, Miller moved lethargically to provide funds authorized by the General Assembly to procure direly needed clothing, blankets, and other necessities for North Carolina militia regiments in the field. As a result, North Carolina's two militia regiments at Norfolk suffered to a greater extreme than they may have had they been provided the needed items. Image courtesy of the North Carolina State Archives.

had authorized Miller to act to alleviate the suffering of the North Carolina detached troops. But as the brutal days of winter slipped by, the bureaucracy of the government—as had so often been the case during this war—failed to act in a timely manner in the best interests of its citizen soldiers. Indeed, Miller was new to the state's top executive position and would have had transition-related and organizational activities to oversee and implement. His request for an accounting had to be sent from Raleigh to Freeman, who in turn had to deliver it to McDonald and Atkinson. The two regimental commanders then had to request each of the captains under their commands to canvass their troops and prepare lists of items. Then the company lists had to be consolidated into regimental lists for approval by McDonald and Atkinson, and finally forwarded to Raleigh.

On January 15 McDonald had received company lists from all ten captains under his command (including Capt. Gavin Hogg, who had replaced James Iredell in command of the predominantly Bertie County company). Maj. John C. Green, the regiment's adjutant general, prepared the consolidated regimental listing. Essentially, hundreds of items of clothing were direly needed by McDonald's troops.

Table 5

Items "Most Needed" by the First Regiment (McDonald's)
North Carolina Militia (Detached), Norfolk, Virginia, January 1815

Item	Total Number Needed by all Companies in the Regiment	Number Needed by Captain Hogg's Company
Blankets	305	40
Shoes	252	50
Shirts	155	30
Stockings	268	70
Hats	66	20
Short coats	202	20
Vests	134	20
Pantaloons (pants)	231	20
Watch coats	25	6

Note: Data was taken from Col. Constant Freeman to Gov. William Miller, January 20, 1815, Miller Letter Books.

The following day McDonald sent the consolidated and individual company listings to Miller, with a copy to Colonel Freeman. McDonald apprised Miller that the lists represented the items his men most needed—but he also let the governor know that the captains under his command had little confidence that the December action by the North Carolina legislature would translate into any meaningful supply of items to the regiment. McDonald wrote that the officers, "fearing that the humane appropriation for the Brigade at this post by the Legislature of our State would be nugatory," had by his directions "purchased a number of articles and became responsible to the sellers" for the amounts owed. He further noted that "the deplorable situation of the men is the only excuse I can offer for the liberty I have taken in anticipating your Excellency's orders." To drive his point home with Miller, he concluded: "the situation of the men are deplorable indeed, and their suffering almost incredible, which they bear with unparalleled fortitude. Our loss since our arrival to this time is about 160. We are to be removed in a few days to Portsmouth."[54]

The regimental site that General Porter had called "a healthy environ" and General Jones had proclaimed as the "the best encampment for health" had transformed itself into a hellhole of suffering and death; yet no officials had seemed sufficiently concerned to take any direct and meaningful actions. The North Carolina troops appeared destined to continue to suffer in their calamitous situation, all in the name of service and patriotism to their country.

The anguished and sickening conditions under which McDonald's regiment of North Carolinians languished were not limited to their camps. The entire Norfolk command was in misery. On January 15 Adjutant General Bankhead, noting that the "afflicted state of the army by sickness demands the utmost exertion of every officer," issued orders stipulating that an officer would be detailed in each regiment with a sufficient party of troops "to remove every kind of filth, to cover the streets between the huts with sand & to have proper sinks . . . constructed." The commanding officers of the regiments were to examine each hut and have them "cleaned and cured," with windows to be made in those huts lacking them for the circulation of air to abet healthier living quarters.[55]

Atkinson's regiment, even though having been at the Norfolk post for only a month, like McDonald's unit, needed significant items of clothing, including 176 blankets, 321 pairs of pants, 152 shirts, 176 coats, and 55 watch coats. Atkinson submitted his lists to Colonel Freeman, who on January 20 sent them to Governor Miller.[56]

Miller received McDonald's and Atkinson's lists on January 23. The following day he wrote Atkinson that "I am truly sorry to hear of the mortality prevailing among the men." He then reminded Atkinson that the appropriation made by the state legislature had been $10,000 and that, inasmuch as three regiments from North Carolina were in the service of the United States—two at Norfolk and one at Wilmington/Beacon Island— "Norfolk is of course entitled to two thirds. . . . I have therefore taken the liberty of enclosing a check on the Edenton Branch Bank for $2,500 and one to Colonel McDonald for $3,500, which makes $6,000 [for the two Norfolk regiments]."[57]

Miller (although unintentionally) had himself treated the regiments inequitably (on a per-soldier basis) in his allocation of the funds to the three organizations. While McDonald's regiment, which consisted of about 800 men by late January, was in the most desperate need of assistance, Miller granted it about $4.37 per man; Atkinson's regiment was likewise suffering significantly but received only $2.40 per member. The third regiment (actually at battalion strength), Lt. Col. Maurice Moore's Third Regiment North Carolina Militia (Detached), consisted of only 500 members and received $4,000—$8.00 per man. Moore's unit, stationed in the more hospitable environment around Wilmington, lost only 4 men to death as a result of sickness and disease during its six-months of service in southeastern North Carolina.

Table 6

Pro Rata Amounts of Funds Allocated by Gov. William Miller
to First, Third, and Fifth Regiments, late January 1815

Regiment	Estimated No. of Men, Jan. 1815	Amount Allocated by Gov. Miller	Per-man Allocation
First Regiment (McDonald's)	800	$3,500	$4.37
Third Regiment (Moore's)	500	$4,000	$8.00
Fifth Regiment (Atkinson's)	1,042	$2,500	$2.40

Note: The author computed the per-man allocation by dividing the amount of money Miller allocated to each unit by the estimated number of men in each, as of late January 1815, per Compiled Service Records of the First Regiment (McDonald's), the Third Regiment (Moore's), and the Fifth Regiment (Atkinson's), North Carolina Militia (Detached).

On January 19 Bankhead disseminated orders for the post's quartermaster general to "procure quarters for the 1st Regt No. Carolina Militia in Portsmouth," across the Elizabeth River from Norfolk, so that the regiment could "be moved over as soon as possible." Bankhead stipulated that the sick would likewise be moved and their infirmary established across the river. He appointed a "Doctor Famford" to tend to the regiment's ill members.[58]

A week later the War Department issued an order for McDonald's regiment to be "forthwith discharged." Department officials, recognizing the rampant sickness prevalent among the regiment's members, stipulated that the "order will be enforced relative" to the constituent companies' sick. The company officers were charged with conveying to their homes all "convalescents" as could "be conveniently removed."[59]

The War Department order reached Colonel Freeman on February 2. He immediately forwarded the order to Colonel McDonald and set about having the necessary arrangements made to expeditiously discharge the members of the First Regiment (McDonald's) North Carolina Militia (Detached). Surely Colonel Freeman felt that the troops had suffered enough. Upon receipt of the order and news that they were "going home," members of the regiment undoubtedly celebrated. Major Green could hardly contain his joy, penning the following letter to a Raleigh newspaper:

Portsmouth, 2nd Feb 1815

This will inform you that I have just copied a general order for the discharge of our Regiment of North Carolina Militia. They are to be discharged on the 4th inst. and will be paid off as soon as muster and pay rolls can be made out; which will take at the fartherest seven days from this date. You can therefore expect to see me in the course of eighteen days.

You may rely on the truth of the regiment . . . being discharged, as I copied the general orders, and they are direct from the war department.

We have lost upwards to two hundred of the men we marched here and there are upwards of three hundred sick; out of which we may calculate one hundred entirely lost to the State of North Carolina. Should they recover they can never be fit for service again.[60]

Coincidentally, Governor Miller's letter to Colonel Atkinson conveying the two bank drafts totaling $6,000 for the purchase of clothing and blankets for his and McDonald's troops arrived in Atkinson's hands on February 1. The colonel replied to Miller that he had already made nearly $250 in expenditures for items that were "absolutely requisite and indispensable, many of the men being barefooted and without any covering. . . . The weather has been remarkably severe at this place for several days." Atkinson admitted that some of his troops were "yet in tents [rather than huts] brought down [from Hillsborough] with them." He ascribed the underlying cause of the lack of adequate shelter as a "want of funds" by the quartermaster's department at Norfolk. Atkinson noted that twenty members of his regiment had died since they arrived at Norfolk and that that day's sick report for his regiment encompassed 282 names, with measles being the prevailing disease and predominant cause of death. He reported that "Great mortality has taken place in the First Regiment," with "upwards of 200 men having died since their arrival at this station and those troops still continue very sickly."[61]

On February 4 Colonel Freeman reported to Secretary of War Monroe that the "orders relative to the discharge of the First North Carolina Regiment of Militia are now in execution; so soon as they shall be mustered and paid they will march from hence, and due attention will be given to the sick, such of them as cannot march will be furnished with transportation."

Freeman added that the troops "in this part of the District have been very sickly, perhaps not more so than the inhabitants of the country in proportion to their numbers; the epidemic which is making cruel ravages in almost all parts of Virginia visited the Troops; they would have been subject to this disease in any other situation. But there have been causes the most aggravating, not under the control of the Commanding Officer which have increased our mortality." He further noted that upon assuming command from General Porter, he had tried to "remedy as far as in my power the evils which have been the subjects of so many complaints. I could not however arrest the disease; I could not furnish clothes to the militia; nor could I compel the Contractor to supply such provisions as was proper for the sick: But everything within my means was given—the means of improving the huts; houses for the infirmaries and straw & fuel when they could be obtained." The colonel concluded by declaring that the "Quarter Master General has been assiduous in the execution of his duties; he has had to struggle against many difficulties."[62]

While Freeman was obviously defending himself (and the Norfolk quartermaster general) from blame for the suffering and deaths among the North Carolina militia, it is quite evident that both the federal and North Carolina governments had failed the men. Indeed, resources—both financial and logistical—were in short supply in late 1814 and early 1815. Nonetheless, long delays in acting (or failing to act) and inattention to troops' needs within the constraints and limitations of available resources (both state and federal) cannot be justified or exonerated. Serving to confirm the dedication to service and patriotism exhibited by the men of the First Regiment North Carolina Militia (Detached) is the enlightening fact that relatively few of them deserted; moreover, they did not mutiny against their commanders, despite intolerable suffering.

February 5, 1815, at Portsmouth, Virginia, was truly a day filled with joy and relief for the members of Colonel McDonald's regiment, as they were mustered, inspected, paid, and discharged from the service of the United States. On that day 767 men were present, of whom 151 men (almost 20 percent) reported themselves sick. Within Captain Hogg's company, 72 men (of whom 60 were Bertie County residents) were present; 13 were reported as sick. During its four months of service, the regiment lost more than 1 in every 4 members. It suffered 212 deaths from illness and disease. Seventeen members of the Iredell/Hogg company died, of whom 11 were Bertie County residents. One hundred forty-eight members of the regiment were discharged for a variety of causes during the

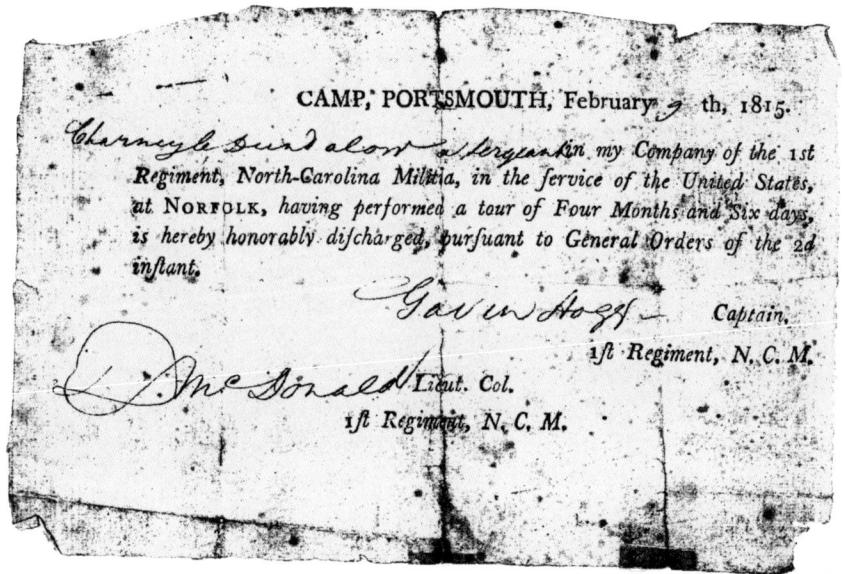

Charney C. Dundelow (Dundalow), more commonly known as Charney Cale, resided in Bertie County and was serving as a private in the Third Regiment United States Infantry when the War of 1812 commenced. Following his discharge from the regular army, he subsequently served as a corporal in the Bertie County militia company whose members were marched to Norfolk, Virginia, in October 1814. As reflected by the document shown above, Dundelow—who had been promoted to sergeant in Gavin Hogg's company of the First Regiment—was discharged at Portsmouth, Virginia, on February 9, 1815. Document from pension file for Charney C. Dundelow (Charney Cale), Federal Pension Application Files, Record Group 15, National Archives.

unit's tour of duty at Norfolk. Thirty-one members enlisted in regular army units, while 4 men transferred. Nineteen men (less than 2 percent of the men who departed Gates Court House in early October) permanently deserted.[63]

Only nine days after the First Regiment was discharged, the secretary of war officially notified the governors of the states that a treaty of peace had been concluded between the United States and Great Britain at Ghent, Belgium, on December 24, 1814. Earlier that day Henry Carroll, secretary of the American legation to Ghent, had delivered a copy of the treaty to President Madison. The secretary was persuaded that if the president found the conditions honorable, the treaty would be ratified. He had hastened to communicate to the states' executives "an event of such high importance to the nation."[64]

On February 16, 1815, the United States Senate ratified the Treaty of Ghent. That same day Secretary of War Monroe informed the commanders of the nation's military districts that he had

the satisfaction to announce . . . that the treaty has been ratified by the President, by and with the advice and consent of the Senate. You will, therefore, suspend all military operations and immediately give information of this event to the officer commanding the forces of his Britannic Majesty in your vicinity. All orders for calling out any additional military force will be immediately countermanded, and the militia now in service discharged forthwith. The district paymasters will be directed to pay off the militia. . . . In discharging the militia, you will return to them the thanks of the President for their patriotism in promptly obeying the call of their country, and for the zeal and perseverance which under great hardships and privations they have so eminently displayed in defence of its rights.[65]

On the following day, British and United States officials exchanged ratifications of the peace treaty, and President Madison declared that the war had ended. The War and Navy Departments immediately began issuing orders and taking actions to deactivate their forces and return the nation's military structure to a "peace establishment."[66]

Col. Richard Atkinson's Fifth Regiment North Carolina Militia (Detached) was discharged at Norfolk on February 22. Of the 934 members present that day, 197 (21 percent) were reported sick. During its two and one-half months of service at Norfolk, the regiment lost 75 members (7 percent) to death by disease and illness. Twenty-nine men deserted. Members of the regiment, like the troops in Colonel McDonald's unit, had suffered and died in substantive numbers while having never fired a shot at a British soldier.[67]

Notes

1. Walter Lord, *The Dawn's Early Light* (New York: W. W. Norton & Company, 1972), 15; *London Times*, April 15, 1814.

2. Joseph Middleton to Charles Gordon, August 16, 1814, Miscellaneous Letters Received by the Secretary of the Navy, 1801–1884 (microfilm, M124), Record Group 45, National Archives, Washington, D.C.; Thomas Swann to Sec. of War John Armstrong, August 17, 1814, Letters Received by the Secretary of War, Unregistered Series, 1789–1861 (microfilm, M222), Record Group 107, National Archives.

3. Lord, *The Dawn's Early Light*, 76.

4. David S. Heidler and Jeanne T. Heidler, eds., *Encyclopedia of the War of 1812* (Annapolis: Naval Institute Press, 1997), 544–545.

5. Heidler and Heidler, *Encyclopedia of the War of 1812*, 31–32.

6. Porter to Sec. of War John Armstrong, August 16, 1814, Letters Received by the Secretary of War, Main Series, 1801–1870 (microfilm, M221), Record Group 107, National Archives (hereafter cited as Secretary of War—Letters Received). The War Department transferred Bvt. Brig. Gen. Moses Porter, a career artilleryman and Revolutionary War veteran, from command of the Third Military District, New York, to command of the Fifth Military District, Virginia (headquarters Norfolk), on April 2, 1814. Porter arrived in Norfolk and assumed command around late April or early May 1814. Adj. Gen. John Walbach to Porter, April 2, 1814, Letters Sent by the Office of the Adjutant General, Main Series, 1800–1890 (microfilm, M565) Record Group 94, National Archives.

7. Porter to Armstrong, August 24, 1814, Secretary of War—Letters Received.

8. Acting Sec. of War James Monroe to Porter and Barbour, September 1, 1814, Letters Sent by the Secretary of War Relating to Military Affairs, 1800–1889 (microfilm, M6), Record Group 107, National Archives (hereafter cited as Secretary of War—Letters Sent).). On August 27, 1814, President Madison and Secretary of State Monroe returned to the nation's capital after vacating it on the verge of the British attack. Two days later, Secretary of War Armstrong reappeared in Washington and encountered open hostility from citizens and militia units for his failure to implement adequate measures to defend the city. Armstrong offered his resignation to Madison, who declined it. Armstrong then took leave and departed the city for his home in Pennsylvania. On August 30 Madison designated Monroe to serve as acting secretary of war in addition to his duties as secretary of state. On September 4, 1814, from his home, Armstrong penned his official letter of resignation to President Madison. Armstrong's resignation became official near the end of September. Monroe was appointed secretary of war on October 1, 1814, and served in that capacity throughout the remainder of the conflict. He also served as acting secretary of state during that period inasmuch as Madison was unable to find a suitable replacement to lead the State Department. See Heidler and Heidler, *Encyclopedia of the War of 1812*, 16, 361, 575.

9. Barbour to Sec. of War John Armstrong, September 4, 1814, Secretary of War—Letters Received. Unbeknown to Governor Barbour at the time he wrote this letter, John Armstrong had departed the nation's capital and James Monroe had been named acting secretary of war and thus received Barbour's missive. Monroe penned the following anecdotal note at the end of Barbour's letter: "The proper provision in this case will be to add a part of N.C. to General Porter's military district. Meantime, a requisition to the Governor of that state may go directly and immediately from the War Dept. with notice thereof to Governor Barbour & Genl Porter. . . . J.M."

10. Porter to Monroe, September 5, 1814, Secretary of War—Letters Received.

11. Monroe to Hawkins, September 6, 1814, Secretary of War—Letters Sent; Bankhead to Hawkins, September 9, 1814, William Hawkins, Governors Letter Books, State Archives, Office of Archives and History (hereafter cited as Hawkins Letter Books). The requisition for North Carolina's militia was made under an act of Congress of February 28, 1795, which provided that "whenever the United States shall be invaded, or be in imminent danger of invasion from any foreign nation . . . it shall be lawful for the President . . . to call forth such number of the militia of the state, or states, most convenient to the place of danger, or scene of action, as he may judge necessary." The provisions of the act of April 10, 1812, to organize, arm, and hold in readiness to march 100,000 of the nation's militia had expired on April 9, 1814. *United States Statutes at Large* 1 (1845): 424, 2 (1845): 705–707.

12. Porter to Monroe, September 10, 1814, Secretary of War—Letters Received.

13. Daniel to commandants of Bertie, Camden, Chowan, Edgecombe, Franklin, Gates, Granville, Halifax, Hertford, Johnston, Martin, Nash, Northampton, Pasquotank, Perquimans, Tyrrell, Wake, and Warren counties, September 15, 1814, Hawkins Letter Books. "Gates Court House," the community in which the militia was to rendezvous, was later officially designated as "Gatesville." William S. Powell and Michael Hill, *The North Carolina Gazetteer: A Dictionary of Tar Heel Places and Their History*, 2nd edition (Chapel Hill: UNC Press, 2010), 201.

14. Hawkins to Slade, September 16, 1814, Hawkins Letter Books.

15. Bankhead to Hawkins, September 17, 1814, Hawkins Letter Books.

16. Williams to Porter, September 19, 1814, Adjutant General Militia Returns, Orders to Officers, 1813–1817 (AG-6), Records of the Adjutant General's Office, State Archives (hereafter cited as Adjutant General Militia Returns and Orders, 1813–1817).

17. Porter to Monroe, September 24, 1814, Secretary of War—Letters Received.

18. In an 1856 deposition relating to a pension application, Hatton William Calloway of Bertie County claimed to have volunteered at Windsor on September 24, 1814. Hatton William Calloway deposition dated November 11, 1856, in Calloway's pension application file, Federal Pension Application Files, Record Group 15, National Archives; Petition of Jonathan S. Tayloe, United States Senate, 42nd Cong., 3rd sess., 1873, Misc. Doc. 76, Library of Congress.

19. Hawkins to Slade, September 26, 1814, Hawkins Letter Books. The General Assembly commissioned Joseph Hunter Bryan as major general on December 24, 1813.

See Annual Return for the North Carolina Militia for 1814 in Roster of Field Officers of Militia, 1813–1842 (AG-7), Records of the Adjutant General's Office, State Archives, Office of Archives and History. In late September—when General Porter was uncertain if he would be able to furnish arms to the North Carolina troops he had requested to be deployed to Norfolk—Acting Secretary of War Monroe advised Governor Hawkins that a battalion (500 men) of the force originally slated to be organized (at Gates Court House) and sent to Norfolk could instead be stationed at Wilmington. The battalion— which was actually designated the Third Regiment North Carolina Militia (Detached)— was organized under the command of Lt. Col. Maurice Moore near Wilmington on October 18. It remained in that area until March 11, 1815, when it was discharged from service. Monroe to Hawkins, September 29, 1814, Secretary of War—Letters Sent; Compiled Service Records of the Third Regiment (Moore's) North Carolina Militia (Detached), Record Group 94, National Archives (hereafter cited as Compiled Service Records, with appropriate unit designation); *Muster Rolls of the Soldiers of the War of 1812 Detached from the Militia of North Carolina, in 1812 and 1814* (Raleigh: Ch. C. Raboteau, 1851; Winston-Salem: Barber Printing Company, 1926), 139.

20. Jones to Hawkins, October 1, 1814, Hawkins Letter Books.

21. Jones to Hawkins, October 1, 1814, Hawkins Letter Books.

22. Jones to Hawkins, October 5, 1814, Hawkins Letter Books.

23. Compiled Service Records of the First Regiment (McDonald's) North Carolina Militia (Detached).

24. Jacocks to Hawkins, October 10, 1814, Hawkins Letter Books.

25. Slade to Hawkins, October 8, 1814, Hawkins Letter Books.

26. The author found no response from Hawkins in the Governors Letter Books or the Governors Papers.

27. Jones to Hawkins, October 5, 1814, Hawkins Letter Books.

28. Porter to Hawkins, October 4, 1814, Hawkins Letter Books; Williams to Porter, October 3, 1814, Adjutant General Militia Returns and Orders, 1813–1817.

29. Slade to Hawkins, October 7, 1814, Hawkins Letter Books.

30. Porter to Hawkins, October 4, 1814, Hawkins Letter Books; Porter to Williams, October 4, 1814, Adjutant General Militia Returns and Orders, 1813–1817; Porter to Slade, October 8, 1814, Hawkins Letter Books.

31. Slade to Hawkins, October 8, 1814, Hawkins Letter Books.

32. Jones to Hawkins, October 8, 1814, Hawkins Letter Books.

33. Slade to Hawkins, October 10, 1814, Hawkins Letter Books.

34. Porter to Monroe, October 3, 1814, Secretary of War—Letters Received; Monroe to Porter, October 12, 1814, Secretary of War—Letters Sent.

35. Porter to Monroe, October 15, 1814, Secretary of War—Letters Received.

36. Porter to Monroe, October 17, 1814, Secretary of War—Letters Received.

37. Compiled Service Records of the First Regiment (McDonald's) North Carolina Militia (Detached).

38. Porter to Hawkins, October 22, 1814, Hawkins Letter Books.

39. *Raleigh Register and North Carolina Gazette*, November 11, 1814.

40. Monroe to Hawkins, October 25, 1814, Secretary of War—Letters Sent.

41. Monroe to Porter, October 25, 1814, Secretary of War—Letters Sent; Bankhead to Williams, October 29, 1814, Adjutant General Militia Returns and Orders, 1813–1817.

42. General Orders, November 10, 1814, Adjutant General's Office, Williams to Atkinson, November 10, 1814; Williams to Jarvis and Brown, November 10, 1814; Williams to Street, November 10, 1814; Williams to Bankhead, November 10, 1814, Adjutant General Militia Returns and Orders, 1813–1817; *Raleigh Register and North Carolina Gazette*, November 11, 1814.

43. Capt. James Iredell to his sister, November 3, 1814, Charles E. Johnson Collection, Private Collections, State Archives, Office of Archives and History.

44. Porter to Monroe, October 9, November 1 and 25, 1814, Secretary of War—Letters Received.

45. Bankhead to Williams, November 19, 1814, Adjutant General Militia Returns and Orders, 1813–1817.

46. Compiled Service Records of the Fifth Regiment (Atkinson's) North Carolina Militia (Detached).

47. Resolution of North Carolina Senate, December 1, 1814, Hawkins Letter Books.

48. Compiled Service Records of Jethro Sowell, James Mizell, John Boyce, William Brown, and James Williams, Compiled Service Records of the First Regiment (McDonald's) North Carolina Militia (Detached).

49. Compiled Service Records of the First Regiment (McDonald's) North Carolina Militia (Detached).

50. Compiled Service Records of Thomas Harrell, Joshua Harrell, Stephen Howell, Bowen Driver, James Williford, Josiah Bird, Zacheus Champion, and David White, Compiled Service Records of the First Regiment (McDonald's) North Carolina Militia (Detached). Zacheus Champion and David White's Courts Martial Records, File AA-4; Joshua Harrell and Stephen Howell's Courts Martial Records, File BB-11; and Bowen Driver and James Williford's Courts Martial Records, File CC-16, Court Martial Case Files, Record Group 153, National Archives.

51. Miller to Monroe, January 11, 1815, William Miller, Governors Letter Books, State Archives, Office of Archives and History (hereafter cited as Miller Letter Books).

52. Compiled Service Records of the Fifth Regiment (Atkinson's) North Carolina Militia (Detached).

53. Freeman to Miller, January 20, 1815, Miller Letter Books.

54. McDonald to Miller, January 16, 1815, Miller Letter Books. Captain Iredell resigned on December 21, 1814. He was commissioned a brigadier general in the militia in 1815.

Compiled service record of Capt. James Iredell, Compiled Service Records of the First Regiment (McDonald's) North Carolina Militia (Detached).

55. General Orders, Adj. Gen. James Bankhead, Fifth Military District, Norfolk, January 15, 1815, James Graham Papers, Private Collections, State Archives, Office of Archives and History.

56. Freeman to Miller, January 20, 1815, Miller Letter Books.

57. Miller to Atkinson, January 24, 1815, Miller Letter Books.

58. General Orders, Adjutant General Bankhead, Headquarters, Norfolk, January 19, 1815, James Graham Papers.

59. General Order, War Department, January 26, 1815, War Department General Orders and Circulars.

60. *Raleigh Minerva*, February 10, 1815.

61. Atkinson to Miller, February 1, 1815, Miller Letter Books.

62. Freeman to Monroe, February 4, 1815, Secretary of War—Letters Received.

63. Compiled Service Records of the First Regiment (McDonald's) North Carolina Militia (Detached).

64. Monroe to Governors of the States, February 14, 1815, Secretary of War—Letters Sent.

65. Monroe to Commanding Officers, Military Districts, February 16, 1815, Secretary of War—Letters Sent.

66. For example, on February 16th, the War Department issued orders to all generals commanding districts and armies to submit to the department "as soon as practicable" description lists of all noncommissioned officers, artificers, musicians, privates, and laborers belonging to the regiments, corps, and detachments within their respective commands. On the 21st the department issued orders regarding, among other topics, granting leave to troops and paying and honorably discharging all noncommissioned officers, musicians, and privates who enlisted to serve during the term of the war. General Orders, War Department, February 16 and 21, 1815, War Department General Orders and Circulars.

The Navy Department soon issued orders to officers to dismantle gunboats and barges, collect and safeguard equipment and munitions, and so forth. To illustrate, see Sec. of the Navy B. W. Crowninshield to Robert Henley, Capt. John H. Dent, Capt. John Cassin, March 9, 1815, Secretary of the Navy—Letters to Officers.

67. Compiled Service Records of the Fifth Regiment (Atkinson's) North Carolina Militia (Detached).

Epilogue

Between June 18, 1812, the date on which the United States declared war against Great Britain, and the formal conclusion of hostilities in mid-February 1815, 241 Bertie County men served in the United States Army and North Carolina detached militia companies called into federal service. The majority of the men served in detached militia units. The following table presents the number of men who engaged in active service.

Table 7

Number of Bertie County Men Who Served
in the Regular Army and Detached Militia

Organizations of Service	Number of Men
Regular army	60
Reg. army and detached militia	14
Detached militia	167
Total	241

Note: The author developed the foregoing statistics from information included in the rosters presented in Appendixes 1 and 2.

In addition to the 74 men who served in the army, another 13 offered their services to the army but were rejected. Existing service records do not include reasons why the men were rejected, but in all likelihood medical or physical factors were the chief causes.

Those individuals who enlisted in the regular army for the duration of the war were discharged in 1815. Twenty-six Bertie County residents—members of the Twentieth and Thirty-fifth Regiment United States Infantry—were discharged at Norfolk in March. Five county residents who were serving in the Forty-third Regiment United States Infantry were discharged at Fort Hampton, Beaufort, North Carolina, in August. Another eight men, who had enlisted for five-year terms of service, were discharged in 1817 (three men) and 1819 (five). Dancy Harrell, the last-serving Bertie County soldier of the war, was discharged on October 31, 1819.

Two companies of the county's detached militia were called into service during the war. Capt. Augustin Pugh's company served two stints in northeastern North Carolina—in July 1813 (at Edenton) and from October 1813 to February 1814 (in Currituck County). A total of ninety-five county residents served under Pugh's command during one or both of the deployments. Capt. Jonathan H. Jacocks's company marched to Gates Court House in late September 1814, and more than eighty of its members were assigned to a company comprised of men from several counties. James Iredell of Chowan County, not Jacocks, was given command of the company, which marched to Norfolk as a constituent unit of the First Regiment (McDonald's) North Carolina Militia (Detached) and served at that post until early February 1815. Eighty-eight Bertie County men (including three who had served in Captain Pugh's company) served in the regiment during its four-month tour of duty at Norfolk.[1]

Captain Pugh and the members of his company, having dutifully answered the country's call to service on two occasions, returned to Bertie County following their discharge from detached service in Currituck County in February 1814 with the understanding that they would be paid for their service. Nevertheless, a year later, when the war ended, Pugh's Bertie County militiamen had not been paid. Days continued to turn into weeks and weeks into months, and still no army paymaster arrived in the county to pay the militiamen. Pugh and his men had become entangled in a bureaucratic quagmire between the state of North Carolina and the federal government.

War Department regulations stipulated that militia detachments called into the service of the United States must be made under the requisition of an officer of the United States who was "regularly authorized" to make such requisitions (such as the commanding officer of a military district) or the executive authority of the state or the territory from which the detachments were to be drawn. Officers making requisitions of the governor of a state or territory were required to stipulate the number of privates, noncommissioned officers, and commissioned officers required. Militia companies called into the service of the United States were to be "mustered, inspected and received into the service of the United States" by an officer duly authorized to perform such duties. Thereafter, the properly mustered and inspected militiamen were placed upon the rolls and reports of the army and were entitled to pay for their time of service. The troops were to be paid by the regimental paymaster "in all cases."[2]

There were no command headquarters situated within North Carolina. The headquarters of the Fifth Military District were at Norfolk, while that of the Sixth Military District (within which North Carolina was situated) were at Charleston. The regular army troops within the state were stationed at Fort Hampton (Beaufort), Fort Johnston (near Wilmington), and the several recruiting rendezvous. In July 1813, in response to the British raid at Ocracoke, Gov. William Hawkins called into service the detached militia companies of various counties in eastern North Carolina, including Bertie County's company commanded by Capt. Augustin Pugh. That call into service was not, however, formally requested by Maj. Gen. Thomas Pinckney, commanding officer of the Fifth Military District. Furthermore, the detached companies called into service were not mustered and inspected by authorized regular army officers, primarily because army officers were not available in the locales where the troops were required (such as Edenton, to which Pugh's company reported). Therefore, the troops called out by the governor's orders were not "officially" in the service of the United States. Other calls made by Hawkins, including sending Pugh's company to Currituck County in October 1813, likewise were not made in accordance with army regulations.

As a result of noncompliance with the pertinent War Department regulations, the militia companies called into service in 1813 in most of eastern North Carolina were not placed on the rolls of the United States and were not paid during or at the conclusion of their terms of service. Captain Pugh's company was not paid for either of its two deployments (Edenton and Currituck County). Additionally, expenses incurred by North Carolina militia officers—such as Gen. Joseph H. Bryan's purchase of lead and other items at Norfolk in July 1813—were not made in accordance with pertinent army rules and regulations; therefore, he too was not paid.

By the fall of 1813, the nonpayment of members of North Carolina's detached militia called into service and the absence of reimbursement of expenses related to that service were matters of concern to state government officials in Raleigh. On September 26 Maj. Gen. Calvin Jones wrote to Secretary of War John Armstrong to request that the militia then in service at Fort Hampton be paid. In Jones's view, "justice" dictated that the federal government pay the troops.[3] On October 9 Governor Hawkins wrote to the War Department regarding the payment of expenses incurred by commanders and others during calls into service. Three weeks later Daniel Parker, chief clerk at the department, informed Hawkins that the "expenses incurred by the militia of North Carolina called into service by the General Government will be defrayed conformably to the laws and regulations for the government of the public agents."[4]

Hawkins, having authorized portions of the state's militia to go into active service and thus incurred expenses that he thought were proper to be paid by the United States government, owed an explanation to the North

Carolina General Assembly, which was to convene in November. On October 19 he wrote to Armstrong that it was of the "utmost importance" that he should be able to communicate to the forthcoming General Assembly "the determination of the President . . . in relation to the expenses already incurred" by the state's militia.[5]

When the General Assembly convened, the state's militia called into service in July still had not been paid. On December 24 the House of Commons approved a resolution that "the local militia when called out to repel invasion, are in the service of the United States, therefore, Resolved, that the Senators from this State in the Congress of the United States be instructed and the Representatives requested to urge upon the Government of the United States the payment of the local militia called out within this State in July last."[6] Hawkins transmitted the resolution to Armstrong on December 27, but the resolution did not move the War Department. More than a month later a Raleigh newspaper reported that detached militia companies recently discharged at Fort Hampton still had not received "a cent of pay."[7]

During a February 1814 meeting between United States senator David Stone and Secretary Armstrong concerning the issue of the nonpayment of North Carolina's militia, Armstrong "assured" Stone that "the General Government pays of course any portion of the detached militia called into service" and that "they also pay the Militia in the neighborhood of an invasion or threatened invasion when called out en masse or in greater proportions than the detachment if the occasion for the call appears to bear a reasonable proportion to the numbers actually called out." Nevertheless, Armstrong informed Stone that no payrolls or demands "of any kind for the pay of the North Carolina militia . . . [had] been transmitted to his Department."[8]

Governor Hawkins, having been advised of the secretary's comments by Stone, replied to the senator that as to the pay of the detached militia called into service, "there certainly ought not to be any question." In his opinion, the North Carolina militia that had been called into service should be paid without question. Nonetheless, Hawkins confided to Stone that the "rules and regulations prescribed by the General Government for calling out the detached militia" were such that it was impossible for the militia to comply fully with them, and he added that ". . . if these rules are not complied with[,] the General Government it has seemed, do[es] not feel bound to pay. Those regulations declare that all companies of the Militia drafts when ordered on duty, will be mustered and inspected by an Inspector General or his Assistant or some other officer of the Army of the United States thereto specially appointed upon whose rolls and reports they will be entitled to pay, etc." Hawkins elaborated:

according to those regulations, if the militia drafts are called into service upon an exigency which should cease and the troops should be discharged before an United States officer, thereto specially appointed musters them and makes his report thereof to the War Department, they would not be considered as entitled to pay. Militia officers are not authorized to inspect them. Nearly every company of the detached militia called into service in July last , except those organized for permanent duty, were discharged without having an opportunity afforded them of being inspected by an officer in the United States Army appointed for that purpose. The fault was not in the Militia but in the General Government, they failed to comply with the essential part of their own regulations to furnish Inspecting officers to inspect the troops and in consequence of their having done so, those troops have not been recognized by the United States.[9]

Capt. Augustin Pugh, back home in Windsor after he and his company had been discharged from their detached service in Currituck County, wrote to Armstrong on March 11. He informed the secretary that in compliance with orders from North Carolina adjutant general Robert Williams, he had assembled and marched his men from Windsor to Currituck, where they remained until Governor Williams ordered him to dismiss the men from service. He informed Armstrong that he reported "from time to time to Major General Pinckney and to the Adjutant General of this state but for some cause yet unknown to me my company has never been mustered [into United States service] nor paid." He concluded: "I give you this information hoping you will in a short time send a paymaster to the County of Bertie to pay off the officers and men."[10]

The pay issue would not die and could not be resolved. Stone again met face-to-face with Armstrong in April, prompting the secretary to prepare a letter documenting the militia payment issue from the War Department's perspective. He wrote: "permit me to observe that in all cases in which detached militia in the service of the United States have been called out by the Authority of the Union—they are promptly paid, provided they have been regularly inspected and mustered, etc. The only body of North Carolina militia of this description known to me is the company of Major Cameron and I am informed by the Paymaster that they have been paid." He next laid out legal and regulatory requirements:

For the payment of militia (other than detached called out by the same authority under the Law of 1795) there are also existing legal provisions; nor is any provision made to pay such militia when called out by a State Authority, if after notice of such call to the War Department the President should think proper to sanction the call.

1st So soon as any State authority has called out a body of militia to repel invasions, either actual or menaced—notice shall be given to the War Department of the number and organization of those so called out and shall be accompanied by an exposition of the cause under which the call has been made. If those be deemed sufficient, the President sanctions the call and the expenses incurred are made chargeable to the United States.

2nd That a similar notice be promptly given to the General Commanding the District within which the call has been made, to the intent that the rules and regulations be executed in relations to inspections and musters, etc. and

3rd That a militia officer so called into service makes regular returns to the General Commanding the District, or to the War Department.

The reasonableness of these rules could readily be questioned. By the first, the President is enabled to judge whether the call be justified by the occasion or otherwise. By the second the Commanding General is enabled to perform a necessary duty. By the 3rd the President is informed how far the call by State authority has been obeyed—and is placed in a condition to direct either a diminution or increase of the force employed. Has either of these rules been observed in the case before us? I am unaware that any report of the number and organization of the Militia in question was sent to the President. I know not that any such report was made to General Pinckney and I do know that no return of any Detachment of North Carolina Militia is to be found in the War Department excepting that of a corps commanded by Major [J. A.] Cameron and which I am informed by Mr. [Robert] Brent has been paid.

From this fact it is evident that the remedy suggested by Governor Hawkins (of completing pay rolls from returns made to this Department) is impracticable. Nor do I know of any substitute (of sufficient character) short of Legislative provisions.[11]

Throughout the remainder of 1814 North Carolina and War Department officials traded letters; all the while no resolution was achieved, and North Carolina's militia companies that Governor Hawkins had called into service in July 1813 did not get paid. In the fall Adj. Gen. Robert Williams communicated multiple times with Robert Brent, paymaster of the army, John K. Bell of the adjutant and inspector general office, and Col. Tobias Lear in the department's accounting office. He forwarded specially prepared muster rolls, receipts, explanations, and other information requested by the officials in Washington, but bureaucracy prevailed: "nothing could be done"—the militia companies were not paid.[12]

In November—more than a year since the nonpayment of the state's militia had become a contentious issue between North Carolina and War Department officials—the General Assembly again met and approved a resolution authorizing Hawkins to transmit to the War Department "a roll exhibiting the amount owed . . . [for] pay, rations and other expenses incurred by the local militias called into service in the months of July and August 1813 when the state was invaded." Hawkins sent the roll to Secretary of War James Monroe on November 15, 1814.[13]

Finally, in December, the state's new governor, William Miller, informed the General Assembly that Governor Hawkins had incurred expenses by ordering out the detached militia in the months of July and August 1813 and that the expenses had "not yet been paid, nor have the claims of individuals who furnished them supplies." Miller informed the legislators that Adjutant General Williams had communicated with the War Department regarding the payment of North Carolina's claims. The General Assembly concluded that a board of auditors should be appointed to resolve the matter, as well as paying the "unliquidated claims of the . . . detached militia."[14]

By April 1815 the members of Captain Pugh's company had not been paid, so a number of them enlisted the services of a Bertie County attorney, William Britton, to seek payment on their behalf. Britton wrote to Governor Miller on April 22, asserting that "many persons" were concerned that "the General Government has aspersed to pay the Detached Militia who served under Capt. Augustin Pugh of this county at Edenton and Currituck in the year 1813." He informed Miller that the claims of the members who had served in the detachment amounted to "eleven hundred odd dollars," and he requested the governor to reply to him regarding the status of the payment of Pugh's troops.[15]

In May 1815 the board of auditors met and approved payments to the members of Pugh's company; Governor Miller likewise approved the payments.[16] Almost two years after they were first called into service, the Bertie County troops appeared to be on the verge of being paid—not by the federal government but by the state of North Carolina. Nevertheless, no paymaster arrived in Bertie County to pay the men.

Finally, in early February 1816—two years after Pugh's men were discharged from detached service at Currituck courthouse and a year after the war had concluded—the Bertie County citizen soldiers were paid. On February 6 William Britton, agent for many of the men, signed a pay and receipt roll in the amount of $2,112.45, a figure that represented the amounts owed to the men for their two 1813 deployments (to Edenton and Currituck Inlet).[17] The men received their long overdue pay, and for them the war was now over.

Notes

1. In January 1851 the North Carolina General Assembly approved resolutions that required the state's adjutant general to publish muster rolls of the state's detached militia units. The document, published later that year, includes rosters for the two companies of detached militia from Bertie County. The first company, detached under terms of the War Department's 1812 requisition, is listed on page 65 of the published muster rolls and includes the names of 108 men. Thirty-six of the men listed did not perform any active service with the company during its two deployments. While they obviously were designated to serve in the detached company at an early muster, for various reasons (including a number of men who apparently departed Bertie County before the company was called into service), they never served. Furthermore, of the ninety-four men who actively served in the company, twenty-two men's names are not listed in the adjutant general's published muster rolls.

Similarly, the 1814 company (Jacocks's) of the county's detached militia is listed on page 77. The list includes 103 names. Of the men listed, thirty-eight did not serve with the unit when it was called into United States service in late September 1814. The names of twenty-one county men who served in the company at Norfolk are not included in the adjutant general's document. See *Muster Rolls of the Soldiers of the War of 1812 Detached from the Militia of North Carolina, in 1812 and 1814* (Raleigh: Ch. C. Raboteau, 1851; Winston-Salem: Barber Printing Company, 1926), 63, 77.

Appendix 1 provides summary service histories of the Bertie County men who saw active service in the state's detached militia during the war. Those men whose names appear on the adjutant general's published muster rolls but who did not deploy with the companies are included in the author's roster.

2. General Orders, War Department, March 19, 1813, General Orders, Adjutant General's Office, War Department, July 4, 1812, General Orders and Circulars of the War Department and Headquarters of the Army, 1809–1860, (microfilm, M1094), Record Group 94, National Archives, Washington, D.C.

3. Jones to Armstrong, September 26, 1813, Letters Sent by the Secretary of War Relating to Military Affairs, 1800–1889 (microfilm, M6), Record Group 107, National Archives (hereafter cited as Secretary of War—Letters Sent).

4. "DPC" [Daniel Parker, Clerk] to Hawkins, October 30, 1813, Letters Received by the Secretary of War, Main Series, 1801–1870 (microfilm, M221), Record Group 107, National Archives (hereafter cited as Secretary of War—Letters Received).

5. Hawkins to Armstrong, October 19, 1813, Secretary of War—Letters Sent.

6. House of Commons Resolutions, December 24, 1813, William Hawkins, Governors Letter Books, State Archives, Office of Archives and History, Raleigh (hereafter cited as Hawkins Letter Books).

7. *Raleigh Minerva*, January 28, 1814.

8. Stone to Hawkins, February 26, 1814, Hawkins Letter Books.

9. Hawkins to Stone, March 11, 1814, Hawkins Letter Books.

10. Pugh to Armstrong, March 11, 1814, Compiled Service Record for Augustin Pugh, Compiled Service Records of the First Regiment (McCotter's) North Carolina Militia (Detached), Record Group 94, National Archives (hereafter cited as Compiled Service Records, with appropriate unit designation).

11. Armstrong to Stone, April 3, 1814, Hawkins Letter Books.

12. Williams to Adjutant and Inspector General, October 7, 1814; John K. Bell, Office of the Inspector General, Adjutant and Inspector General Office to Williams, October 11, 1814; Williams to Brent, October 25, 1814; Williams to Lear, October 25, 1814; Lear to Williams, October 29, 1814; Williams to Lear, November 10, 1814; Lear to Williams, November 17, 1814; Williams to Lear, November 22, 1814; Lear to Williams, November 29, 1814; Williams to Lear, December 5, 1814; and Lear to Williams, December 12, 1814, Adjutant General Militia Returns, Orders to Officers, 1813–1817 (AG-6), Records of the Adjutant General's Office, State Archives.

13. Hawkins to Monroe, November 15, 1814, Hawkins Letter Books.

14. Miller to General Assembly, December 20, 1814, William Miller, Governors Letter Books, State Archives, Office of Archives and History.

15. Britton to Miller, April 22, 1815, William Miller, Governors Papers, State Archives, Office of Archives and History.

16. War of 1812 Pay Vouchers, Capt. Augustin Pugh's company, (microfilm, S.115.137.10), State Archives, Office of Archives and History.

17. Compiled Service Records for members of Capt. Augustin Pugh's company, First Regiment (McCotter's) North Carolina Militia (Detached). On April 1, 1816, Gov. William Miller wrote to Secretary of War William H. Crawford seeking to have the federal government reimburse the North Carolina government for expenses incurred in calling into service various companies of militia during 1813. On April 15, 1816, Crawford informed Miller that Congress had recently authorized an appropriation to discharge the arrearages of the War Department but that "the estimate of the demands exhibited to Congress, [and] upon which the appropriation was made, expressly stated that it did not include any sums advanced by the states to their militia for services rendered during the war, and for which the United States might be responsible; therefore, there is no appropriation made by Congress to meet demands of this nature." In September 1816 Crawford directed the accountant of the War Department to forward to Miller thirty thousand dollars, which was all that could be paid "until the final settlement is made of the accounts of North Carolina." Miller to Crawford, April 1, 1816, Secretary of War—Letters Received; Crawford to Miller, April 15, September 17, 1816, Secretary of War—Letters Sent.

Appendix 1

Roster of Bertie County Militiamen (Detached)
North Carolina Militia (Detached)[1]

FIELD AND STAFF

Bryan, Joseph Hunter, quartermaster general: Appointed quarter-master general for the North Carolina detached militia by Gov. William Hawkins on May 24, 1813. Accepted appointment on May 26, 1813. Commissioned as a major general in the North Carolina militia on December 24, 1813, and appointed commandant of the First Division. Resigned commission on December 2, 1816.

FIRST REGIMENT (McCOTTER'S) NORTH CAROLINA MILITIA (DETACHED) (1812 REQUISITION)

FIELD AND STAFF

Brickell, Thomas M., sergeant: Appointed adjutant to the regiment per muster roll dated October 27, 1813, for Capt. Augustin Pugh's Bertie County company. No further information found regarding this appointment.

BERTIE COUNTY COMPANY (ARTILLERY SERVICE)

OFFICERS

Bryan, Joseph Hunter, captain: Name appears on a muster roll for this company published by the North Carolina adjutant general in 1851. However, he did not serve as captain when the company deployed to Edenton in July 1813 and to Currituck County in October 1813, since he had been appointed quartermaster general for the North Carolina detached militia on May 24, 1813.

Pugh, Augustin, captain: Name, with rank of lieutenant, appears on a muster roll for this company published by the North Carolina adjutant general in 1851. Appointed captain by July 1813, when the company deployed to Edenton, July 19–25. Reported present when the company rendezvoused at Windsor on October 27, 1813, and deployed on detached service to Currituck County. Discharged from detached service at Currituck County Courthouse on February 13, 1814.

Pruden, Lodowick, lieutenant: Name, with rank of ensign, appears on a muster roll for this company published by the North Carolina adjutant general in 1851. Appointed lieutenant by July 1813, when the company deployed to Edenton, July 19–25, 1813. Reported present when the company rendezvoused at Windsor on October 27, 1813, and deployed on detached service to Currituck County. Discharged from detached service at Currituck County Courthouse on February 13, 1814. Deceased by November 21, 1815, when David Pruden was appointed administrator of his estate in Bertie County court.

Caudle, John A., ensign: Name appears as "John A. Cordle" on a muster roll for this company published by the North Carolina adjutant general in 1851. Deployed with the company to Edenton, July 19–25, 1813. Reported present when the company rendezvoused at Windsor on October 27, 1813, and deployed on detached service to Currituck County. Discharged from detached service at Currituck County Courthouse on February 13, 1814.

NONCOMMISSIONED OFFICERS AND PRIVATES

Aaron, Abner, Jr., private: Name appears on a muster roll for this company published by the North Carolina adjutant general in 1851.

Allen, John, private: Name appears on a muster roll for this company published by the North Carolina adjutant general in 1851. Deployed with the company to Edenton, July 19–25, 1813. Pvt. William Hughes reported present as a substitute for Private Allen when the company rendezvoused at Windsor on October 27, 1813.

Baker, Edward B., private: Name appears on a muster roll for this company published by the North Carolina adjutant general in 1851. Deployed with the company to Edenton, July 19–25, 1813. Reported "absent sick at home" when the company rendezvoused at Windsor on October 27, 1813.

Bishop, William M., private: Name appears on a muster roll for this company published by the North Carolina adjutant general in 1851. Reported "absent sick at home" when the company rendezvoused at Windsor on October 27, 1813, and deployed on detached service to

Currituck County. Joined the company on November 17, 1813, and was discharged from detached service at Currituck County Courthouse on February 13, 1814.

Boswell, James, corporal: Name appears on a muster roll for this company published by the North Carolina adjutant general in 1851. Reported present with the rank of corporal when the company rendezvoused at Windsor on October 27, 1813, and deployed on detached service to Currituck County. Discharged from detached service at Currituck County Courthouse on February 13, 1814.

Boswell, Richard, private: Name appears as "Richard Bagwell" on a muster roll for this company published by the North Carolina adjutant general in 1851. Pvt. William Boswell reported present as a substitute for Pvt. Richard Boswell when the company rendezvoused at Windsor on October 27, 1813.

Boswell, William, private: Reported present as a substitute for Pvt. Richard Boswell when the company rendezvoused at Windsor on October 27, 1813, and deployed on detached service to Currituck County. Discharged from detached service at Currituck County Courthouse on February 13, 1814.

Bowers, Richard S., private: Name appears on a muster roll for this company published by the North Carolina adjutant general in 1851. Pvt. William Spivey reported present as a substitute for Private Bowers when the company rendezvoused at Windsor on October 27, 1813.

Brantly, John, private: Name appears on a muster roll for this company published by the North Carolina adjutant general in 1851. Reported "absent out of the state" when the company rendezvoused at Windsor on October 27, 1813. Later served in the Thirty-fifth Regiment United States Infantry.

Brantly, Joshua P., private: Name appears on a muster roll for this company published by the North Carolina adjutant general in 1851. Reported "absent out of the state" when the company rendezvoused at Windsor on October 27, 1813.

Brickell, John M., private: Name appears on a muster roll for this company published by the North Carolina adjutant general in 1851. Absent and reported as having enlisted in the United States Army per muster roll for the company when it rendezvoused at Windsor on October 27, 1813. Enlisted and served in the Tenth Regiment United States Infantry.

Brickell, Thomas M., sergeant: Name appears as "Thomas M. Bickell" on a muster roll for this company published by the North Carolina adjutant general in 1851. Reported "appointed adjutant to the regiment" per muster roll dated October 27, 1813, when the company rendezvoused at Windsor. No further information found.

Brickell, William M., private: Name appears on a muster roll for this company published by the North Carolina adjutant general in 1851. Reported "absent out of the state" when the company rendezvoused at Windsor on October 27, 1813. Served in the artillery service of the United States Army.

Britt, Shadrack ("Shade"), sergeant: Name appears on a muster roll for this company published by the North Carolina adjutant general in 1851. Deployed (with rank of corporal) with the company to Edenton, July 19–25, 1813. Reported present with the rank of sergeant when the company rendezvoused at Windsor on October 27, 1813, and deployed on detached service to Currituck County. Discharged from detached service at Currituck County Courthouse on February 13, 1814. Later served in the Twentieth Regiment United States Infantry.

Brogden, Benjamin, private: Name appears on a muster roll for this company published by the North Carolina adjutant general in 1851. Reported "absent out of the state" when the company rendezvoused at Windsor on October 27, 1813.

Brogden, William, private: Born in Bertie County and served in the Third Regiment United States Infantry from October 21, 1808, until April 6, 1813. Name appears on a muster roll for this company published by the North Carolina adjutant general in 1851. Deployed with the company to Edenton, July 19–25, 1813. Reported present when the company rendezvoused at Windsor on October 27, 1813, and deployed on detached service to Currituck County. Discharged from detached service at Currituck County Courthouse on February 13, 1814.

Bryan, Elijah C., private: Name appears on a muster roll for this company published by the North Carolina adjutant general in 1851. Reported "absent sick at home" when the company rendezvoused at Windsor on October 27, 1813.

Bunch, Cader, private: Name appears on a muster roll for this company published by the North Carolina adjutant general in 1851. Deployed with the company to Edenton, July 19–25, 1813. Reported present when the

company rendezvoused at Windsor on October 27, 1813, and deployed on detached service to Currituck County. Discharged from detached service at Currituck County Courthouse on February 13, 1814.

Calloway, Hatton William, private: Name appears as "Haller Calway" on a muster roll for this company published by the North Carolina adjutant general in 1851. Deployed with the company to Edenton, July 19–25, 1813. Later served in Capts. James Iredell and Gavin Hogg's company, First Regiment (McDonald's) North Carolina Militia (Detached).

Callum, Augustine, private: Name appears on a muster roll for this company published by the North Carolina adjutant general in 1851. Deployed with the company to Edenton, July 19–25, 1813.

Callum, Edward, corporal: Deployed with the company to Edenton, July 19–25, 1813. Reported present when the company rendezvoused at Windsor on October 27, 1813, and deployed on detached service to Currituck County. Discharged from detached service at Currituck County Courthouse on February 13, 1814.

Capehart, Truston, private: Deployed with the company to Edenton, July 19–25, 1813.

Clemmons, Hardy, private: Name appears as "Hardy Clements" on a muster roll for this company published by the North Carolina adjutant general in 1851. Deployed with the company to Edenton, July 19–25, 1813. Reported present when the company rendezvoused at Windsor on October 27, 1813, and deployed on detached service to Currituck County. Discharged from detached service at Currituck County Courthouse on February 13, 1814. Later served in Capts. James Iredell and Gavin Hogg's company, First Regiment (McDonald's) North Carolina Militia (Detached).

Cobb, John, private: Reported present as a substitute for Pvt. David Fleetwood when the company rendezvoused at Windsor on October 27, 1813, and deployed on detached service to Currituck County. Discharged from detached service at Currituck County Courthouse on February 13, 1814.

Cook, Jonathan, private: Deployed with the company to Edenton, July 19–25, 1813. Reported present as a substitute for Pvt. Nathaniel Cullifer when the company rendezvoused at Windsor on October 27, 1813, and deployed on detached service to Currituck County. Discharged from detached service at Currituck County Courthouse on February 13, 1814. Later served in the Twentieth Regiment United States Infantry.

Cook, Lawrence, private: Name appears on a muster roll for this company published by the North Carolina adjutant general in 1851.

Cook, Lazarus, Private: Reported "absent out of the state" when the company rendezvoused at Windsor on October 27, 1813.

Corbett, Thomas, private: Name appears on a muster roll for this company published by the North Carolina adjutant general in 1851. Deployed with the company to Edenton, July 19–25, 1813. Reported present when the company rendezvoused at Windsor on October 27, 1813, and deployed on detached service to Currituck County. Discharged from detached service at Currituck County Courthouse on February 13, 1814.

Cox, George, private: Name appears as "George Core" on a muster roll for this company published by the North Carolina adjutant general in 1851. Deployed with the company to Edenton, July 19–25, 1813. Pvt. Thomas Pearce reported present as a substitute for Private Cox when the company rendezvoused at Windsor on October 27, 1813.

Crumpler, Edmond, private: Deployed with the company to Edenton, July 19–25, 1813. Reported present as a substitute for Pvt. Neal Nichols when the company rendezvoused at Windsor on October 27, 1813, and deployed on detached service to Currituck County. Discharged from detached service at Currituck County Courthouse on February 13, 1814.

Cullifer, Nathaniel, private: Name appears as "Nathaniel Culpeper" on a muster roll for this company published by the North Carolina adjutant general in 1851. Pvt. Jonathan Cook reported present as a substitute for Private Cullifer when the company rendezvoused at Windsor on October 27, 1813.

Early, James, private: Name appears as "James Carley" on a muster roll for this company published by the North Carolina adjutant general in 1851. Deployed with the company to Edenton, July 19–25, 1813. Reported present when the company rendezvoused at Windsor on October 27, 1813, and deployed on detached service to Currituck County. Discharged from detached service at Currituck County Courthouse on February 13, 1814.

Eason, Abner, private: Deployed with the company to Edenton, July 19–25, 1813. Pvt. James Hoggard reported present as a substitute for Private Eason when the company rendezvoused at Windsor on October 27, 1813.

Evans, Dred, private: Name appears on a muster roll for this company published by the North Carolina adjutant general in 1851. Deployed with the company to Edenton, July 19–25, 1813. Reported present when the company rendezvoused at Windsor on October 27, 1813, and deployed on detached service to Currituck County. Deserted on January 2, 1814.

Evans, William, private: Name appears on a muster roll for this company published by the North Carolina adjutant general in 1851. Reported "absent out of the state" when the company rendezvoused at Windsor on October 27, 1813. May have enlisted and served in the Tenth Regiment United States Infantry.

Everitt, John B., private: Name appears on a muster roll for this company published by the North Carolina adjutant general in 1851.

Everitt, Samuel R., private: Reported "absent out of the state" when the company rendezvoused at Windsor on October 27, 1813.

Ferby, Peter D., private: Reported present when the company rendezvoused at Windsor on October 27, 1813, and deployed on detached service to Currituck County. Discharged on December 8, 1813.

Fleetwood, David, private: Name appears on a muster roll for this company published by the North Carolina adjutant general in 1851. Deployed with the company to Edenton, July 19–25, 1813. Pvt. John Cobb reported present as a substitute for Private Fleetwood when the company rendezvoused at Windsor on October 27, 1813.

Fleetwood, Edmond, Jr., private: Name appears on a muster roll for this company published by the North Carolina adjutant general in 1851.

Fleetwood, Edward, private: Deployed with the company to Edenton, July 19–25, 1813. Pvt. William Simons reported present as a substitute for Pvt. Edward Fleetwood when the company rendezvoused at Windsor on October 27, 1813.

Folk, David, private: Name appears on a muster roll for this company published by the North Carolina adjutant general in 1851. Deployed with the company to Edenton, July 19–25, 1813. Pvt. Isom B. Manning reported present as a substitute for Private Folk when the company rendezvoused at Windsor on October 27, 1813.

Freeman, Moses, private: Name appears on a muster roll for this company published by the North Carolina adjutant general in 1851. Deployed with the company to Edenton, July 19–25, 1813. Reported present when the company rendezvoused at Windsor on October 27, 1813, and deployed on detached service to Currituck County. Discharged from detached service at Currituck County Courthouse on February 13, 1814. Later served in the Twentieth Regiment United States Infantry.

Freeman, Seth, private: Reported present as a substitute for Pvt. Cader Mitchell when the company rendezvoused at Windsor on October 27, 1813, and deployed on detached service to Currituck County. Discharged from detached service at Currituck County Courthouse on February 13, 1814.

Gardner, William, private: Name appears on a muster roll for this company published by the North Carolina adjutant general in 1851. Deployed with the company to Edenton, July 19–25, 1813. Reported present when the company rendezvoused at Windsor on October 27, 1813, and deployed on detached service to Currituck County. Discharged from detached service at Currituck County Courthouse on February 13, 1814.

Garrett, David, private: Name appears on a muster roll for this company published by the North Carolina adjutant general in 1851. Deployed with the company to Edenton, July 19–25, 1813. Reported present when the company rendezvoused at Windsor on October 27, 1813, and deployed on detached service to Currituck County. Discharged from detached service at Currituck County Courthouse on February 13, 1814.

Garrett, Jesse, private: Name appears on a muster roll for this company published by the North Carolina adjutant general in 1851. Reported "absent out of the state" when the company rendezvoused at Windsor on October 27, 1813.

Gill, Edward, private: Name appears on a muster roll for this company published by the North Carolina adjutant general in 1851. Deployed with the company to Edenton, July 19–25, 1813. Reported present when the company rendezvoused at Windsor on October 27, 1813, and deployed on detached service to Currituck County. Discharged from detached service at Currituck County Courthouse on February 13, 1814.

Green, Malachi, private: Name appears on a muster roll for this company published by the North Carolina adjutant general in 1851. Reported "absent out of the state" when the company rendezvoused at Windsor on October 27, 1813.

Green, William H., private: Name appears on a muster roll for this company published by the North Carolina adjutant general in 1851. Pvt. Arthur C. Simons reported present as a substitute for Private Green when the company rendezvoused at Windsor on October 27, 1813.

Gregory, Asa, private: Name appears on a muster roll for this company published by the North Carolina adjutant general in 1851. Deployed with the company to Edenton, July 19–25, 1813. Reported present when the company rendezvoused at Windsor on October 27, 1813, and deployed on detached service to Currituck County. Discharged from detached service at Currituck County Courthouse on February 13, 1814.

Gregory, Lemuel, private: Reported present as a substitute for Pvt. Steven Hyman when the company rendezvoused at Windsor on October 27, 1813, and deployed on detached service to Currituck County. Discharged from detached service at Currituck County Courthouse on February 13, 1814.

Harrell, David, private: Name appears on a muster roll for this company published by the North Carolina adjutant general in 1851. Deployed with the company to Edenton, July 19–25, 1813. Reported present when the company rendezvoused at Windsor on October 27, 1813, and deployed on detached service to Currituck County. Discharged from detached service at Currituck County Courthouse on February 13, 1814.

Harrell, Joseph, private: Name appears on a muster roll for this company published by the North Carolina adjutant general in 1851. Deployed with the company to Edenton, July 19–25, 1813. Reported present when the company rendezvoused at Windsor on October 27, 1813, and deployed on detached service to Currituck County. Discharged from detached service at Currituck County Courthouse on February 13, 1814.

Harrell, Simon, private: Name appears on a muster roll for this company published by the North Carolina adjutant general in 1851. Deployed with the company to Edenton, July 19–25, 1813. Reported present when the company rendezvoused at Windsor on October 27, 1813, and deployed on detached service to Currituck County. Discharged November 14, 1813, "sick unable to do duty."

Higgs, William, private: Name appears on a muster roll for this company published by the North Carolina adjutant general in 1851. Deployed with the company to Edenton, July 19–25, 1813. Reported present when the company rendezvoused at Windsor on October 27, 1813, and deployed on detached service to Currituck County. Discharged from detached service at Currituck County Courthouse on February 13, 1814.

Hobbs, Samuel, private: Name appears on a muster roll for this company published by the North Carolina adjutant general in 1851. Deployed with the company to Edenton, July 19–25, 1813. Reported present when the company rendezvoused at Windsor on October 27, 1813, and deployed on detached service to Currituck County. Discharged from detached service at Currituck County Courthouse on February 13, 1814.

Hodder, William, private: Reported "absent out of the state" when the company rendezvoused at Windsor on October 27, 1813. Enlisted in the Tenth Regiment United States Infantry.

Hoggard, James, private: Reported present as a substitute for Pvt. Abner Eason when the company rendezvoused at Windsor on October 27, 1813, and deployed on detached service to Currituck County. Deserted on January 18, 1814.

Hoggard, Thomas, private: Name appears on a muster roll for this company published by the North Carolina adjutant general in 1851. "Volunteered at Windsor" and deployed with the company to Edenton, July 19–25, 1813. Reported present when the company rendezvoused at Windsor on October 27, 1813, and deployed on detached service to Currituck County. Discharged from detached service at Currituck County Courthouse on February 13, 1814.

Holloman, Nathaniel, private: Name appears as "Nathl Wattoman" on a muster roll for this company published by the North Carolina adjutant general in 1851. Reported "absent out of the state" when the company rendezvoused at Windsor on October 27, 1813. Served in the Tenth Regiment United States Infantry.

Holloman, William, private: Name appears on a muster roll for this company published by the North Carolina adjutant general in 1851. Reported "absent out of the state" when the company rendezvoused at Windsor on October 27, 1813.

Holly, John, sergeant: Name appears on a muster roll for this company published by the North Carolina adjutant general in 1851. Deployed as a private with the company to Edenton, July 19–25, 1813. Reported present as a sergeant when the company rendezvoused at Windsor on October 27, 1813, and deployed on detached service to Currituck County. Discharged from detached service at Currituck County Courthouse on February 13, 1814.

Holly, John S., private: Deployed with the company to Edenton, July 19–25, 1813. Reported present as a substitute for Pvt. John West when the company rendezvoused at Windsor on October 27, 1813, and deployed on detached service to Currituck County. Discharged from detached service at Currituck County Courthouse on February 13, 1814. Later served in the Twentieth Regiment United States Infantry.

Hughes, Morris, private: Reported present as a substitute for Pvt. Linus R. Leonard when the company rendezvoused at Windsor on October 27, 1813, and deployed on detached service to Currituck County. Discharged from detached service at Currituck County Courthouse on February 13, 1814.

Hughes, William, private: Reported present as a substitute for Pvt. John Allen when the company rendezvoused at Windsor on October 27, 1813, and deployed on detached service to Currituck County. Discharged from detached service at Currituck County Courthouse on February 13, 1814.

Hunter, Cader, private: Name appears on a muster roll for this company published by the North Carolina adjutant general in 1851. Pvt. Nimrod West reported present as a substitute for Private Hunter when the company rendezvoused at Windsor on October 27, 1813.

Hunter, Hardy, private: Name appears on a muster roll for this company published by the North Carolina adjutant general in 1851. Reported present when the company rendezvoused at Windsor on October 27, 1813, and deployed on detached service to Currituck County. Discharged from detached service at Currituck County Courthouse on February 13, 1814. Later served in the Twentieth Regiment United States Infantry.

Hunter, William, private: Name appears on a muster roll for this company published by the North Carolina adjutant general in 1851.

Hyman, Stephen, private: Name appears on a muster roll for this company published by the North Carolina adjutant general in 1851. Deployed with the company to Edenton, July 19–25, 1813. Pvt. Lemuel Gregory reported present as a substitute for Private Hyman when the company rendezvoused at Windsor on October 27, 1813.

James, Benjamin, private: Name appears on a muster roll for this company published by the North Carolina adjutant general in 1851. Reported "absent out of the state" when the company rendezvoused at Windsor on October 27, 1813.

Jernigan, Ryan, private: Name appears as "Ryan Jonagon" on a muster roll for this company published by the North Carolina adjutant general in 1851. Reported "absent out of the state" when the company rendezvoused at Windsor on October 27, 1813. Later enlisted in the Twentieth Regiment United States Infantry.

Lawrence, Reuben, private: Name appears on a muster roll for this company published by the North Carolina adjutant general in 1851. Pvt. Jesse Qualls reported present as a substitute for Private Lawrence when the company rendezvoused at Windsor on October 27, 1813.

Leonard, Linus R., private: Name appears on a muster roll for this company published by the North Carolina adjutant general in 1851. Deployed with the company to Edenton, July 19–25, 1813. Pvt. Morris Hughes reported present as a substitute for Private Leonard when the company rendezvoused at Windsor on October 27, 1813.

Manning, Isom B., private: Reported present as a substitute for Pvt. David Folk when the company rendezvoused at Windsor on October 27, 1813, and deployed on detached service to Currituck County. Discharged from detached service at Currituck County Courthouse on February 13, 1814.

Martin, Samuel, private: Name appears on a muster roll for this company published by the North Carolina adjutant general in 1851. Deployed with the company to Edenton, July 19–25, 1813. Reported "absent sick at home" when the company rendezvoused at Windsor on October 27, 1813, and deployed on detached service to Currituck County. Joined the company on December 12, 1813. Discharged from detached service at Currituck County Courthouse on February 13, 1814.

Mason, Miles, private: Reported present as a substitute for Pvt. John Ruffin when the company rendezvoused at Windsor on October 27, 1813, and deployed on detached service to Currituck County. Discharged from detached service at Currituck County Courthouse on February 13, 1814.

McGlaughon, Turner, private: Name appears on a muster roll for this company published by the North Carolina adjutant general in 1851. Reported "absent out of the state" when the company rendezvoused at Windsor on October 27, 1813.

McGruder, William, private: Name appears on a muster roll for this company published by the North Carolina adjutant general in 1851. Deployed with the company to Edenton, July 19–25, 1813. Reported present when the company rendezvoused at Windsor on October 27, 1813, and deployed on detached service to Currituck County. Deserted on January 14, 1814. McGruder was deceased by August 10, 1817, when Jeremiah Leggett was appointed administrator of his estate in Bertie County Court.

Miller, Frederick, private: Name appears on a muster roll for this company published by the North Carolina adjutant general in 1851. Deployed with the company to Edenton, July 19–25, 1813. Reported present when the company rendezvoused at Windsor on October 27, 1813, and deployed on detached service to Currituck County. Discharged from detached service at Currituck County Courthouse on February 13, 1814.

Miller, Josiah, private: Name appears on a muster roll for this company published by the North Carolina adjutant general in 1851. Deployed with the company to Edenton, July 19–25, 1813. Reported "absent sick at home" when the company rendezvoused at Windsor on October 27, 1813, and deployed on detached service to Currituck County. Joined the company on November 24, 1813. Discharged from detached service at Currituck County Courthouse on February 13, 1814.

Minor, John, private: Name appears on a muster roll for this company published by the North Carolina adjutant general in 1851. Reported "absent out of the state" when the company rendezvoused at Windsor on October 27, 1813.

Mitchell, Cader, private: Name appears on a muster roll for this company published by the North Carolina adjutant general in 1851. Deployed with the company to Edenton, July 19–25, 1813. Pvt. Seth Freeman reported present as a substitute for Private Mitchell when the company rendezvoused at Windsor on October 27, 1813.

Mizell, George, fifer/musician: Reported present when the company rendezvoused at Windsor on October 27, 1813, and deployed on detached service to Currituck County. Discharged from detached service at Currituck County Courthouse on February 13, 1814.

Nichols, Neal, private: Name appears as "Neal Nicholas" on a muster roll for this company published by the North Carolina adjutant general in 1851. Pvt. Edmond Crumpler reported present as a substitute for Private Nichols when the company rendezvoused at Windsor on October 27, 1813.

Outlaw, David, corporal: Name appears on a muster roll for this company published by the North Carolina adjutant general in 1851. Deployed with the company to Edenton, July 19–25, 1813. Reported "absent sick at home" when the company rendezvoused at Windsor on October 27, 1813, and deployed on detached service to Currituck County. Joined the company on December 7, 1813. Discharged from detached service at Currituck County Courthouse on February 13, 1814.

Outlaw, Levi, private: Name appears on a muster roll for this company published by the North Carolina adjutant general in 1851. Deployed with the company to Edenton, July 19–25, 1813. Reported present when the company rendezvoused at Windsor on October 27, 1813, and deployed on detached service to Currituck County. Discharged from detached service at Currituck County Courthouse on February 13, 1814.

Pearce, Thomas, private: Reported present as a substitute for Pvt. George Cox when the company rendezvoused at Windsor on October 27, 1813, and deployed on detached service to Currituck County. Discharged from detached service at Currituck County Courthouse on February 13, 1814.

Phelps, Lewton K., private: Deployed with the company to Edenton, July 19–25, 1813. Reported present as a substitute for Pvt. Jacob Pruden when the company rendezvoused at Windsor on October 27, 1813, and deployed on detached service to Currituck County. Discharged from detached service at Currituck County Courthouse on February 13, 1814.

Piner, James, private: Reported present as a substitute for Pvt. Jesse Powell when the company rendezvoused at Windsor on October 27, 1813, and deployed on detached service to Currituck County. Discharged from detached service at Currituck County Courthouse on February 13, 1814.

Powell, Jesse, private: Name appears on a muster roll for this company published by the North Carolina adjutant general in 1851. Deployed with the company to Edenton, July 19–25, 1813. Pvt. James Piner reported present as a substitute for Private Powell when the company rendezvoused at Windsor on October 27, 1813.

Pritchard, Elisha, private: Name appears on a muster roll for this company published by the North Carolina adjutant general in 1851. Reported "absent out of the state" when the company rendezvoused at Windsor on October 27, 1813.

Pruden, Jacob, private: Name appears on a muster roll for this company published by the North Carolina adjutant general in 1851. Pvt. Lewton K. Phelps reported present as a substitute for Private Pruden when the company rendezvoused at Windsor on October 27, 1813.

Qualls, Jesse, private: Deployed with the company to Edenton, July 19–25, 1813. Reported present as a substitute for Pvt. Reuben Lawrence when the company rendezvoused at Windsor on October 27, 1813, and deployed on detached service to Currituck County. Discharged from detached service at Currituck County Courthouse on February 13, 1814.

Ramsey, John, private: Name appears on a muster roll for this company published by the North Carolina adjutant general in 1851.

Rawlings, Miles, private: Name appears as "Miles Rollins" on a muster roll for this company published by the North Carolina adjutant general in 1851. Enlisted and served in the Tenth Regiment United States Infantry.

Rawls, William, private: Name appears as "William Roll" on a muster roll for this company published by the North Carolina adjutant general in 1851. Deployed with the company to Edenton, July 19–25, 1813. Reported "absent out of the state" when the company rendezvoused at Windsor on October 27, 1813.

Redditt, Asa, private: Name appears as "Asa Radett" on a muster roll for this company published by the North Carolina adjutant general in 1851. Deployed with the company to Edenton, July 19–25, 1813. Reported present when the company rendezvoused at Windsor on October 27, 1813, and deployed on detached service to Currituck County. Discharged from detached service at Currituck County Courthouse on February 13, 1814. Later served in the Twentieth Regiment United States Infantry.

Rhodes, John, private: Name appears on a muster roll for this company published by the North Carolina adjutant general in 1851. Deployed with the company to Edenton, July 19–25, 1813. Reported present when the company rendezvoused at Windsor on October 27, 1813, and deployed on detached service to Currituck County. Discharged from detached service at Currituck County Courthouse on February 13, 1814.

Robertson, William, private: Name appears on a muster roll for this company published by the North Carolina adjutant general in 1851. Deployed with the company to Edenton, July 19–25, 1813. Reported present when the company rendezvoused at Windsor on October 27, 1813, and deployed on detached service to Currituck County. Discharged from detached service at Currituck County Courthouse on February 13, 1814.

Rogers, Benjamin, private: Name appears on a muster roll for this company published by the North Carolina adjutant general in 1851. Reported "absent out of the state" when the company rendezvoused at Windsor on October 27, 1813.

Ruffin, John, private: Name appears on a muster roll for this company published by the North Carolina adjutant general in 1851. Deployed with the company to Edenton, July 19–25, 1813. Pvt. Miles Mason reported present as a substitute for Private Ruffin when the company rendezvoused at Windsor on October 27, 1813.

Rutland, Johnston, private: Name appears on a muster roll for this company published by the North Carolina adjutant general in 1851. Deployed with the company to Edenton, July 19–25, 1813. Reported present when the company rendezvoused at Windsor on October 27, 1813, and deployed on detached service to Currituck County. Discharged from detached service at Currituck County Courthouse on February 13, 1814.

Rutland, Miles, private: Reported "absent out of the state" when the company rendezvoused at Windsor on October 27, 1813.

Rutland, Redden, private: Name appears on a muster roll for this company published by the North Carolina adjutant general in 1851. Deployed with the company to Edenton, July 19–25, 1813. Reported present when the company rendezvoused at Windsor on October 27, 1813, and deployed on detached service to Currituck County. Discharged from detached service at Currituck County Courthouse on February 13, 1814.

Ryan, James, private: Name appears as "James Ryman" on a muster roll for this company published by the North Carolina adjutant general in 1851. Reported "absent out of the state" when the company rendezvoused at Windsor on October 27, 1813.

Simons, Arthur C., private: Deployed with the company to Edenton, July 19–25, 1813. Reported present as a substitute for William H. Green when the company rendezvoused at Windsor on October 27, 1813, and deployed on detached service to Currituck County. Deserted December 31, 1813. Later enlisted in the Thirty-fifth Regiment United States Infantry.

Simons, James, private: Name appears on a muster roll for this company published by the North Carolina adjutant general in 1851. Reported "absent out of the state" when the company rendezvoused at Windsor on October 27, 1813.

Simons, William, private: Reported present as a substitute for Pvt. Edward Fleetwood when the company rendezvoused at Windsor on October 27, 1813, and deployed on detached service to Currituck County. Discharged from detached service at Currituck County Courthouse on February 13, 1814. Later served in Capts. James Iredell and Gavin Hogg's company, First Regiment (McDonald's) North Carolina Militia (Detached).

Sorrell, Thomas, private: Name appears on a muster roll for this company published by the North Carolina adjutant general in 1851. Deployed with the company to Edenton, July 19–25, 1813. Reported present when the company rendezvoused at Windsor on October 27, 1813, and deployed on detached service to Currituck County. Discharged from detached service at Currituck County Courthouse on February 13, 1814.

Spivey, William, private: Reported present as a substitute for Pvt. Richard S. Bowers when the company rendezvoused at Windsor on October 27, 1813, and deployed on detached service to Currituck County. Discharged from detached service at Currituck County Courthouse on February 13, 1814.

Stewart, John, Jr., corporal: Name appears on a muster roll for this company published by the North Carolina adjutant general in 1851. Deployed with the company to Edenton, July 19–25, 1813. Reported "absent out of the state" when the company rendezvoused at Windsor on October 27, 1813.

Tines, West, private: Name appears on a muster roll for this company published by the North Carolina adjutant general in 1851. Deployed with the company to Edenton, July 19–25, 1813. Reported present when the company rendezvoused at Windsor on October 27, 1813, and deployed on detached service to Currituck County. Discharged from detached service at Currituck County Courthouse on February 13, 1814.

Todd, Levi, private: Name appears on a muster roll for this company published by the North Carolina adjutant general in 1851. Deployed with the company to Edenton, July 19–25, 1813. Reported present when the

company rendezvoused at Windsor on October 27, 1813, and deployed on detached service to Currituck County. Discharged from detached service at Currituck County Courthouse on February 13, 1814.

Turner, Edward, private: Name appears on a muster roll for this company published by the North Carolina adjutant general in 1851. Reported "absent out of the state" when the company rendezvoused at Windsor on October 27, 1813.

Turner, Washington, private: Name appears on a muster roll for this company published by the North Carolina adjutant general in 1851. Reported "absent out of the state" when the company rendezvoused at Windsor on October 27, 1813.

Walton, John, private: Name appears on a muster roll for this company published by the North Carolina adjutant general in 1851. Deployed with the company to Edenton, July 19–25, 1813. Reported present when the company rendezvoused at Windsor on October 27, 1813, and deployed on detached service to Currituck County. Discharged from detached service at Currituck County Courthouse on February 13, 1814.

Ward, George, private: Name appears on a muster roll for this company published by the North Carolina adjutant general in 1851. Deployed with the company to Edenton, July 19–25, 1813. Reported present when the company rendezvoused at Windsor on October 27, 1813, and deployed on detached service to Currituck County. Discharged from detached service at Currituck County Courthouse on February 13, 1814.

West, John, private: Name appears on a muster roll for this company published by the North Carolina adjutant general in 1851. Pvt. John S. Holly reported present as a substitute for Private West when the company rendezvoused at Windsor on October 27, 1813.

West, Nimrod, private: Deployed with the company to Edenton, July 19–25, 1813. Reported present as a substitute for Pvt. Cader Hunter when the company rendezvoused at Windsor on October 27, 1813, and deployed on detached service to Currituck County. Discharged from detached service at Currituck County Courthouse on February 13, 1814. Later served in the Twentieth Regiment United States Infantry.

West, Thomas, private: Deployed with the company to Edenton, July 19–25, 1813. No additional information found.

White, Cader, private: Deployed with the company to Edenton, July 19–25, 1813. Reported present when the company rendezvoused at Windsor on October 27, 1813, and deployed on detached service to Currituck County. Discharged from detached service at Currituck County Courthouse on February 13, 1814.

White, Hardy, private: Name appears on a muster roll for this company published by the North Carolina adjutant general in 1851. Reported absent and having enlisted [in the United States Army] per muster roll for the company when it rendezvoused at Windsor on October 27, 1813. Served in the Tenth Regiment United States Infantry.

Whitehead, Joseph, private: Deployed with the company to Edenton, July 19–25, 1813.

Whitehead, Peggy, wife of Pvt. Joseph Whitehead: Accompanied the company as "cook" on its deployment to Edenton, July 19-25, 1813.

Wiggins, Anthony, private: Name appears on a muster roll for this company published by the North Carolina adjutant general in 1851. Reported "absent out of the state" when the company rendezvoused at Windsor on October 27, 1813.

Wiggins, Isaac, private: Name appears on a muster roll for this company published by the North Carolina adjutant general in 1851. Reported "absent out of the state" when the company rendezvoused at Windsor on October 27, 1813.

Wilkes, Henry, private: Name appears on a muster roll for this company published by the North Carolina adjutant general in 1851. Deployed with the company to Edenton, July 19–25, 1813. Reported "absent out of the state" when the company rendezvoused at Windsor on October 27, 1813. Joined the company on January 24, 1814. Discharged from detached service at Currituck County Courthouse on February 13, 1814.

Wilkes, James, private: Name appears on a muster roll for this company published by the North Carolina adjutant general in 1851. Reported present when the company rendezvoused at Windsor on October 27, 1813, and deployed on detached service to Currituck County. Discharged from detached service at Currituck County Courthouse on February 13, 1814.

Wilkes, John, private: Name appears on a muster roll for this company published by the North Carolina adjutant general in 1851. Deployed with the company to Edenton, July 19–25, 1813. Reported present when the

company rendezvoused at Windsor on October 27, 1813, and deployed on detached service to Currituck County. Discharged from detached service at Currituck County Courthouse on February 13, 1814.

Wilkes, Reuben, private: Name appears on a muster roll for this company published by the North Carolina adjutant general in 1851. Deployed with the company to Edenton, July 19–25, 1813. Reported present when the company rendezvoused at Windsor on October 27, 1813, and deployed on detached service to Currituck County. Discharged from detached service at Currituck County Courthouse on February 13, 1814.

Wilkins, Will, private: Name appears on a muster roll for this company published by the North Carolina adjutant general in 1851.

Wilkinson, William, private: Reported "absent out of the state" when the company rendezvoused at Windsor on October 27, 1813. May have enlisted and served in the Tenth Regiment United States Infantry.

Wilson, George, private: Name appears on a muster roll for this company published by the North Carolina adjutant general in 1851. Deployed with the company to Edenton, July 19–25, 1813. Reported present when the company rendezvoused at Windsor on October 27, 1813, and deployed on detached service to Currituck County. Discharged from detached service at Currituck County Courthouse on February 13, 1814.

Wilson, Isaac, private: Name appears on a muster roll for this company published by the North Carolina adjutant general in 1851. Deployed with the company to Edenton, July 19–25, 1813. Reported "absent sick at home" when the company rendezvoused at Windsor on October 27, 1813. Joined the company on January 1, 1814. Discharged from detached service at Currituck County Courthouse on February 13, 1814.

Wilson, Silas, private: Name appears on a muster roll for this company published by the North Carolina adjutant general in 1851. Deployed with the company to Edenton, July 19–25, 1813. Reported present when the company rendezvoused at Windsor on October 27, 1813, and deployed on detached service to Currituck County. Discharged from detached service at Currituck County Courthouse on February 13, 1814.

Wimberly, Frederick, private: Name appears on a muster roll for this company published by the North Carolina adjutant general in 1851. Deployed with the company to Edenton, July 19–25, 1813. Reported present when the company rendezvoused at Windsor on October 27, 1813, and deployed on detached service to Currituck County. Discharged from detached service at Currituck County Courthouse on February 13, 1814.

Winburn, Benjamin, private: Name appears on a muster roll for this company published by the North Carolina adjutant general in 1851. Reported "absent out of the state" when the company rendezvoused at Windsor on October 27, 1813.

FIRST REGIMENT (McDONALD'S)
NORTH CAROLINA MILITIA (DETACHED)
(1814 REQUISITION)

FIELD AND STAFF

Bozeman, William R. H., quartermaster sergeant: Transferred on October 22, 1814, from Capt. James Iredell's company of this regiment to serve in the Quartermaster Department. Reported present or accounted for until discharged from United States service at Norfolk on February 5, 1815.

Smithwick, Luke, sergeant major: Transferred on October 22, 1814, from Capt. James Iredell's company of this regiment to serve in the adjutant's department. Reported present or accounted for until died on January 18, 1815, at Norfolk.

CAPT. JAMES IREDELL'S COMPANY
(LATER CAPT. GAVIN HOGG'S COMPANY)

OFFICERS

Jacocks, Jonathan H., captain: Resided in Bertie County. Name appears on a muster roll for this company published by the North Carolina adjutant general in 1851. Accompanied company from Windsor to Gates Court House in late September 1814 but was "dismissed" by Brig. Gen. Jeremiah Slade of the North Carolina militia upon the company's rendezvous at Gates Court House on or about September 30, 1814.[2] Slade placed Capt. James Iredell of Chowan County in command of the company, which was composed predominantly of Bertie County men.

Hogg, Gavin, captain: Name appears (with the rank of private) on a muster roll for this company published by the North Carolina adjutant general in 1851. Appointed a lieutenant of this company by Brig. Gen. Jeremiah Slade of the North Carolina militia upon the company's rendezvous at Gates Court House on or about September 30, 1814. Assumed command of the company upon Capt. James Iredell's resignation on December 21, 1814. Appointed to the rank of captain on January 21, 1815. Reported present or accounted for until discharged from United States service at Norfolk on February 5, 1815. As noted in chapter 5, McDonald's regiment (including Captain Hogg's company) was discharged at Portsmouth, Virginia. Nevertheless, the official muster rolls were dated February 5, 1815, and included the name "Norfolk"—the official headquarters of the Fifth Military District.

Clark, Kenneth, lieutenant: Transferred from Capt. Henry G. Williams's company of this regiment on January 19, 1815. Reported present or accounted for until died on January 30, 1815.

Darlett, William M., lieutenant: Name appears on a muster roll for this company published by the North Carolina adjutant general in 1851. Resided in Bertie County and reported present with this company when it rendezvoused at Gates Court House on or about September 30, 1814. Promoted from ensign to lieutenant on December 8, 1814. Reported as "sent on command December 31, 1814," per company muster roll dated January 2, 1815. Reported present or accounted for until discharged from United States service at Norfolk on February 5, 1815.

Harrell, Powell, lieutenant: Name appears on a muster roll for this company published by the North Carolina adjutant general in 1851. Apparently dismissed by Brig. Gen. Jeremiah Slade at Gates Court House on or about September 30, 1814.

King, William P., lieutenant: Name (with the rank of private) appears on a muster roll for this company published by the North Carolina adjutant general in 1851. Resided in Bertie County and reported present with this company as a sergeant when it rendezvoused at Gates Court House on or about September 30, 1814. Promoted from sergeant to ensign on December 8, 1814. Promoted to lieutenant on January 2, 1815. Reported present or accounted for until discharged from United States service at Norfolk on February 5, 1815.

Wilson, James, Jr., ensign: Name appears on a muster roll for this company published by the North Carolina adjutant general in 1851.

NONCOMMISSIONED OFFICERS AND PRIVATES

Baker, Benjamin, sergeant: Name appears on a muster roll for this company published by the North Carolina adjutant general in 1851. Resided in Bertie County and reported present with this company when it rendezvoused at Gates Court House on or about September 30, 1814. Promoted from private to sergeant on January 2, 1815. Reported present or accounted for until died at Norfolk on January 21, 1815.

Baker, Isaac, sergeant: Resided in Bertie County and reported present with this company when it rendezvoused at Gates Court House on or about September 30, 1814. Reported present or accounted for until discharged from United States service at Norfolk on February 5, 1815.

Baker, John, private: Resided in Bertie County and reported present with this company when it rendezvoused at Gates Court House on or about September 30, 1814. Reported present or accounted for until discharged from United States service at Norfolk on February 5, 1815.

Barnes, Reuben, private: Name appears on a muster roll for this company published by the North Carolina adjutant general in 1851.

Bazemore, Cullen, private: Name appears on a muster roll for this company published by the North Carolina adjutant general in 1851. Resided in Bertie County and reported present with this company when it rendezvoused at Gates Court House on or about September 30, 1814. Reported present or accounted for until discharged from United States service at Norfolk on February 5, 1815.

Bazemore, Stephen, private: Name appears on a muster roll for this company published by the North Carolina adjutant general in 1851.

Bird, Josiah, private: Name appears on a muster roll for this company published by the North Carolina adjutant general in 1851. Resided in Bertie County and reported present with this company when it rendezvoused at Gates Court House on or about September 30, 1814. Stated in a bounty land application on December 21, 1815, that he was "drafted in Windsor . . . in the month of August A.D. 1814." Stated in a subsequent declaration that he "volunteered at Windsor." Reported present or accounted for until deserted on an undisclosed date (but likely on December 22, 1814). Returned on December 26, 1814, and, per company muster roll dated January 2, 1815, had been tried by court-martial and was "entitled to pay." Reported "absent sick in general hospital" on February 5, 1815, date of last muster roll for the company.

Blount, Joseph, private: Name appears on a muster roll for this company published by the North Carolina adjutant general in 1851.

Boswell, James, private: Name appears on a muster roll for this company published by the North Carolina adjutant general in 1851. Previously served in Capt. Augustin Pugh's Bertie County militia company, First Regiment (McCotter's) North Carolina Militia (Detached).

Bowen, Benjamin, private: Name appears on a muster roll for this company published by the North Carolina adjutant general in 1851.

Bowen, John, private: Name appears on a muster roll for this company published by the North Carolina adjutant general in 1851.

Boyce, John, private: Reported present with this company when it rendezvoused at Gates Court House on or about September 30, 1814. Reported present or accounted for until died at Norfolk on November 7, 1814. The name "John Boyd," a private, appears on a muster roll for this company published by the North Carolina adjutant general in 1851. "John Boyd" and "John Boyce" were likely recorded names for the same soldier.

Bozeman, William R. H., sergeant: Name appears on a muster roll for this company published by the North Carolina adjutant general in 1851. Resided in Bertie County and reported present with this company when it rendezvoused at Gates Court House on or about September 30, 1814. Transferred to Quartermaster Department, Field and Staff of this regiment on October 22, 1814.

Briscoe, Thomas, private: Reported present with this company when it rendezvoused at Gates Court House on or about September 30, 1814. No further information found. May have been dismissed when Brig. Gen. Jeremiah Slade assembled this company from members of several companies at Gates Court House.

Brown, Jesse, sergeant: Name appears on a muster roll for this company published by the North Carolina adjutant general in 1851. Resided in Bertie County and reported present with this company when it rendezvoused at Gates Court House on or about September 30, 1814. Promoted from private to sergeant on November 16, 1814. Reported "absent sent on command" per company muster roll dated January 2, 1815. Reported as "sent on command 28 December 1814 for 15 days—absent without leave" per last company muster roll, dated February 5, 1815.

Brown, William, private: County of residence not disclosed in compiled military record. Reported present with this company when it rendezvoused at Gates Court House on or about September 30, 1814. Reported present or accounted until died at Norfolk on November 27, 1814.

Bryant, Simon A., private: Name appears on a muster roll for this company published by the North Carolina adjutant general in 1851.

Bunch, Nehemiah, private: Name appears on a muster roll for this company published by the North Carolina adjutant general in 1851. Darius Butler stated in a land bounty application dated November 2, 1850, that he "was substituted in the place and stead of Nehemiah Bunch who was drafted . . . on or about the first of October A.D. 1814."

Butler, Curry, private: Name appears on a muster roll for this company published by the North Carolina adjutant general in 1851. Resided in Bertie County and reported present with this company when it rendezvoused at Gates Court House on or about September 30, 1814. Reported present or accounted for until discharged from United States service at Norfolk on February 5, 1815.

Butler, Darius, private: Resided in Bertie County and reported present with this company when it rendezvoused at Gates Court House on or about September 30, 1814. Stated in a land bounty application dated November 2, 1850, that he "was substituted in the place and stead of Nehemiah Bunch who was drafted" and that he was "mustered into service at Windsor, Bertie County . . . on or about the first of October A.D. 1814." Reported present or accounted for until discharged from United States service at Norfolk on February 5, 1815.

Butler, Jacob, private: Resided in Bertie County and reported present with this company when it rendezvoused at Gates Court House on or about September 30, 1814. Reported present or accounted for until discharged from United States service at Norfolk on February 5, 1815.

Butler, John P., private: Name appears on a muster roll for this company published by the North Carolina adjutant general in 1851. Resided in Bertie County and reported present with this company when it rendezvoused at Gates Court House on or about September 30, 1814. Reported present or accounted for until discharged from United States service at Norfolk on February 5, 1815.

Butler, Ryan, private: Resided in Bertie County and reported present with this company when it rendezvoused at Gates Court House on or about

September 30, 1814. Reported present or accounted for until discharged from United States service at Norfolk on February 5, 1815.

Butler, Silas, private: Name appears on a muster roll for this company published by the North Carolina adjutant general in 1851. Reported present with this company when it rendezvoused at Gates Court House on or about September 30, 1814. Reported present or accounted for until died at Norfolk on January 14, 1815.

Calloway, David, private: Name appears on a muster roll for this company published by the North Carolina adjutant general in 1851. Resided in Bertie County and reported present with this company when it rendezvoused at Gates Court House on or about September 30, 1814. Reported present or accounted for until discharged from United States service at Norfolk on February 5, 1815.

Calloway, Hatton William, private: Name appears as "Hatter Calloway" on a muster roll for this company published by the North Carolina adjutant general in 1851. Resided in Bertie County and previously served in Capt. Augustin Pugh's Bertie County company, First Regiment (McCotter's) North Carolina Militia (Detached). Reported present with this company when it rendezvoused at Gates Court House on or about September 30, 1814. He stated in a land bounty application dated November 11, 1815, that he "volunteered at Windsor . . . on or about 24th day of September A.D. 1814 for the term of six months." Reported present or accounted for until discharged from United States service at Norfolk on February 5, 1815.

Capehart, Truston, private: Name appears on a muster roll for this company published by the North Carolina adjutant general in 1851. Previously served in Capt. Augustin Pugh's Bertie County company, First Regiment (McCotter's) North Carolina Militia (Detached).

Castellow, Cornelius, private: Resided in Bertie County and reported present with this company when it rendezvoused at Gates Court House on or about September 30, 1814. Reported present or accounted for until discharged from United States service at Norfolk on February 5, 1815.

Castellow, William, private: Name appears on a muster roll for this company published by the North Carolina adjutant general in 1851.

Champion, Zacheus, private: Resided in Bertie County and reported present with this company when it rendezvoused at Gates Court House on or about September 30, 1814. Reported present or accounted for until deserted on December 22, 1814. Returned to company about December 26,

1814, and was tried by court-martial in January 1815. Found guilty of the charge of desertion and sentenced to have "one of his eyebrows shaved off, one half of his face black[en]ed with lampblack and oil, and that he be marched before his Regiment in this situation bare headed with the label Deserter pinned to his bust." Appealed his sentence, which was reaffirmed by the court-martial panel and approved by Col. Constant Freeman, commanding officer at Norfolk, on January 30, 1815. Reported present at Norfolk per last company muster roll, dated February 5, 1815, and discharged from United States service.

Cherry, James, Jr., private: Name appears on a muster roll for this company published by the North Carolina adjutant general in 1851.

Clark, Kenneth, private: Name appears (with the rank of private) on a muster roll for this company published by the North Carolina adjutant general in 1851. Served as an officer in Capt. Henry G. Williams's company of this regiment before transferring to this company as a lieutenant (see above).

Clemmons, Hardy, private: Name appears as "Hardy Clements" on a muster roll for this company published by the North Carolina adjutant general in 1851. Resided in Bertie County and previously served in Capt. Augustin Pugh's Bertie County company, First Regiment (McCotter's) North Carolina Militia (Detached). Reported present with this company when it rendezvoused at Gates Court House on or about September 30, 1814. Reported present or accounted for until discharged from United States service at Norfolk on February 5, 1815.

Cobb, John, private: Name appears on a muster roll for this company published by the North Carolina adjutant general in 1851. Previously served in Capt. Augustin Pugh's Bertie County company, First Regiment (McCotter's) North Carolina Militia (Detached).

Cole, John, private: Resided in Bertie County and reported present with this company when it rendezvoused at Gates Court House on or about September 30, 1814. Reported present or accounted for until discharged from United States service at Norfolk on February 5, 1815.

Cook, Elisha, private: Name appears on a muster roll for this company published by the North Carolina adjutant general in 1851.

Cook, Jordan, private: Resided in Bertie County and reported present with this company when it rendezvoused at Gates Court House on or about

September 30, 1814. Reported present or accounted for until discharged from United States service at Norfolk on February 5, 1815.

Cowand, Perry, private: Resided in Bertie County and reported present with this company when it rendezvoused at Gates Court House on or about September 30, 1814. Reported present or accounted for until discharged from United States service at Norfolk on February 5, 1815.

Davidson, Josiah, private: Name appears on a muster roll for this company published by the North Carolina adjutant general in 1851. Resided in Bertie County and reported present with this company when it rendezvoused at Gates Court House on or about September 30, 1814. Reported present or accounted for until discharged from United States service at Norfolk on February 5, 1815.

Douglas, James, private: Name appears on a muster roll for this company published by the North Carolina adjutant general in 1851.

Driver, Bowen, private: Resided in Bertie County and reported present with this company when it rendezvoused at Gates Court House on or about September 30, 1814. Deserted along with Pvt. James Williford on October 28, 1814. Voluntarily returned on an undisclosed date and was charged with desertion. Tried by court-martial in November 1814 and found guilty. Sentenced to hard labor at Fort Nelson (Norfolk) for ten days and to be confined each night of that term in the "Black Hole." Reported present or accounted for until died at Norfolk on February 2, 1815.

Dundelow, Charney C., sergeant: Name appears on a muster roll for this company published by the North Carolina adjutant general in 1851. (This soldier was also known as "Charney Cale.") Resided in Bertie County and previously served in the Third Regiment United States Infantry, from which he was discharged in August 1813. Reported present with the rank of corporal when this company rendezvoused at Gates Court House on or about September 30, 1814. Promoted to sergeant on January 2, 1815. Reported present or accounted for until discharged from United States service at Norfolk on February 5, 1815.

Early, Isaac, private: Name appears on a muster roll for this company published by the North Carolina adjutant general in 1851. Resided in Bertie County and reported present with this company when it rendezvoused at Gates Court House on or about September 30, 1814. Reported present or accounted for until discharged from United States service at Norfolk on February 5, 1815.

Early, James, private: Name appears on a muster roll for this company published by the North Carolina adjutant general in 1851. Previously served in Capt. Augustin Pugh's Bertie County company, First Regiment (McCotter's) North Carolina Militia (Detached).

Early, Seth, private: Resided in Bertie County and reported present with this company when it rendezvoused at Gates Court House on or about September 30, 1814. Reported present or accounted for until discharged from United States service at Norfolk on February 5, 1815.

Ellison, Zachariah, private: Name appears on a muster roll for this company published by the North Carolina adjutant general in 1851. Resided in Bertie County and reported present with this company when it rendezvoused at Gates Court House on or about September 30, 1814. Reported present or accounted for until discharged from United States service at Norfolk on February 5, 1815.

Fleetwood, Hatton, private: Name appears on a muster roll for this company published by the North Carolina adjutant general in 1851.

Fleetwood, Willie, private: Resided in Bertie County and reported present with this company when it rendezvoused at Gates Court House on or about September 30, 1814. Reported present or accounted for until discharged from United States service at Norfolk on February 5, 1815.

Gillam, Miles, sergeant: Name appears on a muster roll for this company published by the North Carolina adjutant general in 1851. Reported present with this company when it rendezvoused at Gates Court House on or about September 30, 1814. Reported present or accounted for until died at Norfolk on December 25, 1814.

Gregory, Asa, private: Name appears on a muster roll for this company published by the North Carolina adjutant general in 1851. Previously served in Capt. Augustin Pugh's Bertie County company, First Regiment (McCotter's) North Carolina Militia (Detached).

Griffin, William, private: Name appears on a muster roll for this company published by the North Carolina adjutant general in 1851. Resided in Bertie County and reported present with this company when it rendezvoused at Gates Court House on or about September 30, 1814. Reported present or accounted for until discharged from detached service at Norfolk on January 20, 1815.

Grimer, Cullen, private: Name appears on a muster roll for this company published by the North Carolina adjutant general in 1851. (Name may have been "Gummer.")

Hale, Joshua, private: Name appears on a muster roll for this company published by the North Carolina adjutant general in 1851.

Harden, Aquilla, private: Name appears on a muster roll for this company published by the North Carolina adjutant general in 1851. Resided in Bertie County and recalled that he "volunteered about the first of August 1814 at Windsor for the term of six months." Reported present with this company when it rendezvoused at Gates Court House on or about September 30, 1814. Reported present or accounted for until discharged from United States service at Norfolk on February 5, 1815.

Harrell, Dancy, private: Name appears on a muster roll for this company published by the North Carolina adjutant general in 1851. Resided in Bertie County and reported present with this company when it rendezvoused at Gates Court House on or about September 30, 1814. Reported present or accounted for until enlisted as a private in the Twentieth Regiment United States Infantry on October 25, 1814.

Harrell, Henry, private: Name appears on a muster roll for this company published by the North Carolina adjutant general in 1851.

Harrell, Joshua, private: Name appears on a muster roll for this company published by the North Carolina adjutant general in 1851. Resided in Bertie County and reported present with this company when it rendezvoused at Gates Court House on or about September 30, 1814. Deserted along with Pvt. Stephen Howell of Bertie County on October 26, 1814, and returned to his home in Bertie County. Apprehended by Sgt. Cullen Sholars at his home and returned to his regiment, where he was charged with desertion. Tried at a court-martial in November 1814 and found guilty. Sentenced to be confined at hard labor at Craney Island for two months and to forfeit portions of his pay to cover one-third of the costs of "retaking" him and two-thirds of the cost of his and Howell's joint court-martial. Reported "absent confined at Craney Island" per company muster roll dated January 2, 1815. Reported present or accounted for until discharged from United States service at Norfolk on February 5, 1815. Harrell had died by August 1816, when Henry White was appointed administrator of his estate in Bertie County Court.

Harrell, Meredith, private: Name appears on a muster roll for this company published by the North Carolina adjutant general in 1851.

Resided in Bertie County and reported present with this company when it rendezvoused at Gates Court House on or about September 30, 1814. Reported present or accounted for until discharged from United States service at Norfolk on February 5, 1815.

Harrell, Thomas, private: Name appears on a muster roll for this company published by the North Carolina adjutant general in 1851. Resided in Bertie County and reported present with this company when it rendezvoused at Gates Court House on or about September 30, 1814. Reported present or accounted for until deserted on or about October 25, 1814.

Hayes, Benton, private: Resided in Bertie County and reported present with this company when it rendezvoused at Gates Court House on or about September 30, 1814. Reported present or accounted for until this company was discharged from United States service at Norfolk on February 5, 1815, at which time Private Hayes was reported as "absent on command." No further information found.

Higgs, John, private: Name appears on a muster roll for this company published by the North Carolina adjutant general in 1851.

Hoggard, Elisha, private: Name appears on a muster roll for this company published by the North Carolina adjutant general in 1851. Resided in Bertie County and reported present with this company when it rendezvoused at Gates Court House on or about September 30, 1814. Reported present or accounted for until discharged from United States service at Norfolk on February 5, 1815.

Hoggard, James, private: Name appears on a muster roll for this company published by the North Carolina adjutant general in 1851. Previously served in Capt. Augustin Pugh's Bertie County company, First Regiment (McCotter's) North Carolina Militia (Detached), from which he deserted.

Howell, Stephen, private: Resided in Bertie County and reported present with this company when it rendezvoused at Gates Court House on or about September 30, 1814. Deserted along with Pvt. Joshua Harrell of Bertie County on October 26, 1814, and returned to his home in Bertie County. Apprehended by Sgt. Cullen Sholars at his home and returned to his regiment, where he was charged with desertion. Tried at a court-martial in November 1814 and found guilty. Sentenced to be confined at hard labor at Craney Island for one month. Reported present or accounted for until died on January 15, 1815.

Hunter, John, private: Name appears on a muster roll for this company published by the North Carolina adjutant general in 1851.

Jenkins, George, private: Name appears on a muster roll for this company published by the North Carolina adjutant general in 1851. Resided in Bertie County and reported present with this company when it rendezvoused at Gates Court House on or about September 30, 1814. Reported present or accounted for until discharged from United States service at Norfolk on February 5, 1815.

Jenkins, Lodowick, private: Name appears on a muster roll for this company published by the North Carolina adjutant general in 1851.

Jenkins, Willie, private: Name appears on a muster roll for this company published by the North Carolina adjutant general in 1851.

Jennings, Levi, private: Name appears on a muster roll for this company published by the North Carolina adjutant general in 1851. Resided in Bertie County and reported present with this company when it rendezvoused at Gates Court House on or about September 30, 1814. Reported present or accounted for until discharged from United States service at Norfolk on February 5, 1815.

Johnson, Littleton, private: Resided in Bertie County and reported present with this company when it rendezvoused at Gates Court House on or about September 30, 1814. Reported present or accounted for until discharged from United States service at Norfolk on February 5, 1815.

Johnson, William W., private: Name appears on a muster roll for this company published by the North Carolina adjutant general in 1851.

Kennedy, Levi, private: Name appears on a muster roll for this company published by the North Carolina adjutant general in 1851. Resided in Bertie County and reported present with this company when it rendezvoused at Gates Court House on or about September 30, 1814. Reported present or accounted for until discharged from United States service at Norfolk on February 5, 1815.

King, Benajah, corporal: Resided in Bertie County and reported present with this company when it rendezvoused at Gates Court House on or about September 30, 1814. Promoted from private to corporal on January 2, 1815. Reported present or accounted for until discharged from United States service at Norfolk on February 5, 1815.

Lassiter, John, private: Name appears on a muster roll for this company published by the North Carolina adjutant general in 1851.

Lawrence, James, private: Resided in Bertie County and reported present with this company when it rendezvoused at Gates Court House on or about September 30, 1814. Reported present or accounted for until discharged from United States service at Norfolk on February 5, 1815.

Lee, Henry, private: Name appears on a muster roll for this company published by the North Carolina adjutant general in 1851.

Leggett, Jeremiah, private: Name appears on a muster roll for this company published by the North Carolina adjutant general in 1851.

Liversage, Thomas, private: Name appears on a muster roll for this company published by the North Carolina adjutant general in 1851.

Malone, Gray, private: Reported present with this company when it rendezvoused at Gates Court House on or about September 30, 1814. No further information found. May have been dismissed when Brig. Gen. Jeremiah Slade assembled this company from members of several companies at Gates Court House.

Mardre, Michael, private: Name appears on a muster roll for this company published by the North Carolina adjutant general in 1851.

Mastin, William B., private: Name appears on a muster roll for this company published by the North Carolina adjutant general in 1851. Served as an officer in Capt. John F. Walker's militia company of this regiment.

Mhoon, John, private: Name appears on a muster roll for this company published by the North Carolina adjutant general in 1851.

Miller, Charles, private: Name appears on a muster roll for this company published by the North Carolina adjutant general in 1851.

Miller, Lewis, private: Name appears on a muster roll for this company published by the North Carolina adjutant general in 1851. Resided in Bertie County and reported present with this company when it rendezvoused at Gates Court House on or about September 30, 1814. Reported present or accounted for until discharged from United States service at Norfolk on February 5, 1815.

Miller, William K., private: Name appears on a muster roll for this company published by the North Carolina adjutant general in 1851.

Minton, Jason, private: Name appears on a muster roll for this company published by the North Carolina adjutant general in 1851. Resided in Bertie County and reported present with this company when it rendezvoused at Gates Court House on or about September 30, 1814. Reported present or accounted for until discharged from United States service at Norfolk on February 5, 1815.

Mitchell, George, private: Resided in Bertie County and reported present with this company when it rendezvoused at Gates Court House on or about September 30, 1814. Reported present or accounted for until died on January 13, 1815. Rachel Mitchell, Private Mitchell's widow, appointed administrator of his estate in February 1815 in Bertie County Court.

Mitchell, King, private: Name appears on a muster roll for this company published by the North Carolina adjutant general in 1851. Resided in Bertie County and reported present with this company when it rendezvoused at Gates Court House on or about September 30, 1814. Reported present or accounted for until discharged from United States service at Norfolk on December 1, 1814.

Mitchell, Reuben, private: Resided in Bertie County and joined this company in Norfolk on December 2, 1814. Reported present or accounted for until discharged from United States service at Norfolk on February 5, 1815.

Mizell, George, private: Name appears on a muster roll for this company published by the North Carolina adjutant general in 1851. Previously served as a musician/fifer in Capt. Augustin Pugh's Bertie County company, First Regiment (McCotter's) North Carolina Militia (Detached).

Mizell, James, private: Name appears on a muster roll for this company published by the North Carolina adjutant general in 1851. Resided in Bertie County and reported present with this company when it rendezvoused at Gates Court House on or about September 30, 1814. Reported present or accounted for until died on October 23, 1814.

Mizell, Lawrence, private: Name appears on a muster roll for this company published by the North Carolina adjutant general in 1851. Resided in Bertie County and reported present with this company when it rendezvoused at Gates Court House on or about September 30, 1814. Reported present or accounted for until discharged from United States service at Norfolk on February 5, 1815.

Mizell, Timothy, private: Name appears on a muster roll for this company published by the North Carolina adjutant general in 1851. Resided in Bertie County and reported present with this company when it rendezvoused at Gates Court House on or about September 30, 1814. Reported present or accounted for until died on December 16, 1814. Jacob Holly appointed administrator of Private Mizell's estate in August 1815 in Bertie County Court.

Morgan, Thomas, private: Name appears on a muster roll for this company published by the North Carolina adjutant general in 1851. Reported present with this company when it rendezvoused at Gates Court House on or about September 30, 1814. Reported present or accounted for until discharged on December 8, 1814.

Murdough, John, private: Name appears on a muster roll for this company published by the North Carolina adjutant general in 1851.

Outlaw, George, private: Resided in Bertie County and reported present with this company when it rendezvoused at Gates Court House on or about September 30, 1814. Reported present or accounted for until discharged from United States service at Norfolk on February 5, 1815.

Outlaw, Noah, private: Name appears on a muster roll for this company published by the North Carolina adjutant general in 1851. Resided in Bertie County and reported present with this company when it rendezvoused at Gates Court House on or about September 30, 1814. Reported present or accounted for until reported as "enlisted Oct. 23, 1814." Enlisted as a private in the Twentieth Regiment United States Infantry on October 26, 1814.

Outlaw, Ralph, private: Name appears on a muster roll for this company published by the North Carolina adjutant general in 1851. Resided in Bertie County and reported present with this company when it rendezvoused at Gates Court House on or about September 30, 1814. Reported present or accounted for until discharged from United States service at Norfolk on February 5, 1815.

Page, James, private: Resided in Bertie County and reported present with this company when it rendezvoused at Gates Court House on or about September 30, 1814. Reported present or accounted for until discharged from United States service at Norfolk on February 5, 1815.

Purvis, Moses, private: Name appears on a muster roll for this company published by the North Carolina adjutant general in 1851. Resided in

Bertie County and reported present with this company when it rendezvoused at Gates Court House on or about September 30, 1814. Reported present or accounted for until discharged from United States service at Norfolk on February 5, 1815.

Redditt, Josiah, private: Name appears on a muster roll for this company published by the North Carolina adjutant general in 1851. Resided in Bertie County and reported present with this company when it rendezvoused at Gates Court House on or about September 30, 1814. Reported present or accounted for until discharged from United States service at Norfolk on February 5, 1815.

Ruffin, Thomas, private: Name appears on a muster roll for this company published by the North Carolina adjutant general in 1851.

Ruffin, Whitmell, private: Name appears on a muster roll for this company published by the North Carolina adjutant general in 1851. Resided in Bertie County and reported present with this company when it rendezvoused at Gates Court House on or about September 30, 1814. Reported present or accounted for until reported as "enlisted Nov. 23, 1814." Records of the Twentieth Regiment United States Infantry indicate that he enlisted as a private in that regiment on October 26, 1814.

Sholars, Cullen, private: Name appears as "Cullen Shoolders" on a muster roll for this company published by the North Carolina adjutant general in 1851. Resided in Bertie County and reported present with this company when it rendezvoused at Gates Court House on or about September 30, 1814. Reported present or accounted for until died on December 25, 1814.

Simons, William, corporal: Name appears on a muster roll for this company published by the North Carolina adjutant general in 1851. Resided in Bertie County and previously served in Capt. Augustin Pugh's Bertie County company, First Regiment (McCotter's) North Carolina Militia (Detached). Reported present with this company when it rendezvoused at Gates Court House on or about September 30, 1814. Promoted from private to corporal on January 2, 1815. Reported present or accounted for until discharged from United States service at Norfolk on February 5, 1815.

Smithwick, Luke, private: Name appears on a muster roll for this company published by the North Carolina adjutant general in 1851. Resided in Bertie County and reported present with this company when it rendezvoused at Gates Court House on or about September 30, 1814.

Reported present or accounted for until transferred to the Field and Staff of this regiment on December 1, 1814.

Sowell, Jethro, private: Reported present with this company when it rendezvoused at Gates Court House on or about September 30, 1814. Reported present or accounted for until died on October 19, 1814.

Tayloe, Jonathan S., private: Name appears as "Jonathan Zaloe" on a muster roll for this company published by the North Carolina adjutant general in 1851.

Terrell, William G., private: Name appears on a muster roll for this company published by the North Carolina adjutant general in 1851.

Todd, Henry, private: Name appears on a muster roll for this company published by the North Carolina adjutant general in 1851. Resided in Bertie County and reported present with this company when it rendezvoused at Gates Court House on or about September 30, 1814. Reported present or accounted for until discharged from United States service at Norfolk on February 5, 1815.

Tulley, Leven, sergeant: Name appears as "Leven McTuller" (with the rank of private) on a muster roll for this company published by the North Carolina adjutant general in 1851. Resided in Bertie County and reported present with the rank of corporal with this company when it rendezvoused at Gates Court House on or about September 30, 1814. Promoted to sergeant on January 21, 1815. Reported present or accounted for until discharged from United States service at Norfolk on February 5, 1815.

Ward, James, private: Resided in Bertie County and reported present with this company when it rendezvoused at Gates Court House on or about September 30, 1814. Reported present or accounted for until discharged from United States service at Norfolk on February 5, 1815.

Ward, Jasper, private: Name appears on a muster roll for this company published by the North Carolina adjutant general in 1851. Enlisted in Thirty-fifth Regiment United States Infantry in September 1814.

Watson, John, sergeant: Name appears (with the rank of private) on a muster roll for this company published by the North Carolina adjutant general in 1851. Resided in Bertie County and reported present with the rank of corporal with this company when it rendezvoused at Gates Court House on or about September 30, 1814. Promoted to sergeant on January 2, 1815. Reported present or accounted for until died on January 25, 1815.

West, Thomas L., private: Name appears on a muster roll for this company published by the North Carolina adjutant general in 1851. A "Thomas West" served in Capt. Augustin Pugh's Bertie County militia company, First Regiment (McCotter's) North Carolina Militia (Detached) in July 1813.

White, David, private: Born in Bertie County, where he resided. Name appears on a muster roll for this company published by the North Carolina adjutant general in 1851. Reported present with this company when it rendezvoused at Gates Court House on or about September 30, 1814. Reported present or accounted for until deserted on December 26, 1814. Returned to the company and charged with desertion. "Suffered" a court-martial in January 1815 and found guilty of the charge by a panel of officers. The panel later reviewed the case and reaffirmed its guilty sentence. Col. Constant Freeman, commanding officer at Norfolk, on January 30, 1815, "disapproved the sentence." Reported present or accounted for until discharged from United States service at Norfolk on February 5, 1815.

White, George, private: Name appears on a muster roll for this company published by the North Carolina adjutant general in 1851.

White, Isaac, private: Name appears on a muster roll for this company published by the North Carolina adjutant general in 1851. Resided in Bertie County and reportedly was "drafted . . . at Windsor, Bertie Co N.C. on or about the first day of October 1814." Reported present with this company when it rendezvoused at Gates Court House on or about September 30, 1814. Reported present or accounted for until discharged from United States service at Norfolk on February 5, 1815.

White, Jesse, private: Resided in Bertie County and reported present with this company when it rendezvoused at Gates Court House on or about September 30, 1814. Reported present or accounted for until discharged from United States service at Norfolk on February 5, 1815.

White, Peter, private: Name appears on a muster roll for this company published by the North Carolina adjutant general in 1851. Resided in Bertie County and reported present with this company when it rendezvoused at Gates Court House on or about September 30, 1814. Reported present or accounted for until discharged from United States service at Norfolk on February 5, 1815.

White, Richard, private: Resided in Bertie County and reported present with this company when it rendezvoused at Gates Court House on or about

September 30, 1814. Reported present or accounted for until discharged from United States service at Norfolk on February 5, 1815.

White, Whitmell, private: Name appears on a muster roll for this company published by the North Carolina adjutant general in 1851.

White, William, private: Resided in Bertie County and reported present with this company when it rendezvoused at Gates Court House on or about September 30, 1814. Reported present or accounted for until discharged from United States service at Norfolk on February 5, 1815.

Whitley, George, private: Resided in Bertie County and reported present with this company when it rendezvoused at Gates Court House on or about September 30, 1814. Reported present or accounted for until discharged from United States service at Norfolk on February 5, 1815.

Wilkes, Kinchen, private: Name appears on a muster roll for this company published by the North Carolina adjutant general in 1851. Resided in Bertie County and reported present with this company when it rendezvoused at Gates Court House on or about September 30, 1814. Reported present or accounted for until died January 16, 1815.

Williams, Benjamin B., private: Name appears on a muster roll for this company published by the North Carolina adjutant general in 1851.

Williford, James, private: Name appears on a muster roll for this company published by the North Carolina adjutant general in 1851. Resided in Bertie County and reported present with this company when it rendezvoused at Gates Court House on or about September 30, 1814. Deserted along with Pvt. Bowen Driver on October 28, 1814. Voluntarily returned on an undisclosed date and was charged with desertion. Tried by court-martial in November 1814 and found guilty. Sentenced to hard labor at Fort Nelson (Norfolk) for ten days and to be confined each night of that term in the "Black Hole." Reported present or accounted for until discharged from United States service at Norfolk on February 5, 1815.

Wimberly, Lewis, private: Name appears on a muster roll for this company published by the North Carolina adjutant general in 1851.

CAPT. JOHN F. WALKER'S COMPANY

OFFICER

Mastin, William B., lieutenant: Resided in Bertie County. Reported present with the rank of ensign with this company when it rendezvoused at Gates Court House on or about September 30, 1814. Promoted to lieutenant on October 12, 1814. Left the company's camp during the evening of December 2, 1814, in violation of a standing general order. Charged with disobedience of general orders and subjected to a court-martial on December 12, 1814. Pleaded guilty to the charge and sentenced to be reprimanded by Lt. Col. Duncan McDonald, First Regiment North Carolina Militia (Detached). Reported present or accounted for until discharged from United States service at Norfolk on February 5, 1815.

PRIVATE

Powell, Asa, private: Resided in Bertie County and previously served in the Tenth Regiment United States Infantry. Reported present with this company when it rendezvoused at Gates Court House on or about September 30, 1814. Deserted on January 1, 1815, for four days. Charged with desertion and tried at a court-martial in January 1815. Found guilty of the charge and sentenced to "have one half of his head shaved, one half of his face black[ene]d with lampblack and oil, to have one month of his pay stop[pe]d, and with a ball and chain on his leg to be compelled to perform hard labor at one of the public works, to be assigned by the commanding officer [Col. Constant Freeman] of this post [Norfolk], during the balance of his term of service." Reported present or accounted for until discharged from United States service at Norfolk on February 5, 1815.

CAPT. HENRY G. WILLIAMS'S COMPANY

OFFICER

Clark, Kenneth, lieutenant: Resided in Bertie County and joined this company on November 20, 1814, with the rank of ensign. Promoted to lieutenant on December 20, 1814. Reported present or accounted for until transferred to Capt. Gavin Hogg's company of this regiment on January 19, 1815.

Notes

1. Bertie County's detached militiamen were identified from *Muster Rolls of the Soldiers of the War of 1812 Detached from the Militia of North Carolina, in 1812 and 1814* (Raleigh: Ch. C. Raboteau, 1851; Winston-Salem: Barber Printing Company, 1926), and Compiled Service Records of North Carolina's detached militia, Record Group 94, National Archives, Washington, D.C. Supplementary information was obtained from selected Court Martial Case Files, Record Group 153, National Archives; Federal Pension Application Files, Record Group 15, National Archives; and William Hawkins, Governors Letter Books, State Archives, Office of Archives and History, Raleigh.

2. According to Maj. Gen. Calvin Jones's letter to Gov. William Hawkins dated September 30, 1814, Captain Jacocks and his Bertie County company had not yet arrived at Gates Court House. Therefore, the company could not have rendezvoused at that location on that date. Compiled service records for Lt. Col. Duncan McDonalds's regiment indicate that the companies rendezvoused on September 30, even though not all companies had arrived at Gates Court House. Therefore, the author has chosen to note the company's rendezvous at Gates Court House as "on or about September 30, 1814." Apparently, muster rolls and inspection reports were dated September 30, even though Brig. Gen. Jeremiah Slade and his staff clearly organized some companies in the first days of October and marched them to Norfolk (see chapter 5).

Appendix 2

Roster of Bertie County Soldiers in the United States Army[1]

THIRD REGIMENT UNITED STATES INFANTRY

Brogden, William, private: Born in Bertie County, where he resided as a laborer prior to enlisting for five years on October 21, 1808, at the age of 21. Place of enlistment and original company commander not disclosed per extant records. Per an order issued at Camp Washington, Mississippi Territory (M.T.), on March 3, 1810, Private Brogden was transferred to Capt. John Darrington's company.[2] Later transferred to Capt. William Butler's company on an undisclosed date. Reported to have been serving as a waiter in the hospital at Washington, Mont., in the fall of 1811. Attached to the general hospital at Baton Rouge, La., on February 27, 1812. Reported sick in the hospital at Pass Christian, Mont., from August 18, 1812, to January 2, 1813. Discharged from the army on April 5, 1813, at Pass Christian for "inability." Later served in Capt. Augustin Pugh's Bertie County company, First Regiment (McCotter's) North Carolina Militia (Detached).

Cale, Charney, private: Born and resided in Bertie County prior to enlisting for five years on August 23, 1808; location of enlistment not disclosed per extant regimental and service records. Served in Capt. Mossman Houston's company until Houston resigned on December 31, 1810. The company was subsequently commanded by Capt. James E. Dinkins, under whose command Private Cale served until transferred to Capt. Duncan L. Clinch's company on July 11, 1812, at St. Tammany, La. No additional information found regarding his service in this regiment, but presumably Cale was discharged on August 22, 1813, upon the expiration of his term of enlistment. Later served under the name of Charney C. Dundelow in Capts. James Iredell and Gavin Hogg's company, First Regiment (McDonald's) North Carolina Militia (Detached).

FOURTH REGIMENT UNITED STATES INFANTRY

Harrell, Dancy, private: Previously served in Capt. James Iredell's company, First Regiment (McDonald's) North Carolina Militia (Detached) and then the Twentieth Regiment United States Infantry. Transferred from the Twentieth Regiment to Lt. William Ligon's company of this regi- ment on or before July 1, 1815, when he was reported "present sick in quarters" on a muster roll of that date. Reported present on an inspection return for Capt. Alexander Cumming's company dated August 31, 1815, with the notation "joined from 20th Inf." Also served in Capts. Isaac D. Barnard and George W. Melvin's companies prior to being discharged at Fort Crawford, Ala., on October 31, 1819, his term of enlistment having expired.

Hoggard, Jonathan, private: Previously served in the Eighteenth Regiment United States Infantry. Joined Capt. James E. Dinkins's company of this regiment on August 10, 1815. Deserted on November 22, 1815, from Fort Hamilton, N.Y.

Johnson, John, sergeant: Previously served in the Twenty-fourth and Seventh Regiments United States Infantry. Transferred as a private to Capt. James E. Dinkins's company of this regiment on or before April 30, 1816. Reported present on inspection returns for Dinkins's company dated April 30, August 31, and October 31, 1816. Promoted to corporal on August 19, 1816. Reported "absent on command" per muster roll for Dinkins's company dated February 28, 1817. Reported present per muster rolls dated April 30 and June 30, 1817. Reported present on inspection returns dated December 31, 1818, and February 28, April 30, and June 30, 1819, for Capt. James M. Glassel's company. Promoted to sergeant on March 15, 1818. Discharged at an undisclosed location on August 29, 1819, his term of enlistment having expired.

Outlaw, Noah, sergeant: Previously served in Capt. James Iredell's company, First Regiment (McDonald's) North Carolina Militia (Detached) and the Twentieth Regiment United States Infantry. Transferred from the Twentieth Regiment to Capt. Alexander Cumming's company of this regiment on or before August 31, 1815, when he was reported "present joined from 20th U.S. Inf[antry]." Transferred as a corporal. Reported present on an inspection return dated December 31, 1815, for Capt. Isaac D. Barnard's company. Reported present with the rank of sergeant on an inspection return dated April 30, 1816; date of promotion not disclosed. Reported present on inspection returns dated August 31 and October 31, 1816, for Capt. George W. Melvin's company. Reported sick at Fort Jackson, Mont., per an inspection return dated February 28, 1817. Reported present on inspection returns dated April 30, June 30, and August 31, 1817. Reported "on command at Montpelier," Mont., per an inspection return dated February 28, 1818. Thereafter, reported present on various returns until discharged at Fort Crawford, Ala., on October 25, 1819, his term of enlistment having expired.

Ruffin, Whitmell, sergeant: Previously served in the Twentieth Regiment United States Infantry. Transferred to Capt. Alexander Cumming's company of this regiment at Annapolis, Md., on or before August 31, 1815, when he was reported present on a company inspection return with the notation "joined from 20th US Inf[antry]." Transferred as a private. Reported present on inspection returns dated December 31, 1815, and April 30, 1816, for Capt. Isaac D. Barnard's company. Promoted to corporal on April 4, 1816. Reported present on various inspection returns from August 31, 1816, through June 30, 1817, for Capt. George W. Melvin's company. Promoted to sergeant on June 21, 1817. Present or accounted for until discharged at Montpelier, Mont., on October 25, 1819, his term of enlistment having expired.

SEVENTH REGIMENT UNITED STATES INFANTRY

Dempsey, John, private: Previously served in the Twenty-fourth Regiment United States Infantry. Transferred to Capt. Robert H. Goodwyn's company of that regiment on an undisclosed date but prior to December 1, 1815, when he was reported present on an inspection return of the subject company. Reported present on inspection returns dated December 31, 1816, February 28 and April 30, 1817, for Capt. Francis W. Armstrong's company at Fort Hawkins, Ga. Died at Camp Montgomery, Mont., on May 21, 1817.

Hawkins, Elias, private: Previously served in the Tenth Regiment United States Infantry. Transferred to Capt. John Machesney's company of this regiment on or before June 30, 1815, when he was reported present on an inspection return for the subject company of that date. Subsequently transferred to the Eighth Regiment United States Infantry on an undisclosed date but prior to February 16, 1815.

Hoggard, James, private: Previously served in the Tenth Regiment United States Infantry. Transferred to this regiment on or before June 30, 1815, when he was reported present on a muster roll for Capt. John Machesney's company at Plattsburgh, N.Y. Transferred to Capt. David Riddle's company, Eighth Regiment United States Infantry on or before February 29, 1816.

Johnson, John, private: Previously served in the Twenty-fourth Regiment United States Infantry. Transferred to this regiment on or before December 31, 1815, when he was reported present on a semiannual muster roll for Capt. Francis W. Armstrong's company as being "transferred to a detachment on infantry" on December 23, 1815. Reported present on an inspection return and semiannual muster roll dated December 31, 1815, for Capt. John J. Clinch's detachment. Reported present on an inspection return dated February 29, 1816, for Capt. Samuel Spott's detachment at Fort Hawkins, Ga. Transferred to Capt. James E. Dinkins's company, Fourth Regiment United States Infantry, on or before April 30, 1816.

EIGHTH REGIMENT UNITED STATES INFANTRY

Farmer, Milbourn, private: Previously served in the Twentieth Regiment United States Infantry. Apparently transferred to Lt. William Ligon's company of this regiment in early May 1815, as he was reported as having deserted "from Craney Island," Norfolk, on May 12, 1815, per an inspection return dated July 1, 1815, for Ligon's company.

Hale, Cader, private: Previously served in the Tenth Regiment United States Infantry. Transferred to this regiment on an unspecified date. Served in Capt. Charles B. Hopkins's company. Discharged at Pittsburgh, Pa., on August 19, 1815, "for disease of the breast."

Hawkins, Elias, private: Previously served in the Tenth and Seventh Regiments United States Infantry. Transferred to this regiment on an undisclosed date but prior to February 16, 1815, when he was reported sick on an inspection return for Capt. David Riddle's company. Reported sick on inspection returns dated April 30, 1816, and August 31, 1816, for the same company. Reported "present, joined from Capt. [Lewis B.] Willis's company" on an inspection return dated February 28, 1818, for Capt. James Dormain's company. Deserted at an undisclosed location on April 21, 1818. Re-joined the Eighth Regiment, apparently at Camp Jefferson, Ala., on July 24, 1818. Discharged on June 30, 1819, his term of enlistment having expired.

Hoggard, James, private: Previously served in the Tenth and Seventh Regiments United States Infantry. Transferred to this regiment on or before February 29, 1816. Reported present per a muster roll dated August 31, 1815, for Capt. David Riddle's company. Reported present on an inspection return dated February 29, 1816, for Riddle's company. Next reported present on an inspection return dated April 30, 1816, for Lt. William Ligon's company. Reported present on an inspection return dated June 30, 1816, for Capt. John Nicks's company. Reported present per an inspection return dated June 30, 1817, for Capt. Lewis B. Willis's company. Discharged at Carry's Experiment, near Cypress Creek, Ala., on August 8, 1817, his term of enlistment having expired.

Rawlings, Miles, private: Previously served in the Tenth Regiment United States Infantry. Transferred to Capt. William Davenport's company of this regiment on an undisclosed date, but prior to October 1, 1815, when his name appeared on an inspection return for Davenport's company. Reported present on various company returns until discharged at Pass Christian, Mont., on August 7, 1817, his term of enlistment having expired.

TENTH REGIMENT UNITED STATES INFANTRY

Rhodes, William Speller, first lieutenant: Resided in Bertie County and commissioned on April 30, 1812. Served in Capt. Joseph Bryant's company until he resigned on April 15, 1813, because of chronic illness ("flux").

Avis, William, private: Born in Bertie County, where he resided as a sailor prior to enlisting at Windsor at age 22 on August 11, 1812. Enlisted by Lt. William Speller Rhodes to serve for five years. Reported present with Capt. Joseph Bryant's detachment at Fort Hampton, Beaufort, Carteret County, N.C., on muster rolls dated March 31, May 31, and June 30, 1813. As a member of Capt. George Vashon's company, was wounded in the hand while in the line of duty on July 10, 1814, at Champlain, N.Y. Hospitalized at Plattsburgh, N.Y., on September 7, 1814, with a "lame hand." Released from the hospital on September 30, 1814. Deemed "incapacitated for military duty" by Dr. Edward Purcell, acting hospital surgeon, Ninth District General Hospital, in Burlington, Vt., on December 13, 1814, and discharged the following day. Received disability pension effective December 14, 1814—degree of disability rated as "one half."

Brantly, Josiah, private: Born in Bertie County and enlisted for eighteen months on August 2 or 7, 1812; occupation—tailor. Reported present on muster rolls dated March 31, May 31, and June 30, 1813, for Capt. Joseph Bryant's detachment at Fort Hampton, Beaufort, Carteret County, N.C. Reported present on muster rolls dated August 31, November 30, and December 31, 1813, for Bryant's company. Discharged on an undisclosed date per a muster roll dated February 28, 1814, for Capt. Robert Mitchell's company.

Brickell, John M., private: Enlisted for eighteen months on July 13, 1812; place of enlistment, age, and occupation not disclosed. Reported present on muster rolls dated March 31, May 31, and June 30, 1813, for Capt. Joseph Bryant's detachment at Fort Hampton, Beaufort, Carteret County, N.C. No additional information found regarding his United States Army service. Brickell's name appears on an October 27, 1813, muster roll for Capt. Augustin Pugh's Bertie County company, First Regiment (McCotter's) North Carolina Militia (Detached) with the notation "inlisted."

Burns, Joshua, private: Born in Bertie County and enlisted at Hillsborough at age 18, November 13, 1814; occupation—farmer. Enlisted by Lt. William Pannill for five years. Served in Capt. Hugh H. Carson's company. Reported present on a description roll dated February 16, 1815, at Raleigh. No additional information found.

Douglas, David, private: Born in Bertie County and enlisted in Halifax County at the age of 25, August 12, 1812; occupation—farmer. Enlisted by Capt. Joseph Bryant for five years. Reported present on muster rolls for Captain Bryant's detachment at Fort Hampton, Beaufort, Carteret County, N.C., dated March 31, May 31, and June 30, 1813. Reported as "left sick at Plattsburgh [N.Y.] Aug. 30, 1814" on a description roll for Capt. William Bailey's company dated February 16, 1815, and inspection returns dated "cantonment Camp Buffalo," N.Y., February 28 and April 30, 1815. Name also appears on a description roll of Capt. Philip Brittain's detachment company dated February 16, 1815, and inspection returns dated Plattsburgh, February 28 and April 30, 1815. Apparently, once Private Douglas's health improved to a degree that he could return to duty, he was assigned to Brittain's command at Plattsburgh. However, Douglas's service history as compiled by the adjutant general's office from available records is quite confusing and convoluted, as his name appears on the returns of multiple regiments simultaneously. Following is the remainder of his service information as provided by the adjutant general's "register of enlistments" file: On April 30, 1815, reported present on inspection returns for (1) Lt. William Ligon's company, Eighth Regiment United States Infantry, and (2) Lt. William Arnold's company of United States Rifles. Reported present on an inspection return dated June 30, 1815, for Capt. John Machesney's company, Seventh Regiment United States Infantry. Next reported "on command at Ft. Clark" per a semiannual muster roll dated June 30, 1816, for Lt. Russell B. Hyde's company, Thirtieth Regiment United States Infantry. Reported present on inspection returns for Capt. James McKeon's company, Third United States Artillery, from August 31, 1816, through June 30, 1817. Discharged at Pass Christian, Mont., on August 12, 1817, his term of enlistment having expired.

Garrett, Caleb, private: Born in Bertie County and enlisted for five years at Edenton at the age of 21, June 26, 1812; occupation—farmer. Served in Capt. Jesse Copeland's company and later in Capt. George Vashon's company following Copeland's death in late November 1813. Per a semiannual muster roll dated December 31, 1813, Private Garrett was reported "sick, sent to Burlington [Vt.]." Died at Burlington in March or April 1814.

Hale, Cader, private: Born in Bertie County and enlisted for five years on July 31, 1812, at the age of 23; occupation—farmer. Served in Capt. Thomas N. Nelson's company. Reported "absent left sick at Washington City [D.C.]" on an undisclosed date per a muster roll for Nelson's company dated August 31, 1813. Reported present per muster rolls dated January 31 and April 30, 1814, for Capt. Philip Brittain's company. Reported present on a description roll dated February 16, 1815, and inspection returns dated February 28 and April 30, 1815. Transferred to Lt. Charles B. Hopkins's company, Eighth Regiment United States Infantry, date not specified.

Haste, Zadock, private: Born in Bertie County and enlisted for five years on July 4, 1812; occupation—farmer. Served in Capt. Jesse Copeland's company. Per the *Edenton Gazette* of December 15, 1812, Private Haste—a deserter "belonging to the 10th Regiment"—was "brought into" Edenton and delivered to Ensign Francis Jones, the only army officer at the post in Edenton at the time. Deserted on July 26, 1813, at Elizabeth City. Reported to have "given himself up" at Norfolk on an undisclosed date to Capt. Richard Pollard of the Twentieth Regiment United States Infantry.

Hawkins, Elias, private: Born in Bertie County and enlisted at an undisclosed location for eighteen months on August 8, 1812. His name appears on a recruiting certificate for N.C. dated August 11, 1812. Reported present on muster rolls dated March 31, May 31, and June 30, 1813, for Capt. Joseph Bryant's detachment at Fort Hampton, Beaufort, Carteret County, N.C. Discharged at an undisclosed location on February 24, 1814, as a member of Capt. Robert Mitchell's company (Capt. Bryant having died in late November 1813). Reenlisted at Washington City [D.C.] for five years on March 5, 1814, at age 21 or 22. Served in Capt. Philip Brittain's detachment. Reported "left sick at Plattsburgh," N.Y., on August 28, 1814. Entered hospital on September 7 and was released on

November 10, 1814. Reported present on a description roll for Brittain's detachment dated February 16, 1815, and an inspection return dated April 30, 1815. Transferred to Capt. John Machesney's company, Seventh Regiment United States Infantry, on or before June 30, 1815.

Hodder, William, private: A member of the Bertie County militia who was reported "absent out of the state" when Capt. Augustin Pugh's company rendezvoused at Windsor on October 27, 1813. Hodder had enlisted in this regiment on September 8, 1812, to serve eighteen months. Reported present on muster rolls dated March 31, May 31, and June 30, 1813, for Capt. Joseph Bryant's detachment at Fort Hampton, Beaufort, Carteret County, N.C. Reported present on muster rolls dated August 31, November 30, and December 31, 1813, for Captain Bryant's company (Bryant having died in late November 1813 near Plattsburgh, N.Y.). Reported present on a muster roll dated December 31, 1813, for Capt. William Irvine's ("late Bryant's") company. Reported present sick on a muster roll dated February 28, 1814, for Capt. Robert Mitchell's company. Discharged on an undisclosed date per muster roll dated April 30, 1814.

Hoggard, James, private: Born in Bertie County and enlisted for five years in July or August 1812, at the age of 20; occupation—farmer. Enlisted by Lt. Richard Plummer at an undisclosed location. Reported present on muster rolls dated March 31, May 31, and June 30, 1813, for Capt. Joseph Bryant's detachment at Fort Hampton, Beaufort, Carteret County, N.C. Reported present on muster rolls dated August 31, November 30, and December 31, 1813, for Captain Bryant's company (Bryant having died in late November 1813 near Plattsburgh, N.Y.). As a member of Capt. George Vashon's company, reported as entering the general hospital at Plattsburgh on August 29, 1814. Discharged from the hospital on January 26, 1815. Transferred to Capt. James Machesney's company, Seventh Regiment United States Infantry, on or before June 30, 1815.

Holloman, Nathaniel, private: Born in Bertie County and enlisted for eighteen months on August 11, 1812, at the age of 25; occupation—farmer. Served in Capt. Joseph Bryant's company. Reported present on muster rolls dated March 31, May 31, June 30, and August 31, 1813, for Captain Bryant's detachment at Fort Hampton, Beaufort, Carteret County, N.C. Reported "sick at Burlington [Vt.]" per a muster roll dated November 30, 1813. Reported "absent on command" per a muster roll dated December 31, 1813. Discharged on an undisclosed date per a muster roll dated February 28,

1814, for Capt. Robert Mitchell's company. Name appears on an October 27, 1813, muster roll for Capt. Augustin Pugh's Bertie County company, First Regiment (McCotter's) North Carolina Militia (Detached) with the notation "absent out of state."

Lawrence, Joseph, private: Born in Bertie County and enlisted for five years on July 4, 1812, at the age of 18; occupation—farmer. Per a notice placed by Capt. Jesse Copeland in the *Edenton Gazette* of December 8, 1812, Private Lawrence deserted from the regiment on an undisclosed date. Per the *Edenton Gazette* of December 15, 1812, Private Lawrence—"a deserter belonging to the 10th Regiment"—was "brought into" Edenton and delivered to Ensign Francis Jones, the only army officer at the post at the time. Reported present on a muster roll dated August 31, 1813, for Captain Copeland's company, but deserted at Philadelphia in September 1813, per a semiannual muster roll dated December 31, 1813, for Copeland's company.

Powell, Asa, private: Born in Bertie County and enlisted for eighteen months on August 1, 1812, at the age of 21; occupation—farmer. Reported present on muster rolls dated March 31, May 31, and June 30, 1813, for Capt. Joseph Bryant's detachment at Fort Hampton, Beaufort, Carteret County, N.C. Discharged at Albany, N.Y., on October 31, 1813, for "inability." Later served in Captain John F. Walker's company, First Regiment (McDonald's) North Carolina Militia (Detached).

Rawlings, Miles, private: (Name shown as "Rollins.") Born in Bertie County and enlisted at Edenton at the age of 21, August 7, 1812; occupation—farmer. Enlisted by Capt. Jesse Copeland for five years. Per notice placed by Captain Copeland in the *Edenton Gazette* of December 8, 1812, Private Rawlings had deserted from the regiment while on furlough on an undisclosed date. Obviously returned from desertion, as he was reported present on muster rolls dated August 31 and November 30, 1813, for Copeland's company. Reported present, sick on a semiannual muster roll dated December 31, 1813, for a Captain Brooks's company. Hospitalized on April 14, 1814, and rejoined the regiment on April 29, 1814. Reported present on a description roll dated February 16 and inspection returns dated February 28 and April 30, 1815, for Capt. George Vashon's company at Buffalo, N.Y. Transferred to Capt. William Davenport's company, Eighth Regiment United States Infantry, on an undisclosed date but prior to October 1, 1815.

White, Hardy, private: Born in Bertie County and enlisted for five years on July 24, 1812, at the age of 21; occupation—carpenter. Served in Capt. Jesse Copeland's company. Deserted at Elizabeth City on an undisclosed date prior to December 31, 1813. "Gave himself up" at Norfolk on an undisclosed date to Capt. Richard Pollard of the Twentieth Regiment United States Infantry. Transferred to the Twentieth Regiment by order of Col. Constant Freeman, United States Army, Norfolk; date of transfer not disclosed by extant records. Private White was previously a member of Capt. Augustin Pugh's Bertie County company, First Regiment (McCotter's) North Carolina Militia (Detached). He was reported as having "inlisted" per the muster roll for that company when it rendezvoused at Windsor on October 27, 1813.

Wilkinson, William, private: Enlisted at the age of 17, August 13, 1812; occupation—farmer. Reported as "absent out of the state" on a muster roll dated October 27, 1813, Windsor, for Capt. Augustin Pugh's Bertie County militia company. Reported present with Capt. Joseph Bryant's detachment at Fort Hampton, Beaufort, Carteret County, N.C., on muster rolls dated March 31, May 31, and June 30, 1813. Reported "absent sick at Philadelphia" per a muster roll dated December 31, 1813. Last reported as "absent sick at Phila[delphia] supposed to be discharged" per muster roll dated February 28, 1814, for Capt. Robert Mitchell's company.

EIGHTEENTH REGIMENT UNITED STATES INFANTRY

Crumwell, John, recruit: Born in Bertie County and enlisted at Rockford (state or territory not identified, but possibly Surry County, N.C.) at the age of 34, October 9, 1813; occupation—farmer. Enlisted by Ensign John S. Todd for five years. Name appears on a recruiting return for this regiment dated December 12, 1813.

Harrell, John: Born in Bertie County and enlisted on April 4, 1814, in Kershaw District, S.C., at the age of 32. Name appears on a recruiting return dated "April 1814."

Hoggard, Jonathan, private: Born in Bertie County and enlisted for five years at Camden, S.C., at the age of 20, August 2 or 3, 1814; occupation—farmer. Enlisted by Lt. William Smith; reported as "sick, present" on a description roll dated February 16, 1815, for Capt. Benjamin T. Elmore's company and an inspection return dated May 1, 1815, at Fort Johnson, S.C. Transferred to the Fourth Regiment United States Infantry in August 1815.

TWENTIETH REGIMENT UNITED STATES INFANTRY

Boyce, Matthew, recruit: Born in Bertie County and enlisted by Lt. John H. Howard at Suffolk, Va., at age 21, June 13, 1814, for the war. Name appears on a recruiting return dated "Suffolk, June 1814."

Boyce, William, private: Born in Bertie County and enlisted at Windsor at age 18, March 25, 1814; occupation—farmer. Enlisted by Capt. Charles Gee for the war. Served in Gee's company. Reported present on a description roll dated February 16, 1815, and an inspection return for the company dated March 15, 1815, Norfolk. Discharged at Norfolk on March 20, 1815, his term of enlistment having expired.

Britt, Shadrack ("Shade"), private: Born in Bertie County and previously served in Capt. Augustin Pugh's Bertie County company, First Regiment (McCotter's) North Carolina Militia (Detached). Enlisted by Capt. Charles Gee in that regiment at Windsor at age 24, February 15, 1814, for the war; occupation—cooper. Reported present on a description roll dated February 16, 1815, and an inspection return dated March 15, 1815, for Captain Gee's company, Norfolk. Discharged at Norfolk on March 20, 1815, his term of enlistment having expired.

Butler, Jarvis, private: Born in Bertie County and enlisted at Windsor at age 21, February 16, 1814; occupation—farmer. Enlisted by Capt. Charles Gee for the war. Reported present on a description roll dated February 16, 1815, and an inspection return dated March 20, 1815, for Captain Gee's company, Norfolk. Discharged at Norfolk on March 20, 1815, his term of enlistment having expired.

Cook, Jonathan, private: Born in Bertie County and previously served in Capt. Augustin Pugh's Bertie County company, First Regiment (McCotter's) North Carolina Militia (Detached). Enlisted in this regiment at Windsor at the age of 17, February 11, 1814; occupation—farmer. Enlisted by Capt. Charles Gee for the war. Served in Gee's company; reported present on a description roll dated February 16, 1815, and an inspection return dated March 15, 1815, Norfolk. Discharged at Norfolk on March 20, 1815, his term of enlistment having expired.

Eason, Jesse, sergeant: Born in Bertie County and enlisted at Windsor at the age of 26, February 15, 1814; occupation—farmer. Enlisted by Capt. Charles Gee for the war. Served in Gee's company; reported present on a description roll dated February 16, 1815, and an inspection return dated

March 15, 1815, Norfolk. Discharged at Norfolk on March 20, 1815, his term of enlistment having expired.

Farmer, Milbourn, private: Born in Bertie County and enlisted at Murfreesboro, N.C., at the age of 17, September 13 or 15, 1813; occupation—farmer. Enlisted by Lt. J. H. Howard for five years. Served in Capt. Charles Gee's company until transferred to Capt. Matthew M. Payne's company. Reported present on a description roll dated February 16, 1815, and an inspection return dated March 15, 1815, Norfolk. Reported present on an inspection return for Payne's company dated April 30, 1815. Apparently transferred to Lt. William Ligon's company, Eighth Regiment United States Infantry, in early May 1815. Reported as having deserted "from Craney Island," Norfolk, on May 12, 1815, per and inspection return dated July 1, 1815 for Lieutenant Ligon's company.

Freeman, Moses, private: Born in Bertie County and previously served in Capt. Augustin Pugh's Bertie County company, First Regiment (McCotter's) North Carolina Militia (Detached). Enlisted by Capt. Charles Gee in this regiment for the war at Windsor on February 11, 1814, at the age of 37; occupation—coach maker. Served in Gee's company; reported present on a description roll dated February 16, 1815, and an inspection return dated March 15, 1815, Norfolk. Discharged at Norfolk on March 25, 1815, his term of enlistment having expired.

Harrell, Dancy, private: (Name is also shown as "Dency" and "Dempsey.") Born in Bertie County and previously served in Capt. James Iredell's company, First Regiment (McDonald's) North Carolina Militia (Detached). Enlisted in this regiment at Norfolk for five years on October 25, 1814, at age 21; occupation—planter. Enlisted by Lt. George McLaughlin. Reported present on a description roll dated February 16, 1815, for Capt. Walter G. Hayes's company and an inspection return dated March 15, 1815, Camp Defiance, Norfolk. Reported present on an inspection return dated April 30, 1815, for Capt. Matthew M. Payne's company. Transferred to the Fourth Regiment United States Infantry on or before August 31, 1815.

Harris, William, private: Born in Bertie County and enlisted at Edenton at the age of 31, May 4 or 6, 1814; occupation—seaman. Enlisted by Capt. Charles Gee for the war. Reported present on a description roll dated February 16, 1815, and an inspection return dated March 15, 1815, for Captain Gee's company, Norfolk. Discharged at Norfolk on March 15, 1815, his term of enlistment having expired.

Holly, John S., private: Born in Bertie County and previously served in Capt. Augustin Pugh's Bertie County company, First Regiment (McCotter's) North Carolina Militia (Detached). Enlisted in this regiment at Edenton at the age of 21, March 18, 1814; occupation—farmer. Enlisted by Capt. Charles Gee for the war. Deserted at Norfolk on February 12, 1815. Extant record discloses that this was his "second desertion."

Hunter, Hardy, private: Born in Bertie County and previously served in Capt. Augustin Pugh's Bertie County militia company, First Regiment (McCotter's) North Carolina Militia. Enlisted for the war at Jerusalem (present-day Courtland), Va., on March 26, 1814, at the age of 22. Served in Capt. Charles Gee's company. Died at Camp Defiance, Norfolk, on December 27, 1814.

Jernigan, Ryan, corporal: Born in Bertie County and enlisted by Capt. Charles Gee for the war at Windsor at the age of 21, February 21, 1814; occupation—farmer. Reported present on a description roll dated February 16, 1815, and an inspection return dated March 15, 1815, for Gee's company, Norfolk. Discharged at Norfolk on March 15, 1815, his term of enlistment having expired. Name appears on muster roll for Capt. Joseph H. Bryan's Bertie County militia company (later Capt. Augustin Pugh's company) published by the North Carolina adjutant general in 1851.

Kanady, Ephraim, private: (Name is also shown as "Kanada" and "Kennedy.") Born in Bertie County and enlisted at Windsor at the age of 20, March 5, 1814; occupation—tailor. Enlisted by Capt. Charles Gee for the war. Reported present on a description roll dated February 16, 1815, and an inspection return dated March 15, 1815, for Gee's company, Norfolk. Discharged at Norfolk on March 15, 1815, his term of enlistment having expired.

King, William, private: Born in Bertie County and enlisted at Windsor at the purported age of 21, February 15, 1814; occupation—joiner. Enlisted by Capt. Charles Gee for the war. Deserted on an undisclosed date, but prior to November 1814. On November 26, 1814, John Blount of Windsor wrote to Congressman William H. Murfree seeking a presidential pardon for King on the charge of desertion. Congressman Murfree forwarded Blount's letter to the secretary of war in January 1815. Private King returned to his company at Norfolk on January 14, 1815, and subsequently deserted on February 12, 1815.

Moore, Westley, private: Enlisted by Lt. John H. Howard at Windsor at the age of 24, January 29, 1814; occupation—farmer. Served in Capt. Charles Gee's company. Reported present on muster rolls dated May 31, June 30, August 31 and October 31, 1814. Reported present on a description roll dated February 16, 1815, and an inspection return dated March 15, 1815, for Gee's company, Norfolk. Discharged at Norfolk on March 20, 1815, his term of enlistment having expired.

Outlaw, Noah, corporal: Born and resided in Bertie County and previously served in Capt. James Iredell's company, First Regiment (McDonald's) North Carolina Militia (Detached). Enlisted at Norfolk at the age of 20, October 26, 1814; occupation—planter. Enlisted by Lt. George McLaughlin for five years. Reported present on a description roll dated February 16 and an inspection returned dated March 15, 1815, for Capt. Walter G. Hayes's company, Camp Defiance, Norfolk. Promoted from private to corporal on February 18, 1815. Reported present on an inspection return dated April 30, 1815, for Capt. Matthew M. Payne's company. Reported present as a private on an inspection return dated July 1, 1815, for Lt. William Ligon's company. A notation on the return indicates that his rank was "suspended" for two months on May 1, 1815, and that he was to receive private's pay for the term of the suspension. Reason for suspension not disclosed. Transferred to Capt. Alexander Cumming's company, Fourth Regiment United States Infantry, on or before August 31, 1815.

Reddick, Ebenezer, private: Born in Martin County and enlisted at Windsor at the age of 23, March 15, 1814; occupation—farmer. Enlisted by Capt. Charles Gee for the war. Reported as "left sick in Fredericksburg" on June 13, 1814, per muster roll dated June 30, 1814, for Gee's company. Never returned to the company.

Redditt, Asa, private: Born in Bertie County and previously served in Capt. Augustin Pugh's Bertie County company, First Regiment (McCotter's) North Carolina Militia (Detached). Enlisted in this regiment for the war at Windsor at the age of 28, February 11, 1814; occupation—tailor. Enlisted by Capt. Charles Gee for the war. Deserted from Gee's company at Norfolk on February 12, 1815.

Revels, William, private: Enlisted at Windsor at the age of 22, March 15, 1814; occupation—farmer. Enlisted by Capt. Charles Gee for the war. Reported present, sick in the infirmary at Norfolk on a description roll dated February 16, 1815, for Gee's company. Reported present on an inspection return dated March 15, 1815, for Gee's company, Norfolk. Discharged at Norfolk on March 20, 1815, his term of enlistment having expired.

Ruffin, Whitmell, private: Born and resided in Bertie County. Previously served in Capt. James Iredell's company, First Regiment (McDonald's) North Carolina Militia (Detached). Enlisted in this regiment at Norfolk at the age of 20, October 26, 1814; occupation—planter. Enlisted by Lt. George McLaughlin for five years. Reported present on a description roll dated February 16, 1815 for Capt. Walter G. Hayes's company and an inspection returned dated March 15, 1815, Camp Defiance, Norfolk. Reported present on an inspection return for Capt. Matthew M. Payne's company dated April 30, 1815. Reported present on an inspection return dated July 1, 1815, for Lt. William Ligon's company. Transferred to Capt. Alexander Cumming's company, Fourth Regiment United States Infantry, on or before August 31, 1815.

Simons, Josiah, private: Born in Bertie County and enlisted at Windsor at the age of 17, February 14, 1814; occupation—cooper. Enlisted by Capt. Charles Gee for the war. Reported present on a description roll dated February 16, 1815, and an inspection return dated March 15, 1815, for Gee's company, Norfolk. Discharged at Norfolk on March 20, 1815, his term of enlistment having expired.

Spivey, Moses, private: Born in Bertie County and enlisted at Windsor at the age of 24, February 13, 1814; occupation—farmer. Enlisted by Capt. Charles Gee for the war. Reported present on a description roll dated February 16, 1815, and an inspection return dated March 15, 1815, for Gee's company, Norfolk. Discharged at Norfolk on March 20, 1815, his term of enlistment having expired.

Stone, Solomon, private: Born in Bertie County and enlisted at Windsor at the age of 23, February 11, 1814; occupation—farmer. Enlisted by Capt. Charles Gee for the war. Reported present on a description roll dated February 16, 1815, and an inspection return dated March 15, 1815, for Gee's company, Norfolk. Discharged at Norfolk on March 19, 1815, his term of enlistment having expired.

Thompson, Jesse, private: Born in Bertie County and enlisted at Windsor at the age of 21, January 27, 1814; occupation—farmer. Enlisted by Capt. Charles Gee for the war. Reported present on a description roll dated February 16, 1815, and an inspection return dated March 15, 1815, for

Gee's company, Norfolk. Discharged at Norfolk on March 20, 1815, his term of enlistment having expired.

Todd, Hardy, private: Born in Bertie County and enlisted at the age of 40 on January 21, 1814; occupation—cooper. Enlisted by Capt. Charles Gee for the war. Deserted on September 14, 1814. Re-joined Gee's company on February 27, 1815 (after the end of the war). Pay and bounty stopped at that time by sentence of general court-martial. Dishonorably discharged at Norfolk on March 15, 1815.

Todd, Willis, private: Born in Bertie County and enlisted by Lt. Thomas Howson for the war at the age of 20, October 3, 1814; occupation— laborer. Reported present on a description roll dated February 16, 1815, and an inspection return dated March 15, 1815, for Capt. Walter G. Hayes's company, Norfolk. Discharged at Norfolk on March 15 or 20, 1815, his term of enlistment having expired.

West, Nimrod, private: Previously served in Capt. Augustin Pugh's Bertie County company, First Regiment (McCotter's) North Carolina Militia (Detached). Enlisted in this regiment at Windsor at the age of 24, March 25, 1814; occupation—carpenter. Enlisted by Capt. Charles Gee for the war. Reported present on a description roll dated February 16, 1815, and an inspection return dated March 15, 1815, for Gee's company, Norfolk. Discharged at Norfolk on March 19, 1815, his term of enlistment having expired.

White, Hardy, private: Transferred to this regiment from the Tenth Regiment United States Infantry on an undisclosed date by order of Col. Constant Freeman. Assigned to Capt. Richard Pollard's company and reported present per a muster roll dated April 30, 1814, for the company. Discharged on June 5, 1814, per muster roll dated June 30, 1814, for Capt. Bernard Peyton's company.

Williams, James, private: Enlisted at Windsor on February 12, 1814; occupation—farmer. Enlisted by Capt. Charles Gee for the war. Reported to have also enlisted in the Twenty-ninth Regiment United States Infantry while a member of the Twentieth Regiment. Tried by court-martial in May 1814 and found guilty of the charge of reenlisting in a regiment while a member of another regiment and defrauding the government by inappropriately receiving a $50 enlistment bounty. Sentenced to three months of hard labor with a ball and chain affixed to his leg. Ordered to repay to the government the amount defrauded through deductions from his pay. Reported present on a description roll dated February 16, 1815, and an inspection return dated March 15, 1815, for Gee's company. Norfolk. Discharged at Norfolk on March 19, 1815, his term of enlistment having expired.

Williams, Parker, private: Enlisted at Windsor at the age of 29, March 27, 1814; occupation—farmer. Enlisted by Capt. Charles Gee for the war. Reported present on a description roll dated February 16, 1815, and an inspection return dated March 15, 1815, for Gee's company, Norfolk. Discharged at Norfolk on March 19, 1815, his term of enlistment having expired.

TWENTY-FOURTH REGIMENT UNITED STATES INFANTRY

Dempsey, John, private: Born in Bertie County and enlisted by Capt. Benjamin B. Jones for five years on September 19, 1814, at the age of 20; occupation—farmer. Served in Captain Jones's company until transferred to Capt. James Stuart's company. Joined Stuart's company on March 30, 1815. Reported present on inspection returns dated April 30, June 30, and August 31, 1815, for Capt. James Stuart's company at Camp Russell, Illinois Territory. Transferred to Capt. Robert H. Goodwyn's company, Seventh Regiment United States Infantry, on an undisclosed date, but prior to December 1, 1815.

Johnson, John, private: Born in Bertie County and enlisted by Lt. Benjamin Davis for five years at the age of 20, August 29, 1814; occupation—farmer. Reported present on a description roll dated February 16, 1815, for Capt. Benjamin B. Jones's company. Transferred to Capt. James Stuart's company on March 23, 1815, and reported present on muster rolls dated April 30, June 30, and August 31, 1815, for that company. Transferred to the Seventh Regiment United States Infantry on or before December 1, 1815.

THIRTY-FIFTH REGIMENT UNITED STATES INFANTRY

Baker, Whitmel, private: Born in Bertie County and enlisted at Windsor by Lt. Francis D. Charlton for five years at the age of 19, October 6, 1813. Served in Capt. James H. Belcher's company until he died of "indisposition" in the infirmary at Camp Defiance, Norfolk, on February 2, 1815.

Brantly, John, sergeant: Born in Bertie County and previously served in Capt. Augustin Pugh's Bertie County company, First Regiment (McCotter's) North Carolina Militia (Detached). Enlisted in this regiment at the age of 21 by Capt. Benjamin Hardaway at Richmond, Va., February 24 or 25, 1814, for the war. Rank at which enlisted not disclosed. Reported present on a description roll dated February 16, 1815, and an inspection return for Hardaway's company dated March 15, 1815, at Norfolk. Discharged at Norfolk on March 15, 1815, his term of enlistment having expired.

Brogden, George, private: Born in Bertie County, where he resided prior to enlisting at Windsor at the age of 18, September 13, 1814. Enlisted by Lt. Francis D. Charlton for five years. Reported on a description roll for Capt. James H. Belcher's company as having died in an infirmary at an undisclosed location (but likely at Norfolk) on December 28, 1814, of "indisposition."

Capps, Horatio, private: Born in Bertie County, where he was enlisted by Lt. Francis D. Charlton on December 12, 1814. Joined Capt. Walter F. Cocke's company on January 3, 1815. Died at Camp Defiance, Norfolk, on February 24, 1815.

Carr, Cyrus, fifer: Born in Bertie County and enlisted at Craney Island, Norfolk, at age 22, February 25, 1814; occupation—musician. Enlisted by Lt. William Dunn for the war. Served continuously in Capt. Francis E. Walker's company. Present or accounted for until discharged at Norfolk on March 15, 1815, his term of enlistment having expired.

Evans, Wright, private: Born in Bertie County and enlisted by a Lieutenant Williams for the war on October 23, 1814, at the age of 35; occupation—farmer. Reported present on a description roll dated February 15, 1815, and an inspection return dated March 15, 1815, for Capt. James H. Belcher's company, with the notation "entitled to an hon[orable] Discharge." Discharged at Norfolk on March 15, 1815, his term of enlistment having expired.

Lowe, Ephraim, private: Born in Halifax County and enlisted at Windsor at the age of 40, September 20, 1814. Name appears on a recruiting return dated October 31, 1814, for this regiment.

Mitchell, George, recruit: Born in Bertie County and enlisted at Windsor at the age of 18, October 7, 1814. Enlisted by Lt. Francis D. Charlton for the war. Name appears on a recruiting return dated October 31, 1814, for this regiment.

Simons, Arthur C., private: Born in Bertie County and previously served in Capt. Augustin Pugh's Bertie County company, First Regiment (McCotter's) North Carolina Militia (Detached), from which he deserted on December 31, 1813. Enlisted by Lt. Francis D. Charlton in this regiment at Windsor at the age of 24, August 16, 1814. Served in Capt. James H. Belcher's company until he died at Camp Defiance, Norfolk, on February 2, 1815.

Sowell, John, private: Born in Bertie County and enlisted at Sampson County Courthouse, Clinton, N.C., at the age of 24, September 17, 1813. Reported present on a muster roll dated December 31, 1813, for Capt. John Thorp's company. Transferred to Capt. Isaac T. Preston's company on March 11, 1814. Present or accounted for until discharged on September 17, 1814.

Ward, Jasper, private: Born in Bertie County and enlisted at Windsor at the age of 19 or 21, September 30, 1814. Enlisted by Lt. Francis D. Charlton for five years and served in Capt. James H. Belcher's company until he died in the infirmary at Camp Defiance, Norfolk, on January 31, 1815.

Wesson, Amos, private: (Name is also shown as "Wilson.") Born in Bertie County and enlisted for the war at Norfolk at the age of 23, June 7, 1814; occupation—farmer. Served in Capt. William Allen's company until reported as discharged on December 8, 1814. Apparently reenlisted for the war by Lt. Francis D. Charlton on December 21, 1814. Reported present on a description roll dated February 16, 1815, for Capt. Walter F. Cocke's company and an inspection return dated March 15, 1815, Camp Defiance, Norfolk. Discharged at Fort Norfolk on March 20, 1815, his term of enlistment having expired.

Wesson, Hardy, private: Born in Bertie County, where he enlisted at the age of 18, December 14, 1814; occupation—farmer. Enlisted by Lt. Francis D. Charlton for the war. Reported present on a description roll dated February 16, 1815, for Capt. Walter F. Cocke's company and an inspection return dated March 15, 1815, Camp Defiance, Norfolk. Discharged at Norfolk on March 20, 1815, his term of enlistment having expired.

Williford, Jonas, private: Born in Bertie County and enlisted at Norfolk at the age of 21, October 30, 1814; occupation—farmer. Enlisted by Lt. J. N. B. Cole for the war. Reported present on a description roll dated February 15, 1815, and an inspection return dated March 15, 1815, for Capt. James H.

Belcher's company. Discharged at Norfolk on March 15, 1815, his term of enlistment having expired.

THIRTY-NINTH REGIMENT UNITED STATES INFANTRY

Butler, William: Born in Bertie County and enlisted by Capt. James Davis at Camp Anderson at age 17, February 14, 1814. Name appears on a recruiting return dated "Camp Anderson, February 18, 1814." (Butler may have been rejected for military service because he was under the age of 18.)

Meazles [Mizells], Henry, private: Born in Bertie County and enlisted by Lt. Simpson Payne on January 19, 1814, at the age of 22. Name appears on a recruiting return dated January 22, 1814.

FORTY-THIRD REGIMENT UNITED STATES INFANTRY

Barber, John D., private: Born in Bertie County and enlisted at Plymouth on February 19, 1814, at the age of 23; occupation—sailor. Enlisted for the war by Capt. Henry Garrett, in whose company he served. Reported present on a description roll dated February 16, 1814, and an inspection return dated August 1, 1815, Fort Hampton, Beaufort, Carteret County, N.C. Discharged at Fort Hampton on August 15, 1815, his term of enlistment having expired.

Barber, Kenneth, corporal: Born in Bertie County and enlisted at Plymouth on April 14, 1814, at the age of 22; occupation—sailor. Enlisted for the war by Capt. Henry Garrett, in whose company he served. Reported present on a description roll for Garrett's company dated February 16, 1815, at Fort Hampton, Beaufort, Carteret County, N.C. Reported as having deserted on July 27, 1815, per an inspection return for Garrett's company dated August 1, 1815.

Bentley, Allen, private: Born in Bertie or Martin County and enlisted at Plymouth at the age of 23, May 11, 1814. Enlisted by Capt. Henry Garrett for the war. Reported present on a description roll dated February 16, 1815, Fort Hampton, Beaufort, Carteret County, N.C. Deserted on July 22, 1815, but apparently returned to his company (date not disclosed), as he was discharged on August 26, 1815, his term of enlistment having expired.

Burnham, Thomas, private: Born in Bertie County and enlisted at Plymouth at age 38, June 11, 1814; occupation—farmer. Enlisted by

Capt. Henry Garrett for the war. Reported present on a description roll dated February 16, 1815, and an inspection return dated August 1, 1815, for Garrett's company at Fort Hampton, Beaufort, Carteret County, N.C. Discharged at Fort Hampton on August 1, 1815, his term of enlistment having expired.

Craft, Solomon, private: Born in Bertie County and enlisted at Plymouth at the age of 23, February 22, 1814; occupation—farmer. Enlisted by Capt. Henry Garrett for the war. Reported present on a description roll dated February 16, 1815, and an inspection return dated August 1, 1815, for Garrett's company at Fort Hampton, Beaufort, Carteret County, N.C. Discharged at Fort Hampton on August 1, 1815, his term of enlistment having expired.

Rogers, Frederick, private: Born in Bertie County and enlisted at Plymouth at the age of 36, January 27, 1814; occupation—shoemaker. Enlisted by Capt. Henry Garrett for the war. Reported present on a description roll dated February 16, 1815, for Garrett's company at Fort Hampton, Beaufort, Carteret County, N.C. Discharged at Fort Hampton on August 1, 1815, his term of enlistment having expired.

White, King, private: Born in Bertie County and enlisted for five years at Tarboro at the age of 19, June 25, 1814; occupation—farmer. Reported present on a description roll dated February 16, 1815, for Capt. Henry Garrett's company and an inspection return dated August 1, 1815, for Lt. John S. Smallwood's detachment. Discharged at Fort Hampton, Beaufort, Carteret County, N.C., on November 5, 1815, with the notation "a minor."

UNITED STATES ARTILLERY

Brickell, William M., private: Name appears on an October 27, 1813, muster roll for Capt. Augustin Pugh's Bertie County company, First Regiment (McCotter's) North Carolina Militia (Detached) as "absent out of the state." Enlisted in the United States artillery at Richmond, Va., at the age of 23, January 21, 1814; occupation—tailor. Enlisted by Capt. Thomas B. Randolph for the war. Present or accounted for until discharged on July 22, 1815, his term of enlistment having expired. Place of discharge not disclosed.

Butler, William, private: Born in Bertie County and enlisted at Raleigh at age 23, June 16, 1812; occupation—farmer. Enlisted by Capt. Philemon

Hawkins for five years. Reported "absent on command at Fort Wingaw [S.C.]" per a muster roll dated October 31, 1813, for Captain Hawkins's company. Deserted on an undisclosed date per an inspection return dated April 30, 1815, for Hawkins's company, Castle Pinckney, Charleston Harbor.

SECOND REGIMENT UNITED STATES RIFLES

Johnson, Joseph, private: Born in Bertie County and enlisted at an undisclosed location on July 7, 1813, at the age of 16; occupation—farmer. Enlisted by Capt. Benjamin Johnson for the war. Reported present on a description roll dated February 16, 1815, at Walden, Upper Canada. Discharged on June 30, 1815, his term of enlistment having expired.

FIFTH REGIMENT UNITED STATES RIFLES

Hunter, Allen: Born in Bertie County and enlisted on July 18, 1814, at the age of 30 by Lt. Gadi Crawford at Marion Court House, S.C. Name appears on a recruiting returned dated "S. Carolina August 31, 1814."

UNITED STATES RIFLES (MISCELLANEOUS)

Hale, Elisha, private: Born in Bertie County and enlisted at Louisville, Ky., on November 21 or 23, 1814, age not recorded; occupation—cooper. Enlisted by Capt. Benjamin Desha for five years. Served in Captain Desha's company; reported "present sick in hospital" per a muster roll dated January 20, 1815, Chillicothe, Ohio. Reported present on an inspection return dated April 30, 1815. Reported "present sick in hospital" on an inspection return dated August 31, 1815, for Lt. Llewellyn Hickman's company at Detroit, Michigan Territory. Transferred to Capt. Edmund Shipp's company by June 30, 1816, when he was reported "absent sick at Detroit."

UNITED STATES ARMY ENLISTEES
(REJECTED OR UNASSIGNED)

Buck, Jasper: Born in Bertie County and enlisted for five years at an undisclosed location in N.C., August 13, 1812, at the age of 20; occupation—farmer. Name appears on a recruiting certificate dated "NC, Aug 13, 1812."

Cale, Rian: Born and resided in Bertie County as a farmer before enlisting for five years on August 21, 1812, at the age of 21. Name appears on a recruiting certificate for N.C. dated August 1, 1813.

James, James Frederick: A "man of colour" born in Bertie County, enlisted for five years on August 17, 1813, at the age of 20; occupation—wheelwright. Name appears on a recruiting return dated "NC, August 17, 1813."

Lawrence, Williamson: Born in Bertie County and enlisted for eighteen months on August 13, 1812, at the age of 25; occupation—farmer. Name appears on a recruiting certificate dated "NC, August 13, 1812."

Notes

1. Bertie County's army soldiers were identified from Registers of Enlistments in the United States Army, 1798–1914 (microfilm, M233), Record Group 94, National Archives, Washington, D.C., and from Charles K. Gardner, *A Dictionary of All Officers Who Have Been Commissioned or Have Been Approved in the Army of the United States, 1789–1853* (New York: G. P. Putnam and Company, 1853). Supplementary information was derived from Federal Pension Application Files, Record Group 15, National Archives; Raymond Parker Fouts, *Abstracts from the* Edenton Gazette and North Carolina General Advertiser, *Edenton, North Carolina*, 3 vols. (Cocoa, Fla.: GenRec Books, 1993); and the *Edenton Gazette and North Carolina General Advertiser*.

2. During the early nineteenth century, companies in the United States Army were designated by their commanders' names and not by letters (Company "A," "B," and so on), as later became the convention.

Bibliography

PRIMARY SOURCES

BERTIE COUNTY COURTHOUSE, WINDSOR, N.C.
Deeds and Indexes. Bertie County Register of Deeds Office.
Wills. Bertie County Office of the Clerk of Court.

LIBRARY OF CONGRESS, WASHINGTON, D.C.
Petition of Jonathan S. Tayloe, United States Senate, 42nd Cong., 3rd sess.,
1873, Misc. Doc. 76.

NATIONAL ARCHIVES, WASHINGTON, D.C.
Compiled Service Records of North Carolina's Detached Militia. Record
Group 94.
First Regiment (McCotter's) North Carolina Militia.
First Regiment (McDonald's) North Carolina Militia.
Third Regiment (Moore's) North Carolina Militia.
Fifth Regiment (Atkinson's) North Carolina Militia.
Correspondence of the Secretary of the Treasury with Collectors of
Customs, 1789–1833 (microfilm, M178). Record Group 36.
Court Martial Case Files. Record Group 153.
Federal Pension Application Files. Record Group 15.
"Finding Aid" for Record Group 36.
General Orders and Circulars of the War Department and Headquarters of
the Army, 1809–1860, (microfilm, M1094). Record Group 94.
Letters Received by the Office of the Adjutant General, 1805–1821
(microfilm, M566). Record Group 94.
Letters Received by the Secretary of the Navy from Captains ("Captains'
Letters"), 1805–1861; 1866–1885 (microfilm, M125). Record Group
45.

Letters Received by the Secretary of the Navy from Commanders, 1804–1886 (microfilm, M147). Record Group 45.

Letters Received by the Secretary of the Navy from Commissioned Officers Below the Rank of Commander and from Warrant Officers ("Officers Letters") 1802–1884 (microfilm, M148). Record Group 45.

Letters Received by the Secretary of War, Main Series, 1801–1870 (microfilm, M221). Record Group 107.

Letters Received by the Secretary of War, Unregistered Series, 1789–1861 (microfilm, M222). Record Group 107.

Letters Sent by the Office of the Adjutant General, Main Series, 1800–1890 (microfilm, M565). Record Group 94.

Letters Sent by the Secretary of the Navy to Commandants and Navy Agents, 1808–1865 (microfilm, M441). Record Group 45.

Letters Sent by the Secretary of the Navy to Officers, 1798–1868 (microfilm, M149). Record Group 45.

Letters Sent by the Secretary of War Relating to Military Affairs, 1800–1889 (microfilm, M6). Record Group 107.

Miscellaneous Letters Received by the Secretary of the Navy, 1801–1884 (microfilm, M124). Record Group 45.

Miscellaneous Letters Sent by the Secretary of the Navy ("General Letter Books"), 1798–1886, (microfilm, M209). Record Group 45.

Miscellaneous Lists and Papers Regarding Impressed Seamen, 1796–1814 (microfilm, M1839). Record Group 59.

Navy Department General Orders and Circulars, 1798–1862 (microfilm, M977). Record Group 45.

Registers of Applications for the Release of Impressed Seamen, 1793–1802, and Related Indexes (microfilm, M2025). Record Group 59.

Registers of Enlistments in the United States Army, 1798–1914 (microfilm, M233). Record Group 94.

Sixth Military District, Letters Sent, March 1813–June 1815, Entry 33. Record Group 98.

Southern Department General Orders Received & Orders Issued, June 1812–February 1813. Vol. 2. Record Group 98.

Third Census of the United States, 1810: Bertie County, North Carolina, Population Schedule.

War of 1812 Military Bounty Land Warrants, 1815–1858 (microfilm, M848). Record Group 15.

NORTH CAROLINA STATE ARCHIVES, OFFICE OF ARCHIVES AND HISTORY, RALEIGH, N.C.

Government Records

Adjutant General Letters, Orders, and Returns, 1807–1812 (AG-1).

Adjutant General Militia Returns, Orders of Officers, 1811–1813 (AG-2).

Adjutant General Militia Returns, Orders to Officers, 1813–1817 (AG-6).

Adjutant General Roster of Field Officers of Militia, 1813–1842 (AG-7).

Estates Records, 1730–1920, Bertie County.

Governors Letter Books: Nathaniel Alexander, William Hawkins, William Miller.

Governors Papers: William Hawkins.

War of 1812 Pay Vouchers, (microfilm, S.115.137.10).

Private Collections

Graham, James, Papers.

Johnson, Charles E., Collection.

NEWSPAPERS

Edenton Gazette.

Evening Post (New York).

London *Times.*

New Bedford (Mass.) *Mercury.*

Norwich (Conn.) *Courier.*

Raleigh Minerva (weekly).

Raleigh Register and North Carolina Gazette (weekly).

Raleigh Register and North Carolina Weekly Advertiser (weekly).

Washington (D.C.) *Expositor.*

BOOKS, PAMPHLETS, ARTICLES, AND OTHER PUBLISHED MATERIAL

Ashe, Samuel A., Stephen B. Weeks, and Charles L. Van Noppen, eds. *Biographical History of North Carolina*. 8 vols. Greensboro: Charles L. Van Noppen, 1905–1917.

Axelrod, Alan. *The Real History of the American Revolution: A New Look at the Past*. New York: Sterling Publishing Co., 2007.

Bergh, Albert Ellery, ed. *The Writings of Thomas Jefferson, Memorial Edition*. 20 vols. Washington, D.C.: Thomas Jefferson Memorial Association, 1904.

Broussard, James H. *The Southern Federalists, 1800–1816*. Baton Rouge and London: Louisiana State University Press, 1978.

Dudley, William S., and Michael J. Crawford, eds. *The Naval War of 1812: A Documentary History*. Washington, D.C.: Naval Historical Center, Department of the Navy, 1985.

Eckert, Edward K. "William Jones: Mr. Madison's Secretary of the Navy." *The Pennsylvania Magazine of History and Biography*. Vol. 96, no. 2 (April 1972): 167–182.

Fouts, Raymond Parker. *Abstracts from the* Edenton Gazette and North Carolina General Advertiser, *Edenton, North Carolina*. 3 vols. Cocoa, Fla.: GenRec Books, 1993.

Gardner, Charles K. *A Dictionary of All Officers Who Have Been Commissioned or Have Been Approved in the Army of the United States, 1789–1853*. New York: G. P. Putnam and Company, 1853.

Gilpatrick, Delbert Harold. *Jeffersonian Democracy in North Carolina, 1789–1816*. New York: Octagon Books, 1967.

Heidler, David S., and Jeanne T. Heidler, eds. *Encyclopedia of the War of 1812*. Annapolis: Naval Institute Press, 1997.

_____. *The War of 1812*. Westport, Conn.: Greenwood Press, 2002.

Heitman, Francis B. *Historical Register and Dictionary of the United States Army*. 2 vols. Washington, D.C.: Government Printing Office, 1903.

Hickey, Donald R. *The War of 1812: A Forgotten Conflict*. Champaign: University of Illinois Press, 1989.

_____. *The War of 1812: A Short History*. Urbana: University of Illinois Press, 1995.

Laws of the State of North Carolina. Raleigh: J. Gales, 1821.

Lemmon, Sarah McCulloh. "Dissent in North Carolina during the War of 1812." *North Carolina Historical Review* 44 (April 1972): 103-118.

_____. *North Carolina and the War of 1812*. Raleigh: State Department of Archives and History, 1971.

Lord, Walter. *The Dawn's Early Light*. New York: W. W. Norton & Company, 1972.

Morgan, David T., ed. *The John Gray Blount Papers*. 3 vols. Raleigh: North Carolina Department of Cultural Resources, 1982.

Muster Rolls of the Soldiers of the War of 1812 Detached from the Militia of North Carolina, in 1812 and 1814. Raleigh: Ch. C. Raboteau, 1851; Winston-Salem: Barber Printing Company, 1926.

Pitch, Anthony S. *The Burning of Washington: The British Invasion of 1814*. Annapolis: Naval Institute Press, 1998.

Polk, William Mecklenburg. *Leonidas Polk, Bishop and General*. New York: Longmans, Green and Col, 1893.

Powell, Col. William H., U.S. Army. *List of Officers in the Army of the United States from 1779 to 1900*. New York: L. R. Hamersly & Co., 1900.

Powell, William S., ed. *Dictionary of North Carolina Biography*. 6 vols. Chapel Hill: University of North Carolina Press, 1979–1996.

Powell, William S. and Michael Hill. *The North Carolina Gazetteer*. 2nd ed. Chapel Hill: University of North Carolina Press, 2010.

Purcell, Sarah J. *The Early National Period: An Eyewitness History*. New York: Facts on File, 2004 by author.

Seybert, Adam. *Statistical Views of the United States of America*. Philadelphia: Thomas Dobson & Son, 1818; New York: Augustus M. Kelley, Publishers, 1970.

Skeen, C. Edward. *Citizen Soldiers in the War of 1812*. Lexington: University of Kentucky Press, 1999.

Stagg, J. C. A., et al., eds. *The Papers of James Madison: Presidential Series*. 6 vols. to date. Charlottesville: University of Virginia Press, 1999–.

Thompson, Harry L. *The Windsor Story—1768–1968*. Windsor, N.C.: Windsor Bicentennial Commission, 1969. Bertie County NCGenWeb Project Page. www.rootsweb.ancestry.com/~ncbertie/windsor.htm.

Tyler, John E. "Sandy Run Baptist Church, Roxobel—A History in Recognition of Its Bicentennial, 1759–1950." Roxobel, N.C.: the author, 1950.

United States Statutes at Large.

Wheeler, John H. *Historical Sketches of North Carolina from 1584 to 1851.* 2 vols. Philadelphia: Lippincott, Grambo and Col, 1851.

Wood, Gordon S. *Empire of Liberty: A History of the Early Republic, 1789–1815.* Oxford: Oxford University Press, 2009.

World Book Encyclopedia, The. 2000 edition.

OTHER SOURCES

Officers of the Continental and U.S. Navy and Marine Corps, 1775–1900. Naval Historical Center, Washington, D.C. www.history.navy.mil/books/callahan/reg-usn.

Official War of 1812 Bicentennial Website, The. www.visit1812.com/history/USMusket.html.

Taylor, Melanie Johnson. "David Stone: A Political Biography." Master's thesis, East Carolina University, 1968.

Index

T

Tallmadge, Benjamin, 16

Tarboro, N.C.: recruiting rendezvous at, 64, 65

Tayloe, Jonathan S., **183**

Taylor, James, 85

Taylor, Robert B., 79, 88, 95

Tecumseh (Shawnee Indian), 6

Tenskwatawa (Shawnee Indian better known as "The Prophet"), 6

Tenth Regiment United States Infantry, xi, 19, 20, 61, 62, 65, 66, 67, 68, 69, 72, 77n. 30; enlistees in, from Bertie (1812), enumerated, 63; members of, enumerated, 192–197

Terrell, William G., **183**

Third Regiment North Carolina Militia (Detached), 127, 134n. 19

Third Regiment United States Infantry, 49, 62, 63, 67; members of, enumerated, 188

Thirteenth Brigade, North Carolina Militia, 13, 22

Thirty-fifth Regiment United States Infantry, 74; enlistees in, from Bertie, enumerated, 78n. 38; members of, enumerated, 204–207

Thirty-ninth Regiment United States Infantry: enlistees in, from Bertie, enumerated, 78n. 38; members of, enumerated, 207

Thompson, Jesse, 72, **202**

Thorp, John: infantry company of, mentioned, 206

Tines, West, **163**

Tippecanoe, battle of, 6

Tisdale, Nathan, 89

Todd, Hardy, 72, 73, **203**

Todd, Henry, **183**

Todd, John S.: mentioned, 197

Todd, Levi, **163**

Todd, Willis, **203**

Treaty of Ghent, 130, 131

Tulley, Leven, **183**

Turner, Edward, **164**

Turner, James, 25, 82

Turner, Simon, 2

Turner, Washington, **164**

Twelfth Congress. *See* "War Congress"

Twentieth Regiment United States Infantry, 72, 74; enlistees in, from Bertie, enumerated, 78n. 38; members of, enumerated, 198–204

Twenty-fourth Regiment United States Infantry: members of, enumerated, 204

Tyrrell County detached militia, 92

U

United States Army: enlistees in, from Bertie, 74; expanded by congressional action (December 1811), 19; rejected or unassigned enlistees in, from Bertie, enumerated, 209–210

United States Artillery: members of, enumerated, 208

United States Navy: condition of (1812), 21

United States Rifles (Miscellaneous): member of, named, 209

United States War Department: announces lenient policy of desertion, 78n. 40; designates N.C. as distinct recruiting district, 67; discontinues recruiting rendezvous at Tarboro, Fayetteville, 67; establishes recruiting departments, districts, 61, 75n. 3; and recruitment, 64

V

Vashon, George: infantry company of, mentioned, 192, 194, 195, 196

W

Walker, Francis E.: infantry company of, mentioned, 205